CONTACT!
EARLY US NAVAL AND MARINE CORPS AVIATION, 1911–18

ALAN C. CAREY

Published by Key Books
An imprint of Key Publishing Ltd
PO Box 100
Stamford
Lincs PE9 1XQ

www.keypublishing.com

The right of Alan C. Carey to be identified as the author of this book has been asserted in accordance with the Copyright, Designs and Patents Act 1988 Sections 77 and 78.

Copyright © Alan C. Carey, 2023

ISBN 978 1 80282 647 0

Front cover design: Myriam Bell Designs

All rights reserved. Reproduction in whole or in part in any form whatsoever or by any means is strictly prohibited without the prior permission of the Publisher.

Typeset by SJmagic DESIGN SERVICES, India.

Acknowledgements

This project has been a rewarding, surprisingly enjoyable, and sometimes frustrating journey through the annals of naval aviation history and the research process. I want to acknowledge the researchers, archivists, and librarians at the Naval Historical Center in Washington, DC; Naval History and Heritage Command and its digital archives; the National Archives in College Park, Maryland; and the Marine Corps University Historical Records Branch, its digitalized archives, and Yale University's F. Trubee Davison papers, manuscripts, and archives. A special thank you to Key Publishing Ltd and Nicholas Veronico, who made the publication of this work possible. Photographs are public domain unless otherwise noted.

Note: The original quoted text is in its original form and will contain grammatical and spelling errors.

Contents

Introduction 7
Terminology 9

PART ONE: GROWING PAINS

Chapter 1	The Rise of Aviation	13
Chapter 2	Glenn Curtiss and Eugene Ely	32
Chapter 3	The Birth of Naval Aviation	50
Chapter 4	The Birth of Marine Corps Aviation	78
Chapter 5	Fleet Operations (1913–14)	95
Chapter 6	The United States Naval Reserve Flying Corps ...	121
Chapter 7	Pushers Versus Tractors	148
Chapter 8	Naval Aviation Training (1915–18)	170

PART TWO: NAVAL AND MARINE CORPS AVIATION AT WAR

Chapter 9	Wartime Aircraft Production (1917–18)	197
Chapter 10	Naval Aviation at War	218
Chapter 11	Naval Air Operations in Britain and France	246
Chapter 12	Naval Air Operations in Italy	264
Chapter 13	The First Marine Aviation Force	283
Chapter 14	The Northern Bombing Group: Marine Corps Operations	302

Chapter 15	Lighter-Than-Air Operations	334
Chapter 16	Impact and Legacy of Early Naval Aviation	343
Appendix A	Course of Instruction for Naval Aviators, Dated May 1, 1917	349
Appendix B	Major Naval Aircraft Production Models (1916–18)	351
Appendix C	US Naval Air and Marine Corps Stations	352
Appendix D	Overseas Naval Air Stations	354
Selected Bibliography		356
Notes		363
Index		380

Introduction

This work is a historical narrative encompassing the formation and development of US Navy and Marine Corps aviation from 1911 through World War One. It includes prewar organization, wartime training, aircraft development, operations, and personalities such as the Navy's Theodore "Spuds" Ellyson and Marine Alfred A. Cunningham. Both were pioneers of military aviation who continuously fought to maintain and promote their service's air arms. Their resolve would, within seven years, lead to the organization of wartime scouting, pursuit, and bombing operations during World War One. In addition, individuals in early aviation, such as John Towers, Marc Mitscher, and Roy Geiger, would become significant leaders in the Pacific during World War Two. Metaphorically, United States naval aviation barely made it off the ground. Individual tenacity and an unwillingness to fail drove early naval aviation pioneers such as Ellyson, who became Naval Aviator No. 1 when he soloed in an aircraft made of bamboo, wood, canvas, and wire. Alfred Cunningham would follow a year later when he became the Marine Corps' first aviator. However, the future of naval aviation was much in doubt, especially during its formative years between 1911 and 1914.

The Navy establishment questioned whether primitive aircraft had any role within the service, since those in command looked upon the flying machines as experimental toys. However, the minuscule aviation section played a small but important role during the Veracruz Crisis in 1914, using seaplanes as reconnaissance platforms. Unfortunately, a lack of interest by those in power offered little in allocations. Thus, little growth in the number of qualified aviators and aircraft occurred during the prewar years. The lack of both interest and distribution of money for aviation began changing in 1916 when it became clear the United States would, in all probability, enter the war in Europe. Nevertheless, the naval and marine air sections were woefully unprepared for warfare when the United States declared war against the Central Powers and had to rely on its European Allies to provide bombers and pursuit aircraft throughout the conflict.

There was initial tension between the Navy and Marine Corps as the naval hierarchy saw no need to provide land-based aircraft for the Corps. Instead, the aviation duty was to scout and carry out anti-submarine operations using seaplanes and flying boats. Negotiations brought forth the concept of the Northern Bombing Group (NBG), a land-based unit equipped primarily with British and Italian aircraft. However, it took until October 1918 for that unit to become fully operational. In the meantime, the Navy and Marine Corps farmed out personnel to British and French squadrons to obtain training and combat experience. Groups of American pilots and observers began training in the fall of 1917; still, it was not until March 1918, nearly a year after the United States declared war, that the First Naval Aeronautical Company and the First Naval Aviation Force deployed overseas.

Consequently, the Navy did not form an independent naval air force during the war. Meanwhile, the First Marine Aeronautical Force under the command of Alfred Cunningham did not arrive in France until July 1918; dozens of pilots and observers of that force, like that of the Navy, were sent to British and French units for additional training and to gain combat experience. Finally, the NBG, comprising naval and marine personnel, became an independent fighting force when an adequate number of DH-4 and DH-9 biplane bombers reached the group in October 1918 – a month before the end of hostilities. The wartime experiences of naval aviation in World War One made it an essential arm of the United States Navy and the Marine Corps. Its growth continued, albeit gradually, during the 1920s and '30s, which saw the development and rise of aircraft carriers as part of the fleet and overall naval planning, which would become vital when the United States entered World War Two.

Terminology

Aerodrome: An antiquated term for an airfield.

Aeroplane: An antiquated term for airplane/plane.

Archie: German antiaircraft fire from machine guns and artillery directed against aircraft.

BuAer: Bureau of Aeronautics.

BuC&R: Bureau of Construction and Repair.

BuNav: Bureau of Navigation.

BuOrd: Bureau of Ordnance

BuShips: Bureau of Ships

BuY&D: Bureau of Yards and Docks

Contact: A nostalgic verbal cue for a mechanic to manually rotate the propeller(s) to start an airplane's engine.

CNO: Chief of Naval Operations

FNAF: First Naval Aeronautic Force

Huns: A term for Germans.

Hydroplane/Hydroaeroplane: An antiquated term for an amphibious airplane fitted with pontoons or a hull, which can land and take off from water.

Lt/Lieut: An abbreviation for lieutenant. A naval lieutenant is equal to a Marine Corps or Army captain.

Lieutenant (jg): The Navy's term for a lieutenant junior grade, which is equal to a second lieutenant in the Marine Corps or Army.

NAS: Naval Air Station.

NBG: Northern Bombing Group.

RFC: Royal Flying Corps (replaced by the Royal Air Force on April 1, 1918).

RAF: Royal Air Force

RNAS: Royal Naval Air Service

U-boat: German submarine

USMC: United States Marine Corps

USNAF: United States Naval Air Force

USNR: United States Naval Reserve

PART ONE
GROWING PAINS

Chapter 1

The Rise of Aviation

The earliest history of humans attempting flight is probably the Greek myth of Icarus, written circa 1500 BCE. Daedalus and his son, Icarus, fashioned wings made of feathers and wax to escape King Minos, who had imprisoned them. However, Daedalus warned his son to neither fly too low nor too high. Unfortunately, Icarus ignored his father's advice and flew too close to the sun, where the wax melted, and the lad fell into the sea and drowned. Nearly 3,600 years later, humans' flying attempts continued in the last decade of the 19th century, and the early part of the 20th century.

Lighter-than-air ballooning had been around since the 1780s, and its first military use began during the French Revolution. Dirigibles and balloons remained stylish for the rich but, at the time, had little military application; they were slow and cumbersome, but military powers, including the United States, would primarily use them as observation platforms. Germany would be an exception, using Zeppelins in strategic bombing – mainly civilian targets in Britain and France during World War One. However, the invention of the heavier-than-air flying machine proved to be a more complex undertaking. The earliest documented case of powered flight was that of Frenchman Clement Ader, in which historians give him credit for an uncontrolled flight of his machine, the *Éloe*, flying approximately 161ft. However, the Wright brothers conducted the first controlled flight of a heavier-than-air machine. Very few individuals, if any, in those times imagined how the development of controlled flight had become a paradigm on a monumental scale. Individuals such as Glenn

Curtiss probably did not understand they had begun a process that would change the world – a world in which aircraft would be used for peaceful purposes and in armed conflict.

Military interest in heavier-than-air flying machines in the United States preceded the Wright brothers by five years when Professor Samuel Pierpont Langley constructed an airplane model equipped with a steam engine that was successfully launched on May 6, 1896. The model with tandem wings measured 13ft by 16ft. On March 25, 1898, the Assistant Secretary of the Navy, Theodore Roosevelt, requested that the Secretary of the Navy appoint two naval officers to examine Langley's unmanned flying machine and report whether such a contraption could have naval applications. Impressed with the model, the officers gave Roosevelt a positive review. On November 11, 1898, the War Department granted $50,000 while the Smithsonian Institute provided another $20,000 to develop a heavier-than-air flying machine Langley called the *Aerodrome A*. On August 8, 1903, a second model with a gasoline engine was flown, followed by a one-quarter-size model which tested successfully, indicating a full-size version was possible. The full-size version weighed 830lb with a pilot, and had a wing area of 1,040sq ft. Langley attempted to fly the machine on September 7 and December 3, 1903. Both attempts were unsuccessful, and he abandoned the program. By then, the Wright brothers were about to complete successful flights of their aircraft design.

On a windy day, a northerly 27mph freezing wind kicked up a thick haze of sand as it blew across a stretch of beach at Kill Devil Hills, North Carolina. Overlooking the Atlantic on December 17, 1903, the two brothers prepared their heavier-than-air flying machine. Their craft was constructed of wood, bamboo, fabric, and metal, had a weight of 830lb with a pilot, a wing area of 1,040sq ft, and was powered by a water-cooled 52.4hp engine. The Wright brothers possessed remarkable intelligence, guts, grit, perseverance, and possibly some insanity to design and operate a heavier-than-air flying contraption without killing themselves. Finally, they put theory into practice. Orville Wright conducted the first of four powered flights that day with a heavier-than-air power-driven airplane named the Wright Flyer I. It seems unremarkable today as the first flight lasted 12 seconds, covering 20ft, while the last flew 852ft in 59 seconds. Aircraft design and construction had little to do with science or engineering; trial and error pushed aeronautics during the early years. Stresses in flight and the understanding of balance, stability and control aerodynamics were largely unknown or only faintly understood. Contemporary scientists and engineers hardly noticed the groundbreaking flights, and many scoffed at the notion that such a machine existed and could fly.

The brothers continued redesigning the plane and improving their piloting skills in relative secrecy for the next two years, testing the Flyer II and III between 1904 and 1905. Both distance and duration increased significantly between September 26 and October 5, 1905, with the last flight reaching a distance of 24 miles in 39 minutes at a speed near 40mph.

Langley's full-size man-carrying aerodrome on a houseboat in the Potomac River, October 7, 1903. Two tests failed in October and December 1903, and he gave up on creating the first successful heavier-than-air flying machine. (Courtesy of the US Naval History and Heritage Command)

Amazingly, military aircraft would triple this speed and range within a decade. During 1905, the brothers flew successful flights in Ohio with the Wright Flyer III at Huffman Prairie and Dayton, during which time they offered to demonstrate their machine to the Army, free of charge. The Army politely refused as it remembered Langley's debacle just a few short years before when the War Department paid $50,000 for the professor's machine. The Wright brothers would stir worldwide interest in experimenting and developing similar contraptions, along with competitors, by 1906. The appeal of planes to European governments and international companies finally caught the attention of President Theodore Roosevelt, who showed a keen interest in the possibilities of the airplane. He, therefore, requested that the Army's Bureau of Ordnance and Fortifications notify the service to investigate such machines.

Meanwhile, as the Wrights continued tinkering with their machines, European pioneers advanced in aviation in an era known as the period of

The Wright brothers' first powered flight took place in Kitty Hawk in December 1903. Several years later, the US Army decided to take an interest in heavier-than-air aircraft. The US Army's Signal Corps purchased its first plane from the Wright brothers. (Courtesy of the Library of Congress)

inventors. Brazilian-born Santos Dumont, in France on August 26, 1906, brought about genuine public interest in powered flight by exhibiting his design powered by Léon Levavasseur Antoinette's V-8 50hp engine. The 645lb contraption, with a wing area of 650sq ft, flew 32ft at a speed of 23mph, followed by a second exhibition on November 12 when the aircraft flew 723ft. That flight was the first successful public demonstration in Europe and earned Dumont the first certification by the Fédération Aéronautique Internationale (FAI). The following year, the British–French aviator Henri Farman flew his design 2,559ft during a public demonstration on October 27, 1907. Farman, in 1908, also conducted the first circular route of an airplane.

The two brothers knew they had to publicly prove their aircraft would be successful as they now had competition. Still, due to their secrecy, they failed to communicate their success to the public. Finally, they did so in 1908. In September that year, Orville Wright made the first exhibition flight

Alberto Santos-Dumont took his Demoiselle monoplane out to the practice grounds for a flight in 1909. He, Henri Farman, and Louis Blériot were the Wright brothers' primary European competitors. (Courtesy of the Library of Congress)

of one hour in the air with a passenger at Fort Myer, Virginia. Henri Farman countered that demonstration a month later, in October, by conducting the first cross-country flight from Chalon to Rheims, France – a distance of 16 miles in 20 minutes. That December, Wilbur Wright attained an altitude of 361ft at Le Mans, France.

Europeans continued challenging the Wrights, with Louis Blériot crossing the English Channel, from Calais to Dover, in 37 minutes in July 1909. In September of that year, Wilbur Wright flew around the Statue of Liberty and over naval ships anchored in the harbor. While Europeans surpassed the Wrights, the military became seriously interested in the Wright Flyer's potential for military application.

In mid-1907, Army lieutenant Frank P. Lahm asked President Roosevelt to have the War Department purchase the Flyer he witnessed in Dayton, Ohio. At around the same time in June 1907, Lahm wrote a letter to the Board of Ordnance and Fortifications to purchase the aircraft. The board agreed to buy the machine, but the Wright brothers told them they did not want payment until they produced an updated design.

Henri Farman, a British–French inventor, after winning the Deutsch prize in aviation circa 1908–1909. He broke altitude and endurance records before the Wright brothers. He flew a cross-country flight of 27 miles on October 30, 1908. (Bain News Service, courtesy of the Library of Congress)

The Rise of Aviation

Louis Blériot with his monoplane circa 1908–09. He became the first aviator to fly across the English Channel in a heavier-than-air monoplane in July 1909, flying a type XI at an altitude of 200ft at 45mph. (Courtesy of the Library of Congress)

Wilbur and Orville Wright with their second powered plane, the Wright Flyer II, built in 1904, at Huffman Prairie, Dayton, Ohio. It had a maximum speed of 35mph and a range of 5.0 miles. It developed into the Wright Flyer III. (Courtesy of the Library of Congress)

Wright Flyer over Fort Myer, Virginia, during a public demonstration circa 1907–08. The US Army chose to purchase its first Wright plane in 1909, two years before the Navy purchased its own. (Courtesy of the Library of Congress)

However, upon interviewing Wilbur Wright, the board seemed unimpressed with his proposal – enough to solicit bids from other parties interested in developing a heavier-than-air flying machine for $25,000.

The board received 41 bids, including Wright's two-page proposal dated January 27, 1908, which was accepted. The contract was issued on February 10, 1908, marking the birth of US Army aviation, followed by the Army's first fatal aircraft crash seven months later. That sad distinction went to Lieutenant Thomas E. Selfridge, who flew aboard a Wright Flyer A with Orville, which crashed on September 17, 1908. However, the crash did not deter the Army's interest as it saw the potential of such a machine. The US Army Signal Corps saw the military potential of aircraft by establishing an aeronautical division on August 1, 1907, but waited until 1909 to purchase a Wright plane. The Army's interest in the military possibilities of the airplane increased during the aviation competition at Fort Myer, Virginia, in September 1908. Spectators saw Orville Wright carry passengers, and twice they saw him set the world record for endurance by staying in the air for over an hour. By that time, the Army had three certified pilots.

Lieutenant Lahm and Glenn Curtiss watch a flight by Orville Wright at Fort Myer, Virginia. Lahm was instrumental in establishing the US Army's aviation section of the Signal Corps. (Courtesy of the Library of Congress)

The Army found it much easier to incorporate airplanes since an aeronautical section with balloons had been part of the Army Signal Corps since the 1890s. Moreover, the Army was organized to suit the military occupational specialty of each soldier, divided into infantry, signal corps, artillery, and cavalry. The Navy, meanwhile, was and still is divided into bureaus such as the Bureau of Navigation (BuNav), Bureau of Ordnance (BurOrd), Bureau of Yards and Docks (BuY&D), etc. In addition, the Navy formed bureaus for supporting combat ships, with each subsection responsible for maintaining those vessels. Therefore, it would have been less difficult to establish the Marine Corps section of aeronautics, as the corps organization was, and still is, very much like the Army's. Yet, slowly, the Navy established an independent aeronautical department that would evolve into the Bureau of Aeronautics, but such a concept would be in the future.[1]

However, the Navy saw little practicality in establishing a Marine Corps land-based aviation section until 1918.

The Navy officially investigated the possibilities of aviation in September 1908 when Lieutenant George C. Sweet and Assistant Naval Constructor William McIntee, with the Bureau of Construction, were detailed to observe the Wright's plane during a demonstration at Fort Myer, Virginia, on November 3, 1909. The Army's Lieutenant Frank P. Lahm piloted the aircraft; Sweet accompanied him as a passenger and is credited as the first naval officer to fly in an airplane. Sweet would become one of his service's leading supporters of aviation.[2]

Sweet and McIntee wrote an enthusiastic report on the Wright Flyer to Rear Admiral William Cowles, commanding officer of the Bureau of Equipment

Seen here are doctors attending to either Orville Wright or Lieutenant Selfridge when the Wright Flyer crashed on September 17, 1908, killing Selfridge. Wright suffered severe injuries, including a fractured femur and broken ribs. (Courtesy of the Library of Congress)

(BuEquip), who, in turn, forwarded it to the Secretary of the Navy, Victor H. Metcalf. This report included specifications for an airplane that would be useful to the Navy in relaying messages, as a spotter, and a reconnaissance platform. However, the secretary took no action on Sweet's report. After the Army accepted the Wright Flyer, Cowles requested authority to purchase two airplanes for the Navy.[3] The Navy establishment declined to buy an aircraft, with the acting Secretary of the Navy stating, "The Department does not consider that the development of airplanes has progressed sufficiently to warrant their purchase at this time for use in the Navy."[4]

The Navy continued to pay little attention to "flying machines" until the Wright brothers began conducting additional public performances. Then, finally, a demonstration in New York on October 4, 1909, caught the attention of Captain Washington Irving Chambers and Commander William L. Sims. The Wright Flyer flew over the United States battleship *Louisiana* (BB-19) and passed over the *Minnesota* (BB-22). Commander Sims, the future commander of US Naval Forces in Europe during World War One, observed Wilbur's exhibition from the bridge of *Minnesota*.

Lieutenant Commander George C. Sweet, USN (Retired). A World War One period portrait photograph was taken after March 1915, when he retired. He was instrumental in establishing naval aviation. His awards included the Distinguished Service Cross, Spanish War Medal, Samoan Campaign Ribbon, Chevalier of the Legion of Honor, and Officer de L'Instruction, Republique of France. (Courtesy of the US Naval History and Heritage Command, NH 44185)

Meanwhile, Chambers did not think much of it at first and categorized it as a publicity stunt. Likewise, Commander Sims initially held a reserved opinion about the future of aircraft in warfare and told a reporter: "At the height, Mr. Wright was flying, the ship would probably be able to get the range and destroy the airplane. At a greater altitude and going at the speed Wright flew, the aviator's chance of dropping anything on a battleship would be small."[5]

Sims' pronouncement that the Wright flying machine was vulnerable to naval gunfire, and would have trouble with accuracy in an aerial bombing, became a widely accepted criticism of the military value of the airplane. The machine was seen as having no practical naval use. However, Sims would become an essential advocate in the years to come when the Navy's use of seaplanes became evident during the Tampico Affair in 1914. Meanwhile, the Allies and Central Powers used seaplanes for anti-submarine duty, aerial reconnaissance, and as bombers and fighters during World War One. However, that was in the future; before then, a typical statement was made by the new Secretary of the Navy, George von L. Meyer, who replaced Metcalf, in response to a newspaper reporter's question about the airplane in 1911: "That they will be used as fighting machines is very doubtful. It has been suggested that they could drop explosives on war vessels and forts. There are some barbarities, however, that are prohibited even in war. Besides, Germany has a gun that pumps lead into the air as thick as rain, and an aeroplane could be shot to pieces before it got near enough to do any damage."[6]

Hence, airplanes were useless to the navy brass in an era of dreadnaughts. Unfortunately, Secretary Meyer made a valid statement at the time as there was no practical use for aircraft in the Navy. Still, he and others failed to understand that advances in aeronautics in the coming years would prove the practicality of aircraft in peacetime and war.

Yet, in the case of the doubtful Washington Irving Chambers, his attitude quickly evolved, as did his standing within the service. He graduated from the Naval Academy in 1876, standing 27th out of a class of 41. Promotions in the fleet were slow, but he earned the dream of many line officers – to command a warship. When he saw the Wright airplane, he was 53 years

The Rise of Aviation

Above left: Lieutenant William McEntee, USN Naval Constructor, photographed circa 1902 by H. Pierre Smith. McEntee and Sweet were the first naval officers to investigate the feasibility of planes having a role in the Navy. (Courtesy of the US Naval History and Heritage Command, NH 47970)

Above right: This is a 1909 copyrighted portrait by the Moffett Studio of Chicago of Secretary of the Navy George von Meyer, who served from March 1909 to March 1913. He initially saw no positive military use of aircraft. (Courtesy of the US Naval History and Heritage Command, NH47838)

old with 33 years of service. Unknown to him, his days of commanding a warship would soon end, replaced by becoming the de facto commander of an insignificant naval aviation program.

In December 1909, he became the assistant to Captain Frank F. Fletcher, who, in turn, was the aide to the Bureau of Material under the Secretary of the Navy; some months later, in 1910, he found himself handling mail regarding aviation – a far drop from commanding a warship. An individual who found Wright's contraption "uninteresting" became a naval librarian immersed in finding everything he could read on aeronautics and absorbed information regarding the mechanical aspects of it. He found it quite exciting and became an ardent supporter

Captain Washington Irving Chambers, USN. In 1910, while in charge of aviation-related correspondence in the office of the Secretary of the Navy, he became convinced of the value of airplanes to the fleet and worked tirelessly to see them introduced. (Courtesy of the National Archives, 80-G-424786)

of eliciting pilots, funds, and planes for naval use while at a tournament at Belmont on October 22, 1910.

Besides Sweet and Chambers, supporters within the Navy saw the potential viability of aeronautics within the Navy but were hesitant to discuss it openly. Rear Admiral Richard Wainwright's views evolved when he voiced his opinion that the Navy "enter actively into the subject of securing satisfactory airplanes or kites for observation purposes at sea." Likewise, Admiral George Dewey recommended "that aeroplanes for use in naval warfare should be investigated without delay…"[7]

Captain Bradley A. Fiske concurred but spoke of expanding the use of airplanes as an integral part of the future Navy. Fiske was a veteran of the Battle of Manila during the Spanish–American War and a member of the war planning committee; he saw the planning for a potential war with Japan as inadequate for defending the Philippines. An individual who may have never seen an airplane suggested to the committee that the Navy establish four air stations with 100 planes each to protect the Philippine islands. Admiral Wainwright told Fiske to drop such a preposterous idea. However, the captain's

The Rise of Aviation

Above left: Admiral George Dewey was an early supporter of naval aviation and headed the Navy's General Board. He passed away on January 16, 1917, before the full potential of American naval aviation was realized. (Estate of Lieutenant C. J. Dutreaux; courtesy of the US Naval History and Heritage Command, WHI.2014.05)

Above right: In 1914, the Naval Aide for Operations, Rear Admiral Bradley Fiske, wrote that the Navy was not ready for war but would be unable to avoid it. In this, he was at odds with Secretary of the Navy Josephus Daniels, who, along with President Woodrow Wilson, wished to avoid involvement in the European War. He strongly urged the creation of a strong naval aviation force. (Painting, Oil on Canvas; by Orlando Lagman; 1965. Courtesy of the US Naval History and Heritage Command, 65-033-AA)

support of aviation never wavered. He also foresaw the concept of torpedo planes and would receive a patent for related mechanisms two years later.[8]

Chambers' and Fiske's interest coincided with that of Admiral Dewey, chief Navy board member, who recommended to the Bureau of Steam Engineering and Construction and Repair a scouting vessel with space for airplanes. Hutchinson Cone, the engineer in chief, used Dewey's recommendation to suggest the Secretary of the Navy purchase an aircraft for the USS *Chester*, along with instructions to show officers how to operate such a machine. In addition, Dewey suggested Cone and Chief Constructor

R. M. Watt appoint aides to Chambers. As a result, the Bureau of Engineering established Lieutenant H. N. Wright and the Bureau of Construction and Repair named William McEntee as aides for Chambers.[9]

A few days after the board's meeting, Beekman Winthrop, Assistant Secretary of the Navy and Acting Secretary during Meyer's absence, sent orders to Chambers and his aides to go to New York for an aviation tournament held at Belmont Park between October 22 and 31. The tournament provided Chambers with a review of the latest aeronautical technology. The French Blériot machines impressed him the most, as the Wright and Curtiss aircraft suffered from mechanical issues. Conceivably, the first US Navy plane could have been a Blériot.

Afterward, the captain sent a report to the General Board of the Navy, stating that planes would develop rapidly and had the potential to land, take off from ships, and become aerial scouts. Chambers then wrote the first original work on aviation, "Aviation and Aeroplanes," in the March 1911 issue of the *United States Naval Institute Proceedings*. The article detailed explicitly how the Navy could establish an aeronautical section, the need for the Naval Library to collect all literature about aeronautics, how the Navy

Hutchinson Cone, Chief of the Bureau of Steam, was instrumental in establishing naval aviation and voiced his opinion that aviation would become a requisite part of the Navy. He would remain a staunch supporter during World War One. (Courtesy of the US Naval History and Heritage Command)

could construct and train pilots of its own, and the merit in establishing an Office of Aeronautics. Many of his findings would become a reality in the years to come. However, he knew there were limits to what, at the time, airplanes could accomplish. The article and the official report to the board converted some skeptics. Still, many critics believed aviation would have no role within the service and that such a program would waste money and personnel. The Navy Board's only power was to advise the different bureaus. Still, capital to allocate for various projects fell to Congress and the Secretary of the Navy, a hurdle that would last until the onset of World War One. It must be remembered that the first generation of planes were primitive flying machines constructed of wood, bamboo, fabric, and steel wire, with a top speed of 40mph. They had no practical use outside of entertainment. Chambers understood when he wrote:

> Many writers on aviation are predicting all sorts of dire disasters to battleships from aerial warfare, with much of the same sort of enthusiasm and abandon as actuated the early prophets of torpedo warfare, but conservative writers believe that it is yet too early to forecast the full development of aerial warfare, although they admit that it will play an important part in future wars. It may be assumed, however, that the present state of development will limit the use of aeroplanes, in the navies of the immediate future, to reconnaissance or scouting duty.[10]

He saw planes as simple devices that could provide aerial scouting for the fleet, while others looked at the potential value of flying machines as attack platforms. Most understood aeronautics would advance beyond their understanding, but those in power could not see beyond the here and now. That is what proponents were fighting: an entrenched hierarchy of captains and admirals barely agreeing to allow or fund aviation. Even Chambers' views were somewhat simplistic. He believed an airplane was analogous to boats; therefore, construction would not be problematic for the Bureaus of Steam Engineering and Construction and Repair. Planes were simple machines that would be no more troublesome than building a small boat.

Beekman Winthrop, Assistant Secretary of the Navy and Acting Secretary of the Navy, during the absence of Meyer, ordered the Bureau of Engineering and Bureau of Construction and Repair to aid Captain Chambers in investigating the use of aviation for the Navy. (Courtesy of John H. Chafee, 1974; held by the US Naval History and Naval Heritage Command, NH 82510)

However, his drive continued by expanding the need for a future aerial scouting force and Chambers envisioned fields in which students learned to fly before the service procured its first machine. Glenn Curtiss explained to Chambers the method of training students but accomplished naval pilots took over training in 1914. One point of contention was the establishment of a quasi-independent department, as Chambers suggested: "One of the earliest steps recommended, is the establishment of an Office of Naval Aeronautics in the Department, and the detailing of a representative from each of the Bureaus of Construction and Repair, Steam Engineering, Navigation, and Ordnance to study the subject of aviation and to recommend the measures to be taken, from time to time, for its development in the Navy."

Those officers would constitute a council or board to meet at the Office of Naval Aeronautics, whenever required, to consider recommendations and consult the literature collected or to discuss the many questions involved: "A library of standard aeronautical works, current aeronautical literature, small models, plans and all available information on the subject should be systematically collected at this office and kept up to date under the directions of the senior officer detailed to preside and to attend to the correspondence."[11]

Some within the naval bureaucracy saw Chambers as an interloper attempting to establish a new bureau that would cut into naval appropriations from their fiefdoms. They believed Chambers was building like-minded individuals within the Navy and those of wealthy financiers and politicians. Meanwhile, Dewey and Fiske continued to advocate for the Navy to purchase planes by working endlessly to awaken interest in aviation by primarily concentrating on developing adequate machines as naval scouts. They knew such aircraft could increase intelligence and aid in more effective gunnery by producing greater accuracy from naval guns. Others were pragmatic, seeing airplanes as fragile and too slow to avoid defensive fire from ships, even by rifles. This era was the age of dreadnaughts, and such ships were viewed as the decisive weapon in naval warfare. As the primary spokesman, Chambers kept pushing to have an airplane land aboard a vessel to exhibit the versatility of such a machine and asked the Wright brothers to conduct such an event, but they flatly turned him down. Chambers needed somebody to prove the practicality of airplanes for naval use. Glenn Curtiss and Eugene Ely were two such individuals.[12]

It may have been another air event, at Halethorpe, Maryland – seeing Curtiss pilots dropping sacks filled with flour on a target – that expanded his views on how planes, in the future, could have a broader role in warfare. Chambers returned to Washington "deeply impressed with what he saw."[13] Curtiss was no mere mechanic. Instead, Chambers found him an interesting and intelligent individual who had, by trial and error, understood the fundamental physics and mechanical aspects of aviation; Curtiss, like the Wright brothers, was a self-made engineer. At the same time, he viewed the pilots as daredevils who did not understand the "why" of flying and how an airplane flies; few had formal flight training.[14]

Chambers saw Curtiss as the future of naval aviation. At the time, he had begun experiments to fit pontoons on planes, enabling them to land and depart from water; he was also in the early stages of creating a flying boat. Landing and taking off from water were crucial abilities for a seagoing scouting aircraft and critical for acceptance by the Navy and Congress, which would fund such an endeavor.

Chapter 2

Glenn Curtiss and Eugene Ely

Glenn Curtiss was 25 years old when the Wrights conducted their first successful flight in 1903. By 1907, Curtiss, like the Wrights, was a self-made engineer, and owned a bicycle shop. He progressed from selling and repairing bicycles when he fitted a motor on a bike to climb the hills around Hammondsport, New York, which proved successful. Others wanted to purchase such a mode of transportation, and Curtiss found himself selling motorized bicycles in what became known as motorcycles. With his dark hair receding and sporting a mustache common to most men at that time, he built a motorized bike and rode it, reaching an astonishing 137mph during a race in Florida. He then found himself, in 1907, selling modified motors to the wealthy blimp and dirigible owners. Alexander Graham Bell, Curtiss, Lieutenant Selfridge, and two Canadian engineers later established the Aerial Experiment Association to design planes at Curtiss' hometown of Hammondsport, New York.

Selfridge created the first such plane, and one of the Canadian engineers, F. W. Baldwin, flew it 300ft before crashing. In May 1908, Curtiss took Selfridge's design, rebuilt the plane, and flew it some 1,000ft. He then designed and flew his first airplane, *June Bug*, earning him a prize from *Scientific American* in 1908. With limited experience in flying and design, he set up his own company offering planes for sale, with flight training included. Afterward, Curtiss began an unsuccessful experiment by mounting pontoons on *June Bug*. On May 29, 1909, he won $10,000 by flying from Albany to New York City, a trip of 137 miles in 152 minutes, with two stops along the way to refuel.

Glenn Curtiss and Eugene Ely

In an undated photograph from the Bain News Service, aviation pioneer Glenn Curtiss is seen here at the pilot's control wheel of a pusher plane. Note the radiator and engine behind him, which was a standard configuration at the time. (Courtesy of the Library of Congress)

Afterward, a significant problem arose in aviation as the Wrights, by 1910, looked upon other aircraft designers as cheats who swindled them out of paying license fees for not building Wright-licensed planes. The licensing issue would lead to lawsuits on patent infringement owned by the brothers against such individuals as Curtiss. Ultimately, the Wrights would win and create a schism between early naval aviators.

Captain Chambers met Curtiss when the inventor was 32 in 1910, only two years after the latter flew for the first time. The man from Hammondsport was reserved, quiet, and somewhat lacking in interpersonal skills unless he spoke to like-minded aerial enthusiasts. Nevertheless, the captain asked the inventor whether he could design the machine to take off and land on water. Curtiss attempted this the year before and acknowledged the possibility, leaving Chambers believing Glenn was the right individual for such a program. If anything, the aircraft inventor was a businessman and understood the potential for tremendous profits from training and selling planes to the Navy. Chambers additionally found one of Curtiss' aviators, Eugene Ely, the most personable flyer he had met; he was knowledgeable in the field, with a keen interest in every aspect of aviation, including the mechanical.

Interestingly, Chambers found the Wright planes better constructed by using semi-scientific methods. However, all the designers he spoke to used trial-and-error methods: if it did not work the first time, then they would try another design. Based upon speaking to every designer that day, and the perceived reservations from the Wrights, he felt Curtiss would soon succeed in building a hydroaeroplane (hydroplane). Curtiss agreed to create such a machine and enlisted the company's representative, 24-year-old Eugene Ely, a former race car driver turned aviator, to take the chance. Curtiss hoped that a successful exhibition might sway the Navy into allocating money for his aircraft and saw a tremendous business opportunity to fund the purchasing of his planes.

Chambers met the flyer and his wife, Mable, at their hotel in Baltimore after a rainstorm, along with heavy wind gusts, had halted an air tournament. They met Chambers and began conversing on aviation when he told the flyer he had asked Wilbur Wright if it was possible for a plane and pilot to take off from a ship and if he would be interested. Wilbur had turned him

Glenn Curtiss won the Scientific American Trophy with his plane named *June Bug*, at his hometown of Hammondsport, New York on July 4, 1908. He only began flying an airplane a year earlier. The first American naval aviator would later be trained on *June Bug*. (Courtesy of the Library of Congress)

down. Chambers was stunned, as Orville, in 1908, had suggested the idea. Ely asked for the job. "I've wanted to do that for a long time," Ely quickly told him. Chambers wanted Curtiss' approval, but Ely said no, as he signed contracts individually. Curtiss saw this as too dangerous, not wanting his company to be tarnished by the aviator's death, should it happen.[1]

Chambers returned to Washington after speaking with Curtiss and Ely, where Wainwright and Fletcher turned down what they considered dangerous stunts, telling them the Navy would not fund such an endeavor. Captain Chambers then sent Ely to discuss it with Secretary Meyer, who coldly rejected the idea as pure nonsense. So, it became time to illicit funding from private sources. One such individual was John Barry Ryan, a multimillionaire publisher interested in aviation, especially for the military. Ryan offered $1,000 to the first person to fly an airplane from a ship to the shore; he expected Chambers to have Ely do it. Meyer rejected Ryan's offer. However, Ryan was politically connected, and the secretary began feeling pressure; he relented by offering a warship for the experiment but

Eugene Ely in flying gear, standing by his Curtiss pusher biplane, circa 1911. Note the rubber inner tubes worn as a life preserver in case of a forced water landing. (Eugene B. Ely scrapbooks; courtesy of the US Naval History and Heritage Command, NH 77599)

would not provide any funding. Meyer left the decision on which ship to use to his acting Secretary Winthrop, who quickly signed orders to send the cruiser *Birmingham* (CL-2) to the Norfolk Navy yard to have a ramp built on the ship, which Constructor McEntee had designed. The 83ft ramp was built on the ship's forecastle, sloping down 5°, with the forward edge 37ft above the water line.[2]

Ely would depart from this makeshift ramp in a plane recently constructed and never tested; he had no clue whether it would fly. Yet, the young aviator knew success was the only option, or the secretary would never give him a second chance. Naval aviation's birth and future relied on this one test. Reporters gathered inside the Monticello Hotel to ask the flyer if he would succeed. He answered, "Everything is ready, if the weather is favorable. I expect to make the flight tomorrow without difficulty." Ely felt the pressure: he was about to take a flight in an untested airplane and land on a ship, but his wife had faith in him.[3]

After Ely and his mechanic had the biplane raised onto *Birmingham*'s ramp, the ship headed out from Norfolk into Hampton Roads. Heavy rain

The first aircraft take-off from a warship occurred on November 14, 1910. Sailors and civilians crowd around Eugene Ely's Curtiss pusher airplane as a floating crane places it on board USS *Birmingham* (Scout Cruiser #2). Photographed at the Norfolk Navy Yard, Virginia, shortly before the flight. (Eugene B. Ely scrapbooks; courtesy of the US Naval History and Heritage Command, NH 77562)

squalls and hail initially delayed an attempt at a flight until mid-afternoon on November 14, 1910. Ely may have been apprehensive about the weather as he did not know how to swim; his lifesaver was an inner tube. Intermittent rain squalls continued until the sky cleared momentarily. Ely rolled down the ramp, dropping out of sight over the bow; the propellers hit the water briefly, splintering the edges of them, but he kept the plane in the air.

"The front push rod," Ely explained, "was a little longer than the one I am used to, and I didn't handle it quite right…[and] the fact that the ship was not underway was a great disadvantage to me."[4]

Gradually it gained altitude as Ely headed toward the nearest land he could see through the rain squalls: Willoughby Spit. He had planned to fly to the naval station at Norfolk, but water spots on his goggles and low visibility caused him to lose his sense of direction, forcing him to seek out the nearest land.[5]

Eugene Ely's Curtiss pusher airplane rests on the flying-off platform built over the foredeck of USS *Birmingham*. The photograph was taken at the Norfolk Navy Yard, Virginia, shortly before the flight. The floating crane that had lifted the airplane onto the ship is visible at the extreme left. (Eugene B. Ely scrapbooks; courtesy of US Naval History and Heritage Command, NH 77551)

He landed on a beach, not at the navy yard as expected, smashing the propeller upon landing. Ely thought the flight was a failure and continued to think so as a boat carrying Chambers and Captain William B. Fletcher, commanding officer of *Birmingham,* arrived. He still thought he had failed, even when both men congratulated him. His apprehension finally subsided when a party was held that evening in his honor. The following day papers in the United States and abroad flashed headlines on his accomplishment. Speculation from around the world pondered whether the US Navy would begin building ships with ramps for airplanes. Naval experts were more conservative as such ramps would make a ship's guns inoperable, and the range of such aircraft would be of no use for scouting. Nevertheless, his successful flight, five minutes and three miles long, impressed those attending, comprising Navy dignitaries and a few young naval officers interested in learning how to fly such a contraption.

Not long after Ely departed *Birmingham,* he set about another groundbreaking flight. Chambers sent a letter to the aviator asking him

Eugene Ely's aircraft on the USS *Birmingham* in Hampton Roads, Virginia, on November 14, 1910. (Eugene B. Ely scrapbook collection, S-005; courtesy of the US Naval History and Heritage Command, NH 77545)

if he could land aboard a warship. Ely, without hesitation, accepted the challenge. Secretary Meyer now saw the Navy's opportunity in aviation and appeared with instructions not to spend more than $500 to build another ramp on an undetermined warship; actually, the money for *Birmingham's* ramp came from John Ryan. Secretary Meyer's tacit approval for the test allowed Rear Admiral Edward Barry, commander of the Pacific Fleet, to loan out the cruiser *Pennsylvania* (ACA-4). This warship was 100ft longer than *Birmingham* and had four times the tonnage.

Chambers arranged to have a rudimentary platform 30ft wide and 120ft long constructed on the ship's stern. Ely and others on the scene gradually worked out a mechanical means for stopping the airplane before it overran the length of the landing platform; thus, the first arresting system was born by rigging the lines raised several inches off the deck at 3ft intervals across the ramp. Three hooks were mounted on the landing carriage of Ely's plane to the ship's lines to stop the forward momentum of the aircraft.

Eugene Ely flies his Curtiss pusher airplane from USS *Birmingham* (Scout Cruiser #2), in Hampton Roads, Virginia, during the afternoon of November 14, 1910. USS *Roe* (Destroyer #24), serving as plane guard, is visible in the background. (Eugene B. Ely scrapbook collection, S-005; courtesy of the US Naval History and Heritage Command, NH 77545)

Each line across the platform was weighted with 50lb sandbags to ensure the lines would halt the aircraft's forward momentum. Following this first take-off from a warship, Ely scored another aviation first when he landed on a slightly inclined platform on the stern of the cruiser *Pennsylvania* on January 18, 1911.[6]

Curtiss was asked by reporters for his opinion the night before Ely attempted to land aboard the warship: "This is the first time an aviator has attempted to land on board a battleship. Ely will alight on the *Pennsylvania*. I'm willing to guarantee that much. The only question is can he do it without damaging his machine?"

Once again, Curtiss was apprehensive regarding the event. His prestige, company, and the future of naval aeronautics were at stake. He urged the young pilot not to try it. Yet, flying was in Ely's blood.

Eugene Ely with Captain Charles F. Pond, USN, Commanding Officer of USS *Pennsylvania*, shortly after landing his airplane on board the ship, in San Francisco Bay, California, January 18, 1911. Ely's wife, Mabel, is standing on the left. (Eugene B. Ely scrapbooks; courtesy of the US Naval History and Heritage Command, NH 77528)

His wife and Curtiss knew it. Each flight could be his last, and he recognized it.

It was a cool day with a 3kt breeze; Captain Charles "Frog" Pond, commander of the ship, placed crews in lifeboats and swimmers out at the ship's tail to rescue the flyer if the plane plunged into the water. Hundreds of people aboard tugboats and ferries surrounded the ship to watch history in the making.

Twelve miles from the vessel at Tanforan, located in San Bruno, California, mechanics made the plane ready. At 10.48am, Ely lifted his 1,000lb Curtiss pusher from a temporary airfield near San Francisco Bay at 10.45am. In his own words:

> As I came out over the bay above Hunters Point, I was about 1200 feet up. It was cloudy, smoky, and hazy. I could not see the ships at first and did not locate them until I was within about two miles of them.
>
> I was spinning along at about 60 miles an hour with the winds directly behind me, and when I sighted the *Pennsylvania*, I saw that the stern was pointed into the wind, and when about a mile away I veered off to pass over what I supposed was the flagship *California*. As I neared her, I dropped down from 1,000 to about 400 feet in salute to the admiral. This ship, however, proved to be the *Maryland*, as the *California* was not in the bay, and I swung around the *West Virginia*, coming down to about 100 feet above the water, and pointed my machine for the *Pennsylvania*. I then made a sharp turn about 100 yards astern of that ship, gradually dropping down. But there was an appreciable wind blowing diagonally across the deck of the cruiser and I had to calculate the force of this wind and the effect it would have on my approach to the landing.
>
> I found that it was not possible to strike squarely toward the center of the landing, so I pointed the aeroplane straight toward the landing, but on a line with the windward side of the ship. I had to take the chance that I had correctly estimated just how many feet the wind would blow me out of my course.
>
> Just as I came over the overhang at the stern, I felt a sudden lift to the machine, as I shut down the motor, caused by the breaking of the wind

around the stern. This lift carried me a trifle further than I intended going before coming in actual contact with the platform.

The arresting gear caught the plane and stopped it as designed at 11.01am. Ely's landing and using a primitive arresting gear system were revolutionary. Captain Pond quickly became a proponent as he watched as the aircraft neared the vessel and landed. Ely recalled:

> When about 75 yards astern… [the plane] straightened up and came on board at a speed of about 40 miles an hour, landing plumb on the center line, missing the first 11 lines attached to the sand bags-but catching the next 11, and stopping within 30 feet with 50 feet to spare, nothing damaged in the least, not a bolt or brace started, and Ely the coolest man on board. Hardly two minutes had elapsed from the time the aeroplane was first sighted, and no one had imagined he would make the landing on the first turn. The sandbags worked perfectly, stopping the machine, with the aviator, about 1,000 lbs., with a speed of 40 miles an hour, within 30 feet, and, as Ely stated, with no perceptible jar. Six pairs of bags did the work, being hauled in over the guide rails dose to the machine, the other five pairs being only slightly disturbed. The bags were caught, four on the first set of hooks, three on the second, and four on the third set. As the aeroplane came on board, the upward draft from the wind striking the starboard quarter of the ship lifted it bodily and gave it a slight list to port…Three feet more of elevation would have forced him to plunge directly into the canvas screen, and three to ten feet less elevation would have caused him to strike the fantail with consequences which can only be surmised.[7]

He landed a plane aboard a ship for the first time in history. Cheering sailors and officers ran to the plane. Among the crowd, his wife threw herself in Eugene's waiting arms, shouting at him, "Oh boy! I knew you could do it." Pond pumped Eugene's hand before guiding his guests to the captain's cabin for lunch. At the hatch leading to the room, the captain issued an order to the officer of the day that has become unforgettable to

In his Curtiss pusher biplane, Ely is ready to take off from *Pennsylvania* for his return to land on January 18, 1911. The ship was then at anchor in San Francisco Bay, California. (Eugene B. Ely scrapbooks; courtesy of the US Naval History and Heritage Command, NH 77525)

those serving aboard aircraft carriers: "Mr Luckel, let me know when the plane is respotted and ready for take-off." Thus, the term "Respot the deck" was born.[8] None of those who witnessed the event could have foreseen the birth and rise of aircraft carriers. However, eight years later, the British converted an ocean liner into the carrier HMS *Argus*, the first aircraft carrier. Two years after *Argus*' commissioning, the US Navy converted the collier *Jupiter* into the carrier *Langley*.

On *Pennsylvania*, at 11.58am, Ely lifted his plane off the ship's deck and returned safely to San Francisco. Upon viewing Ely's flight, Captain Pond was convinced of aviation's value in modern warfare: "I desire to place myself on record as positively assured of the importance of the aeroplane in future naval warfare."[9] Afterward, Chambers told Ely he was needed for future testing and told the young aviator to halt exhibition flying. The request went unheeded, and Ely, who desired to become a member of the Navy and thus become the first naval aviator, died in a plane crash in Macon, Georgia, on October 19, 1911; he was 25 years old. The Navy posthumously awarded him the Distinguished Flying Cross as a civilian awardee.

Curtiss' willingness to provide an aircraft for experimental work and Ely's successful flights showing that a plane could take off and land aboard a ship, led to additional acceptance and support of naval aviation by a growing number of naval officers. Chiefs of different bureaus between 1910 and 1911, such as Hutchinson Cone, Chief of the Bureau of Steam Engineering, made similar requests. Cone foresaw aircraft as a valuable tool in scouting ahead of the fleet. His letter caught the attention of Secretary of the Navy

Eugene Ely flies his Curtiss pusher biplane off the aircraft platform on USS *Pennsylvania* to return to Tanforan Field, San Francisco, California, on January 18, 1911. (Eugene B. Ely scrapbooks; courtesy of the US Naval History and Heritage Command, NH 77517)

Meyer, who passed it along to his aides. They, in turn, saw minimal benefit in pursuing aircraft purchases at that time but passed Cone's letter to the Navy's General Board for consideration.

There, it received support from Admiral George Dewey, a proponent of aviation and the Navy Board's president. He wrote: "The General Board believes that the value of aeroplanes for use in naval warfare should be investigated without delay and recommends that the [Navy] Department approve the request of the Engineer-in-Chief [Cone]."[10]

Beekman Winthrop, Acting Secretary of the Navy, ordered the Bureau of Engineering and Bureau of Construction and Repair to assign officers to coordinate efforts with Captain Chambers. The latter handled all aviation-related correspondence, placing him as the unofficial naval aviation chief. Putting Chambers in that position became necessary in

Eugene Ely's Curtiss pusher biplane leaves the aircraft platform on USS *Pennsylvania* on the return flight to Tanforan Field, San Francisco, California, January 18, 1911. Ely had landed on the ship earlier in the day. Note the boats in the foreground, with several photographers working from them. (Eugene B. Ely scrapbooks; courtesy of the US Naval History and Heritage Command, NH 77520)

assigning the first naval officers for flight instruction. Although Chambers, Curtiss, and Ely showed that an airplane could feasibly operate from a warship, did such flights convince Secretary Meyer? Aeronautics caught the attention of the secretary, who applauded Ely's flights in the Navy's annual report and a letter to the aviator:

> This experiment and the advances which have been made in aviation seem to demonstrate that… [aviation] is destined to perform some part in the naval warfare of the future.[11]
>
> You are the first aviator in the world to have accomplished this feat, and I congratulate you…The fact that you made this flight under adverse conditions of weather, with a comparatively old aeroplane, and while the ship was not underway, increases the information sought and the satisfaction of the Department with your efforts.[12]

Ely had scoffed at the letter; Meyer had every intention to crush the idea of naval aeronautics, and Ely knew it. By the spring of 1911, Chambers

Eugene Ely's plane has successfully departed from the *Pennsylvania* and is heading toward Tanforan Field on January 18, 1911. His flying stunts would convince a few within the Navy of the naval potential of aircraft. (Courtesy of the Naval History and Heritage Command, UA 450.07)

was considered a leading expert in the military use of aviation, but he vocally expressed that airplanes would become scouting tools for the fleet and nothing more; using airplanes as offensive weapons of war seemed impossible. His view countered that of future naval aviators who foresaw airplanes as more than scouts and possibly as offensive weapons of war.

> It has been demonstrated that an aeroplane can leave a ship and return to it in flight; that aeroplanes may be stowed on board ship in suitably dimensioned crates or boxes and readily assembled for use in less than an hour; that it is possible to hoist a hydro-aeroplane out like a ship's boat after the plane pulled alongside the vessel, have it raised from the water and then placed back into the water where it would fly to shore. The water in this case need not be altogether smooth… observations can be made and photographs taken from great altitudes… reconnaissance can be made over land or sea… and… flights may now be made in high winds and during rainy weather.[13]

He did not, or could not, envision that airplanes would become a significant component of naval warfare. He, like Sims, saw that aircraft had limitations. Planes at the time, such as the Wright Flyer III, were made of bamboo, wood, fabric, and wire, with a top speed of 35mph – hardly a dangerous platform, and such aircraft could not carry a bomb load or defensive weapons. When the Bureau of Construction and Repair proposed using planes to bomb ships, Chambers stepped in and crushed the idea. He told his boss, the Chief of the Bureau of Navigation, Rear Admiral Reginald Nicholson, "To utilize the few aeroplanes now owned by the Navy in bomb-dropping experiments… would, in my opinion, be a waste of valuable time."[14] As mentioned, it is interesting to note that Chambers witnessed a bomb-dropping exercise at Halethorpe, Maryland, by a Curtiss aviator and may have realized the significance but knew aviation was too primitive at the time for such operations. Still, Ely's taking off and landing aboard warships brought further interest in the practical application of aviation for the Navy. Yet, many saw the impracticality of ship-based planes, believing they would interfere with gunnery.

Eugene Ely's showmanship with the *Birmingham* and *Pennsylvania* provided Chambers with proof of the applicability of aviation for the Navy. The number of supporters grew, and it appeared Secretary Meyer was also on board. Functionality became a problem as Curtiss' planes were elemental land planes with skids or landing gear. He needed functional planes for the Navy, ones that could take off and land on water and be retrieved by a ship's hoist – a hydroplane. By late January 1911, Curtiss had solved problems in designing such an aircraft and proved it by landing a hydroplane next to the *Pennsylvania*, hoisting aboard, and then lowering it back into the water. This showmanship showed that a seaplane could maneuver close to a naval vessel and be hauled aboard and unloaded into the water, thus allowing warships to operate such aircraft for long-range scouting.

The Navy assigned Chambers to the Bureau of Navigation, but the department said there was no room for him. He then went to the former

Aviator Eugene Ely receives an award at Tanforan Field shortly after his flights to and from USS *Pennsylvania* on January 18, 1911. The noted opera star Luisa Tetrazzini is presenting the award, as several Army officers and a Navy officer serve as an honor guard. The aviator's wife, Mabel (Hall) Ely, stands to the left. Captain Charles Pond, CO of *Pennsylvania*, is directly behind the flagstaff, wearing civilian clothes. (Eugene B. Ely scrapbooks; courtesy of the US Naval History and Heritage Command, NH 77526)

State, War, and Navy building and, an ingenious individual with over 30 years in the Navy, found a room in the basement. Room 67 became the unofficial Office of Aeronautics. For the next three years, he continued to suggest the establishment of an "Office for Aeronautics," which the Secretary of the Navy rejected; however, Chambers became a member of the General Board as the service's expert on aviation. Infighting among the different naval bureaus began as planes proved their viability to be part of the service. Each wanted ownership of naval aviation, and bureau chiefs became alarmed that Chambers was trying to establish an aviation office. They all wanted aviation as part of their bureaus and the appropriations that went with it. The champion of naval aviation began making as many enemies as supporters.

Nevertheless, he kept pushing for funding and establishing a naval aviation component, and the willingness of officers to volunteer for aviation training grew. However, budgeting proved troublesome for years, although finding brave souls to operate airplanes proved easier. Chambers characterized such an individual as "young, technically inclined, energetic, preferably with athletic ability, enthusiastic, and mature." Thus, the future of naval aviation fell to a naval officer that displayed all those characteristics, a 25-year-old named Theodore Gordan Ellyson, Annapolis class of 1905.[15]

Chapter 3

The Birth of Naval Aviation

R ed-headed Theodore "Spuds" Ellyson was the third son of Henry and Lizzie Ellyson of Richmond, Virginia, born into an upper-middle-class family on February 27, 1885. Henry Theodore Ellyson was quiet and reserved and served as the treasurer of the *Richmond Dispatch*, the family newspaper. Also red-headed, Lizzie was vocal, energetic, overbearing, and in charge of most family decisions. She would become very protective of her youngest son and attempted, unsuccessfully, to keep her son out of the Navy. Still, Theodore grew into an independent teenager enamored with reading about the US Navy's victories at Manila and Santiago during the Spanish–American War.

Lieutenant Theodore G. Ellyson became the first naval aviator in 1911. The aviation pioneer's nickname "Spuds" came from his appetite for potatoes. (Courtesy of the US Naval History and Heritage Command, Catalog, NH 49634)

He graduated from the Naval Academy in 1905, and by 1910, Ellyson had served aboard cruisers and submarines and seemed to have no serious thought of becoming an aviator. Then, his friend and fellow naval officer, Kenneth Whiting, who would become Naval Aviator No. 16, asked him if he knew anything about flying. Ellyson did not but became interested in the idea due to his growing impatience waiting for his next command. He felt no obligation to stay at the Newport News Shipyard waiting for the submarine USS *Seal* (SS-183) to be built and commissioned. Therefore, on December 10, 1910, Ellyson sent a written request for flying duty. He wrote:

> From: Lieutenant T. G. Ellyson
> To: The Secretary of the Navy
> Subject: Request duty in connection with aeroplanes.
> I request that I be assigned duty in connection with aeroplanes as soon as such duty becomes available.
> T. G. Ellyson[1]

However, individuals like Ellyson and Whiting found little support from the naval establishment as several naval officers, including Ken Whiting, had previously sent letters requesting flight training. By chance, Ellyson's letter reached Chambers' desk at the most reasonable time, as a month earlier, in November, he had received a letter from aviation pioneer Glenn Curtiss offering a deal to train an officer free of charge. He understood the Navy was not inclined to involve itself in aviation but, as an astute businessman, he knew the word "free" would coax the service's interest. He wrote: "As I am fully aware that the Navy Department has no funds for aviation purposes, I am making this offer with the understanding that it involves no expense to the Navy Department other than the cost of detailing an officer to the aviation grounds in southern California."[2]

Curtiss elaborated on November 29 in a letter to Secretary of the Navy Meyer, two weeks before Ellyson sent his correspondence to Chambers about the viability of the future of aeronautics based on his experimentation and the successful flights attained by his pilots. Curtiss wrote: "…justify me in venturing to prophecy that the military branches of the government, in the very near future will find an aeroplane equipment absolutely essential."[3]

What drove Ellyson into such a vocation remains a mystery; maybe Ken Whiting sold him on the idea, providing a temporary reprieve from the boredom of waiting for the *Seal*'s commissioning. On the other hand, he knew nothing about aviation outside of what Whiting told him. He, therefore, spent his time reading and absorbing what he could on aeronautics while aboard a train heading across the country toward Curtiss and destiny. Navy Secretary Meyer was tired of replying to letters from young officers like Ellyson who wanted to become flyers. Therefore, he told Captain Chambers to respond to Ellyson and others who wanted to fly. Eager officers requesting aviation training were duly noted, but nothing more came of it until Ellyson's letter, dated December 10, 1910, was placed on top of the stack. Thus, two days before Christmas 1911, Chambers

Lieutenant Ellyson seated in a Curtiss pusher airplane, possibly the A-1, circa 1911 before the plane's tricycle landing gear was removed and floats attached. (Courtesy of the National Archives, 80-G-186886)

selected him as the first naval aviator, ordering him to report for duty with the Curtiss Company winter headquarters at North Island, California, in San Diego Bay. Why was Ellyson selected? Chambers told him, "You were selected because you were not considered a crank but a well-balanced man who would be able to assist in building up a system of aviation training in the Navy."[4]

The first naval aviator trainee immersed himself in every aspect of aeronautics, with Glenn Curtiss guiding him along the design and mechanics of aeronautics, since students had to be able to maintain, repair, and rebuild an aircraft before soloing. While teaching Ellyson the intricacies of aeronautics, Ellyson was a spectator of Eugene Ely's successful landing aboard the *Pennsylvania*. It is interesting that Ellyson viewed Ely's landing aboard a warship as merely an exhibition and saw no practical application at the time.

A week after Ely's display, Curtiss and Ellyson perfected a float attachment, thus developing the floatplane (then termed a hydroaeroplane), which he successfully tested on January 26, 1911, lifting off the water near San Diego and landing safely alongside the ship. Crew members aboard the ship

Glenn Curtiss took off from Glorietta Bay, North Island, California, in the first seaplane flight on January 26, 1911. His flight was successful and all three of the first planes purchased by the Navy had pontoons attached to them. (Courtesy of the Naval History and Heritage Command, NH 113530)

hoisted the aircraft onto the vessel and inspected it for any damage before hoisting it out again, and Curtiss flew back to North Island. Ellyson saw waterborne aircraft fitted with pontoons as the future of naval aviation. Flight instruction for early aviators was largely informal but followed the Aero Club of America (ACA), a chapter of the FAI. However, the Navy would not develop a more formal training syllabus until 1916. Therefore, to become a certified pilot, Ellyson had to qualify according to the American Aero Club, following the FAI standards.

> Applicants must have passed the three following tests:
> Two distance tests, each consisting of covering, without touching the ground, a closed circuit of not less than five kilometers in length.
> An altitude test consisting in rising to a minimum height of 50 meters above the starting point.
> The (B) test may be made simultaneously with one of the (A) tests.

Glenn Curtiss landed in the hydroplane beside USS *Pennsylvania* in 1911, demonstrating the feasibility of a plane and pilot landing safely beside a warship. Curtiss is lowered back onto the plane. (Courtesy of the US Naval History and Heritage Command, UA 41.01.07)

The course over which the aviator shall accomplish the afore said circuits must be indicated by two posts situated not more than 500 meters from each other.

After each turn around a post, the aviator will change his direction to leave the other post on his other side. The circuit will thus consist of an uninterrupted series of figure eights, each circle of the figures alternately encircling one of the posts. The distance credited over the course covered between the two turns shall be the distance separating the two posts.

For each of the three tests, the landing shall be made:

Stop the motor no later than when the machine touches the ground. At a distance of fewer than 50 meters from a point designated by the applicant before the test.[5]

On the first day of Ellyson's actual flight training, Ellyson made four runs over the ground at about 20mph. This exercise included nothing but taxiing along the airfield four times. The following day, he made five runs, and on the third day, he made six runs. The purpose of the runs was to accustom the student to the aircraft and the use of its rudder. Ellyson pointed out two factors limiting the number of runs: wind, and the number of individuals training on any particular day. Nevertheless, Ellyson continued with his ground runs, gradually increasing speed to cause the aircraft to become light without flying and draw the student's attention to all the controls.

On his seventh training day, Ellyson rose from the ground in short hops of 10 to 15ft. These hops were long enough to require coordinated use of the ailerons and throttle to bring the aircraft back to earth. Before the end of February, he had soloed. By March 5, he was making flights of a mile-and-a-half at an altitude of 15ft. On 31 March, Ellyson wrote the Navy Department stating, "… in my opinion and in that of Mr. Curtiss, I have qualified in practical aviation."[6]

On the last day of March 1911, he sent a report to the Secretary of the Navy stating, "I have qualified to fly a standard eight-cylinder Curtiss biplane [named "Lizzie"] under favorable conditions, but more practice

Above: Curtiss flyers – Army, Navy, and civilian – next to the Curtiss A-1, 1911. Lieutenant Theodore Ellyson is second from right. This photograph was probably taken during the summer at Hammondsport, New York. (Courtesy of the US Naval History and Heritage, Command, UA 41.01.13)

Left: Painting of Rear Admiral Richard Wainwright, USN, Aide for Naval Operations, who was one powerful individual that opposed funding for naval aviation. (Orlando Lagman, 1965; courtesy of the US Naval History and Heritage Command, NH 42784-KN)

must be had before I will be capable of flying in strong winds, making accents in limited space, or landing on a designated spot. I have no practice in flying the hydro aeroplane."[7]

He qualified for the ACA seaplane certification on July 6, 1911, flying the Curtiss model A-1, which would become the Navy's first aircraft; subsequently, he officially became Naval Aviator No. 1 on March 4, 1913. The early flights observed by naval officials between 1909 and 1910 were not enough to convince Congress or the Navy, as aviation had not progressed far enough to request money in the Navy's budget allocation for what seemed like an experimental endeavor, but that changed in 1911 before Ellyson's solo. Two days before Ely landed aboard the *Pennsylvania*, Secretary Meyer requested $25,000 before the House Committee on Naval Affairs to fund aeronautics. He testified before the committee that funding "would be of incalculable value."[8]

Congress listened and appropriated the money requested. Now Chambers envisioned an independent aeronautical section and continued asking the Secretary to establish an Office of Aeronautics. He hoped such an office, headed by a senior officer, would be found; however, several bureaus were jockeying for position to take over the fledgling idea of naval aviation.

The Curtiss flying boat A-2 was one of three purchased by the Navy in 1911. The others were the Curtiss A-1 and the Wright B-1. All three experienced major mechanical problems. (Courtesy of the Naval History and Heritage Command, UA 41.01.29)

An additional section under one or more bureaus' jurisdiction meant more power and appropriations. Chambers concluded that aviation would fall into the following categories if not afforded to become an independent entity. The Bureau of Construction and Repair would undertake experimentation and development of aircraft fuselages and pontoons; the repair of aircraft engines would be carried out by the Bureau of Steam Engineering; pilot training would fall under the Bureau of Navigation, and aircraft weapons under the Bureau of Ordnance. Chambers soon found out his hunch regarding solid opposition to an autonomous aviation bureau was true. The Bureaus of Construction and Repair and Steam Engineering were vehemently opposed, as was Rear Admiral Richard Wainwright, Aide for Naval Operations. Chambers' vision of an independent aviation section would not come to fruition until the Navy established the Bureau of Aeronautics (BuAer) in 1921.[9]

Two weeks before Ellyson's solo flight, on March 13, 1911, Secretary Meyer sent Chambers a directive outlining the establishment of an unofficial aviation department:

> You are hereby directed to keep informed of the progress of aeronautics, especially in this country, and of the development of aircraft generally, with a view to advising the department concerning the adaptability of such material for naval warfare, especially for purposes of naval scouting and the steps required, from time to time, to gradually provide the Navy with suitable equipment for aerial navigation and to instruct the Navy personnel in its use.
>
> You will consult with the librarian of the Navy Department concerning the collection of standard works and periodical literature on the subject, and will recommend the purchase of such literature as may be necessary to keep fully informed on the subject of aeronautics.
>
> You will also consult the bureaus of the department having cognizance of the various branches of the work, calling together for discussion, whenever necessary, the officers designated by the chiefs of these bureaus to represent them and will prepare for action by the department such

letters or correspondence as may be approved by the bureaus concerned. The enforcement of the recommendations thus made, when approved by the department, will rest entirely with the bureaus having cognizance of the details.[10]

Meyer's memorandum allowed Chambers, on May 8, 1911, to write requisitions to purchase two Curtiss aircraft and one Wright biplane. This date marks the official birth of US Naval Aviation. He released the specifications for the dual purpose: "The aircraft would be equipped for arising from or alighting on land or water, with a metal-tipped propellor designed for at least 45 miles per hour, with provisions for carrying a passenger alongside the pilot, and controls that either the pilot or passenger could operate."[11]

The Navy purchased a landplane from the Wrights, designated the B-1, and two Curtiss model As. The Curtiss plane would later become dual-use with the Curtiss model E-1 (designated A-1).

> The pilot sat in the open, the motor behind, and had a top speed of approximately 45 miles per hour. Curtiss and Ellyson had worked on the A-1 at San Diego; by February 1911, the aircraft had proven to be aerodynamically stable in favorable weather conditions. The aviation pioneer, speaking to journalists, said, "for a long time I have believed that I ought to make the aeroplane a particle machine for the use of the navy, and for that purpose it must be able to fly from the water and land on the water."[12]

Some six months later, on September 6, 1911, several bulky crates arrived at the United States Naval Academy from Dayton, Ohio. At Dahlgren Hall, a small working party went to work uncrating and laying out the packaged materials consisting of a few bicycle-type wheels, a gasoline motor, wooden propellers, fabric-covered wings, struts, and braces. When assembled, the pieces were that of the Wright B-1 and represented one of the three planes ordered for the Navy, the A-1, A-2, and B-1. Unfortunately, the first planes delivered were all pusher planes, with the engine and radiator behind the pilot. This design would prove deadly for some future naval aviators.

Ellyson was somewhat skeptical about the A-1 but acknowledged the aircraft's potential and voiced his opinion: "… with stronger construction… and substitution of metal for [a] wooden propeller, I am confident that the aeroplane can be operated from the water under any weather conditions that could be operated from [on] land."[13]

The two Curtiss pushers were initially land-based with tricycle landing gear, but pontoons were fitted, converting the A-type and Wright B-1 into hydroplanes. They were single pontoons with wing tip floats. The A-2 sported the single pontoon until August 1911, when two sheet metal pontoons replaced the single version. All these seaplanes gave a reasonably good performance, considering the state of development at that time. Though they were all very lightly constructed, there were no major structural failures initially. The Navy would choose Curtiss planes over the Wrights' and purchase 14 A-1 variants. This class laid the groundwork for amphibians to become integral to naval aviation for nearly 60 years.[14] While Curtiss and Ellyson tinkered on the A-1, Captain Chambers looked for a location to establish the first naval aviation camp.

Lieutenant John Rodgers prepares for a flight in the Wright type B-1 at the US Naval Academy circa 1912. He became the second certified ACA naval aviator in August 1911. (Courtesy of the *Evening Capital*, Annapolis, US Naval History and Heritage Command, NH 44374)

He settled on Greenbury Point, near Annapolis, Maryland, in the summer of 1911.

A small group of naval officers waited, hoping to learn to fly them; however, there was a shortage of qualified instructors for the aircraft. Winter forced Chambers to relocate the aviation cadre from the Greenbury Point aviation camp to the Glen Curtiss Flying School in San Diego, California, in the winter of 1911. The aspiring students quickly became aviators over the winter months. The unit returned to the Greenbury Point facility in the summer of 1912. They continued their practice flights with the three aircraft on hand and experimented with various float designs developed by the newly established aerodynamics laboratory at the Washington Navy Yard.[15]

By the summer of 1911, Ellyson and Curtiss were no longer the only ones actively engaged in aviation training for the Navy, as two additional naval officers would complete training during 1911. The preceding March, the Wright brothers offered to train a naval officer to fly, provided the Navy would purchase an aircraft from them. The Navy responded to this offer by detailing Lieutenant John "Jang" Rodgers, Academy class of 1903. He came from a long line of naval officers beginning in the War of 1812. His father, Rear Admiral John A. Rodgers, graduated from the academy in 1861 and served in the Civil War. Jang arrived at Dayton, Ohio, on March 17, 1911, to begin flight training under the famous brothers. The following year, his devotion to the brothers would become an area of contention. He received ACA Certificate No. 48 on August 3, 1911. He became Naval Aviator No. 2 retroactively.[16]

Lieutenant Rodgers soon displayed his flying ability a month after his certification when he established a new Navy record by flying to Havre de Grace, Maryland, and returning to Annapolis. Ellyson continued working with Glenn Curtiss at his factory in Hammondsport in May 1911, working on aircraft stability issues and training student pilots. One of them, John H. "Jack" Towers, Academy class of 1906, arrived at Hammondsport on June 27 to become a student pilot but nearly killed himself in the process. Before aviation entered his mind, he served aboard USS *Kentucky* for the required two years of sea duty. He attended the Curtiss School at

Hammondsport for initial training, with Ellyson as his instructor, using the Curtiss training syllabus for the four-cylinder, underpowered training plane known as "Lizzie." Unfortunately, the 25-year-old former gunnery officer nearly killed himself when a gust of wind propelled the aircraft 20ft into the air. Tower had no idea how to fly or land the machine and it crashed, the student suffering a broken ankle. While on the mend, he was ordered to Aviation Camp at Annapolis to complete his training, where he received ACA Certificate No. 62 on September 14, 1911, becoming Naval Aviator No. 3.

After completing flight school, the Navy detailed Towers to the Curtiss Flying School at North Island, where he assisted Curtiss in experimental work. A week before Towers arrived at Hammondsport, Ellyson sent a letter to Chambers implying the A-1's engine problems appeared to be solved, and informed his boss that he and Towers would attempt to fly from Annapolis to Washington. He stated, "… for I think that it will establish the world's record, certainly the American record for overwater flight, and will call attention to the hydroplane safety features."[17] To test the A-1's

Lieutenant John Towers, here in 1920, became the third American naval aviator and would play a vital role in the Pacific during World War Two as the Commander of the Fifth Fleet, among other duties. (Courtesy of the US Naval History and Heritage Command)

Lieutenant Ellyson with Captain W. I. Chambers, USN (First Officer in Charge, Naval Aviation), as a passenger in a Curtiss Navy trial of the A-2 at Hammondsport, New York, in September 1911. (Courtesy of the US Navy History and Heritage Command, NH 1386)

durability, Towers undertook a flight from Annapolis to Hampton Roads. The trip on October 10 covered approximately 110 miles. Two weeks later, on October 25, they attempted a round-trip flight from Annapolis to Fort Monroe, Virginia, with a new engine. Still, a leaking radiator shut down the trip after covering 122 miles in 122 minutes. A fractured carburetor ended a third trip on November 2. Increasingly poor weather halted further flights from Annapolis. Chambers chose once again to move the aviation camp to North Island.

Mechanical issues with the A-1 continued to frustrate the team during the winter of 1912, leaving only the B-1 operational. The A-2 had been cannibalized for parts to keep the A-1 in operation and thus needed a rebuild. Ellyson and Towers took turns flying the Wright plane and found it underpowered but rugged and reliable. Patrick Bellinger said of aviation: "Aviation development followed the pattern of build, fly, wreck, rebuild and fly again." He further elaborated, "You don't know how to fly until you've walked away from a crash."[18]

Left to right are Lieutenant Theodore G. Ellyson, Lieutenant John H. Towers, and 1st Lieutenant John W. McClaskey, USMC (Ret.) seated on a dock at Hammondsport, while at the Curtiss aviation facility in summer 1911. (Courtesy of the US Naval History and Heritage Command, NH 95640)

Curtiss A-1 (left) and possibly the Wright B-1 at Hammondsport, circa 1911. Both planes were the first purchased by the US Navy via Chambers, who led early naval aviation. The A-1 was nicknamed the Triad; it was 28ft long and had a wingspan of 37ft. It had dual controls for the pilot and passenger. The plane had a top speed between 55 and 60mph. (Author's collection)

Leaving the B-1 as the only training craft used to certify the only naval officer in 1912, Victor D. "Vic" Herbster, earned ACA Certificate No. 103 upon graduating on February 28, 1912. After that, he served at the Naval Academy in aviation-related duties and conducted experimental work at Hammondsport. At North Island, two of the three Navy aircraft were out

Ellyson and Towers flew the Curtiss A-2 aircraft, the second purchased by the Navy, at Hammondsport, in August 1911. This aircraft was fitted with two cigar-shaped pontoons. It was 27ft 8in long, with a wingspan of 37ft and a maximum speed of 65mph. It became known as the OWL and was redesignated as the E-1 and later the AX-1 (Courtesy of the Naval Historical Foundation, Collection of Commander T. G. Ellyson, US Naval History and Heritage Command, NH 95638)

Ellyson testing the Curtiss flying boat A-3 at Hammondsport. This plane continued to be part of the Navy's inventory through 1914 and was later designated as the AH-3. It was used for the first catapult launch in 1912. (Courtesy of the US Naval History and Heritage Command, UA 41.01.24)

Left: Victor "Vic" Herbster, Naval Aviator No. 4, served with the first aviation camp during fleet exercises in 1913. Some of his fellow pilots called him egotistical. He went on to command NAS Wexford, Ireland, during World War One. (Courtesy of the US Naval History and Heritage Command, NH 49121)

Below: Greek Seaplane *Nautilos* of the Greek Navy circa 1912, piloted by Lieutenants Moraitinis and Moutousis. It is believed to be the first aircraft to have delivered attacks against enemy warships in the Balkan War of 1912, when the US Navy and Marine Corps aviation had hardly begun. (Courtesy of the Greek Navy 1976 and the US Naval History and Heritage Command, NH 85316)

Theodore Ellyson in a Navy A-3 ready for launching from a catapult, October 1912. The A-3 was redesignated the AH-3 and used for aviation experiments through 1914. (Courtesy of the US Naval History and Heritage Command, UA 41.01.01)

of commission; Chambers wanted positive results to request additional funding to purchase more planes, and non-flyable machines meant doom for the service's fledgling air service. Moreover, Chambers believed Curtiss was an excellent self-made engineer and aircraft designer. Still, he worried that Curtiss' methodology was troublesome and could impede progress in ensuring that airplanes met naval standards. He sent the right individual, Holden "Dick" Richardson – a 200lb naval constructor, engineer, and graduate of the Academy, class of 1912. He arrived at North Island in March 1912 as a non-aviator to work out the deficiencies of Curtiss' aircraft, and to become an aviator himself.[19]

Before Richardson qualified, Ellyson nearly killed himself while flying the A-2, which was now "airworthy." The weather on March 14 seemed perfect for flying that day: the air still, a cloudless day, and cool. Spuds decided to take the plane for a few test flights. He made two flights before lunch and found the air bumpy: no flights for the novice. So Ellyson went on a third hop, which Towers recorded later:

> … he went down alright but got badly tossed about. He had gotten about a third of the way back when he took a sudden drop, recovered, them a second one caused him to shoot straight into the ground at an angle of about 45 degrees and from a height of about twenty-five feet. It was so sudden that he did not have time to do anything and there was not enough room to recover anyway. The machine plowed an awful hole in the field, then turned over. A near as I could tell from conditions, Ellyson was thrown from his seat through the forward controls to the ground, striking on his helmet, then over and striking on his back and hips. The machine sort of scooped him up when it turned over. I fortunately had my motorcycle there and when I got to the wreck, he was lying half in the wreck, the lower part of his body on the top engine section and his head and shoulders just a few inches from the radiator. The helmet and his face were completely covered with earth and the first thing he said when he regained consciousness, which was three or four minutes after I got there, was that he couldn't see, which was no wonder for his eye sockets were completely filled [with dirt].

The A-1 Triad hydroaeroplane is in the launching position at the top of the inclined wire cable. Lieutenant Ellyson is about to take a test flight from an elevated platform along a wire cable at Hammondsport, in the summer of 1911. John Towers is holding the guidelines to the right wing. (Courtesy of the US Naval History and Heritage Command, UA 41.01.03)

Towers washed Ellyson's eyes out with water from the radiator and checked whether the pilot had broken any bones; it did not appear so, but he kept going in and out of consciousness. Finally, he was transferred to a nearby home, and a doctor from the repair ship *Iris* came over and tended to Ellyson. Towers continued in his report: "All day yesterday and most of last night they gave him morphine to ease the pain in his neck and back… The other damage are multiple bruises and badly skinned places, and also a sprained ankle."

Ellyson suffered a severe concussion, and it took several weeks to get out of bed. He returned to flying after recovering from the near-fatal crash and, on June 21, took the A-1 out at Annapolis, climbing to 900ft in three minutes and 30 seconds – a stunning performance for 1912. On October 6, 1912, Lieutenant Towers, flying the Curtiss A-2, took off from the water at Annapolis at 6.50am and remained in the air for six hours, ten minutes, and 35 seconds, setting a new American endurance record for planes.

Within two years, pilots were doubling the length of air time. Ellyson and Towers conducted the first "long-distance" flight by naval aviators from Annapolis, Maryland, to Milford Haven, Virginia, on November 3, covering 112 miles in 2 hours and 2 minutes. Ellyson rejoined the fleet in April 1913 as a member of the USS *South Carolina*. He would not return to aviation until January 1921 and served in the experimental development of aviation in the years before and after World War One. He also spent several years before the war as part of the Navy's submarine service. A recipient of the Navy Cross for his anti-submarine service in World War One, Ellyson died in 1928 when his aircraft crashed into the Chesapeake Bay.

Complications within the naval aviation community appeared before Ellyson left aviation. The significant antagonists were Ellyson and Rodgers. The latter's grievances may have begun with the issue of naval precedence since Spuds viewed himself as the senior aviator, to which he was entitled, but Rodgers outranked him. The latter assumed he should be the commander of the aviation camp due to his rank; therefore, he saw himself as the senior aviator. Ellyson, however, would win the argument.[20]

Contact!: Early US Naval and Marine Corps Aviation, 1911–18

The C-2 flying boat on a folding car on the catapult launch from a barge in Pensacola. The invention of the catapult proved to be successful and subsequent tests aboard ships proved the viability of having planes aboard warships. (Courtesy of the US Naval History and Heritage Command, UA 41.01)

The C-1, with Ellyson piloting, was launched from the catapult on a barge at the Washington Navy Yard in November 1912. The AB-1, 2, and 3, redesignated as C-1, 2, and 3, were used extensively in experiments, thus, they had to be rebuilt several times. (Courtesy of the US Naval History and Heritage Command, UA 41.01.05)

The Birth of Naval Aviation

A Navy A-1 wrecked by Lieutenant John Towers at Annapolis on November 16, 1911. The A-1 Triad had been rebuilt several times before this accident. (Courtesy of the US Naval History and Heritage Command, UA 41.01.41)

Early naval aviation pioneers Lieutenant Ellyson, Naval Aviator No. 1 (right) and Lieutenant Towers, Naval Aviator No. 3 (left) on a Curtiss or Wright biplane, possibly taken at Hammondsport. (National Archives; courtesy of the US Naval History and Heritage Command, 80-G-427990)

At some point, aviators of the fledgling force broke into two camps: pro-Wright and pro-Curtiss, which stemmed from legal issues concerning patents. However, both were frustrated about Chambers being a non-flyer and not understanding the intricacies of flying. Additionally, Ellyson and Rodgers agreed that naval aviation could advance if the public knew about them through demonstrations. However, Chambers axed the idea because he feared a fatal crash would set back, and possibly end, the program. He, like Curtiss, feared bad publicity.

However, the primary issue was that Chambers was not only a non-flyer but he was an engineer. His playing that role frustrated the pilots. They knew the intricacies of flying, but Chambers did not. The flight control system was one example of the disagreements between Chambers and the aviators. Early planes used a steering wheel for control, but one flyer suggested trying Deperdussin controls (the now familiar stick-and-rudder pedals) in an airplane; Chambers resisted. He felt that steering with the feet would be awkward for a sailor and, in any case, was just a "European vogue" that would pass. He also objected to the stick, believing that a wheel (as on the Curtiss controls) would be more

Lieutenant Ellyson, with a Curtiss AH seaplane, piloted the catapult mechanism that Richardson developed. This photograph was probably taken during June or July 1912. (Courtesy of the US Naval History and Heritage Command, NH 44380-A)

natural to a navy man. The aviators also felt that Chambers was ordering new planes without considering their opinions. As an engineer, Chambers brushed aside the pilots' views in developing new aircraft designs. Then, out of frustration, one of the pilots jumped the chain of command and, in a letter, asked the Secretary of the Navy to assign an aviator to select new designs.[21]

Two months later, in August, Rodgers left aviation. Several factors may have led him to make the decision: first, his dislike of Ellyson, regarded as the senior aviator, and Chambers' seeming preference for the first aviator; second, his distaste for Chambers as an ill-informed non-aviator; and third, the Navy's new regulation where considered promotions relied on the amount of sea duty a naval officer acquired. The death of his cousin in an airplane crash may have also played a part, or becoming a newlywed with a wife who wanted her new husband out of the dangerous sport of flying. Whatever may have been the case, Rodgers did not return to aviation duties until July 1922 when he became commanding officer of Pearl Harbor and would remain in aviation as Assistant Chief of the Bureau of Aeronautics until his death in an airplane crash on August 27, 1926.

Eugene Ely proved that airplanes could land and take off from ships, but such methods placed gun turrets out of action. Lieutenant Richardson understood the problem and devised a third method of launching

A Curtiss C-type flying boat crossing the bow of USS *Rhode Island* (Battleship #17), off Annapolis, circa 1913. Note the typical Chesapeake Bay schooner in the left distance. (From the album of Francis Sargent; courtesy of Commander John Condon, 1986; US Naval History and Heritage Command, NH 101065)

Lieutenant Towers and Lieutenant Godfrey de Chevalier are in the Navy's first Curtiss F flying boat, circa 1913. The F boats were superior to early Curtiss pushers in design and construction. (Courtesy of the US Naval Heritage and History Command, NH 52828)

aircraft from a catapult system. He developed a compressed air system using a torpedo tube. Unfortunately, the system failed twice in June and August 1912, the last destroying the A-1.

At the Naval Gun Factory, Ellyson tested the catapult under the supervision of Captain Chambers. The first and second attempted shots proved unsuccessful. Navy Contractor Richardson redesigned the catapult, resulting in Lieutenant Ellyson's first successful catapulting on November 12. On that day, with Ellyson at the controls of the A-3 (later designated the AH-3), he conducted the first successful catapult launching of an airplane at the Washington Navy Yard. The following month, Ellyson made a second successful launch in the flying boat C-1. Glenn Curtiss called it, "The greatest aviation advance since wheels replaced skids for aeroplane landing gear."[22]

Through 1912, Ellyson continued testing aircraft and aided in the establishment of the Naval Aviation Camp in San Diego in June 1912. On October 6, 1912, Lieutenant Towers, flying the Curtiss A-2, took off from the water at Annapolis at 6.50am, and remained in the air for six hours, ten minutes, and 35 seconds. Within two years, pilots were doubling the length of air time. Then, in the late fall of 1912, the first Curtiss F-1 flying boat was delivered. In 1913 four more planes were produced: two Curtiss flying boats, one Curtiss amphibian boat (OWL), and one Wright 60hp seaplane.[23]

A Curtiss A-1 hydroplane with Lieutenant Ellyson at Hammondsport. Testing of aircraft took place at Hammondsport during the spring and summer, while the winter months were spent in California. (Courtesy of the US Naval History and Heritage Command, UA 41.01.36)

Curtiss Navy A-1 hydroplane piloted by Ellyson for testing at Hammondsport – the hometown of Glenn Curtiss and where aircraft testing was conducted in the spring and summer months. (Courtesy of the US Naval Heritage and History Command)

The Curtiss A-2/AH-2, during a training flight at Coronado, California, winter 1912. The cruiser USS *West Virginia* (AC-55) is in the background. (Courtesy of the US Naval History and Heritage Command, NH 1583)

Lawrence B. "Gyro" Sperry (left), Naval Aviator No. 345, and Lieutenant Junior Grade Patrick N. L. Bellinger, USN, in the cockpit of a Curtiss model "F" flying boat, at Hammondsport during testing of the Sperry gyroscope in 1913. (Courtesy of the Sperry Gyroscope Co and the US Naval History and Heritage Command, NH 95634)

Pioneer pilot Richard C. Saufley, Naval Aviator No. 14, at the controls of a Curtiss AH pusher hydroplane. On December 3, 1915, Lieutenant Saufley, flying the Curtiss AH-14, set the American altitude record for a hydroplane, reaching an altitude of 11,975ft over Pensacola. (Author's collection, US Navy photograph)

An unknown Curtiss flying boat, either an A1 or an A2, on the ramp at Hammondsport. Lieutenant Patrick Bellinger and Lieutenant Holden C. Richardson are on opposite sides of the hull. (Courtesy of the US Naval History and Heritage Command, UA 41.01.40)

Chapter 4

The Birth of Marine Corps Aviation

Ellyson, on the mend from a broken foot in San Diego, was not at Annapolis to witness the birth of Marine Corps aviation. An event that might never have occurred as there were calls for the abolishment of the Corps during the post-Spanish–American War years. Secretary of the Navy Metcalf and others, including the President of the United States, questioned the very existence of the Marine Corps. Army Chief-of-Staff General Leonard Wood suggested the Marine Corps be absorbed into the Army. President Theodore Roosevelt, a friend of Woods since the Spanish–American War, accepted this idea.

Meanwhile, the Navy concluded naval ships no longer needed Marines aboard, a historical tradition since the Revolutionary War. However, Marines fought tenaciously during the Spanish–American War, capturing Guantanamo Bay on June 10, 1898, which started the invasion of Cuba, and the Corps survived. It had solid allies and funding continued with the appropriations act of 1910. However, a sense of paranoia set in with the belief that a pen stroke would terminate the Corps' existence. The Marines needed to keep it from becoming a footnote in history; the Advance Base Force and aviation were the concepts the Marine Corps needed to keep it viable.[1]

The Navy thought of the Marine Corps as a section of naval landing forces throughout its existence, and it seemed plausible that such a service's abolishment would occur at some point in time. However, structurally, the Marines were understaffed and ill-equipped to be effective. By the 1890s, the force consisted of only 75 officers and 2,100 enlisted men, and could barely arrange funding for target practice. As a result, the Corps was hard-pressed to muster a complete battalion at the onset of the Spanish–American War. Nevertheless, Lieutenant Colonel Charles Heywood, commandant of the Marine Corps, managed to scrape enough personnel and arms for the makeshift battalion that secured Guantanamo Bay. Heywood quickly seized the potential mission for his Marines as it showed how important and valuable it was to have a body of troops that can rapidly be mobilized and sent aboard transports, thoroughly equipped for service ashore and afloat.[2]

The General Board of the Navy saw the potential use of an advanced force comprising a Marine battalion; the concept of the Advanced Base Force was born. A student of the force concept was Second Lieutenant Alfred A. Cunningham, whom the Navy assigned to the Advanced Base School in November 1911, where he conceived a potential role for aviation. Cunningham wrote on the feasibility of aviation becoming an integral part of the Advance Base concept: "… that could defend advance bases in support of naval forces and freeing the Sailors to remain on the ships instead of being added to the landings. The Advanced Base Force concept, as it was known, stated that the Marines were the most suited for immediate needs of establishing advanced bases, creating quick defenses, gun emplacements, and laying mines."[3]

Cunningham forwarded his concept of the Advanced Base assisted by aircraft in a letter on February 12, 1912, to the commandant of the Marine Corps, General William Biddle. The Corps had no funding for purchasing aircraft for the force, even though he foresaw that airplanes would become an essential component of that force. However, Biddle believed in Cunningham's recommendation that a sufficient number of Marine officers would train in aviation for conducting reconnaissance work for the Advance Base force.[4]

Biddle recognized that airplanes would significantly improve the defense of an Advance Base and recommended that eligible Marine officers be trained to fly, "so that a sufficient number of expert aviators… may be available."[5]

Pre-1915 photograph of Lieutenant Alfred Cunningham who, in 1912, became the first Marine Corps pilot. The plane is unidentified but is probably one of the earlier A/AH series. (Official USMC photograph, USMC Digital Archives)

Chambers agreed with Biddle and informed him that two Marines at a time would be trained at Annapolis, without funding within the Corps. Cunningham reported for aviation duty on May 22, 1912, with Bernard Smith following on September 18. The introduction of Marines created tension among naval and marine aviators as the Navy saw the arrival of Marines as an additional strain on limited resources. Nevertheless, Secretary of the Navy Winthrop approved the flight training. Through the actions of Biddle and Chambers, Cunningham would become the Marine Corps' first aviator.

The foresighted and ambitious Alfred "Cunny" Austell Cunningham was born on March 8, 1882, in Atlanta, Georgia, to a middle-income family. An adventuresome lad served at age 16 with the 2nd and 3rd Georgia Infantry Volunteers in Cuba during the Spanish–American War. Upon being mustered out of the Army, he attended the Gordon Military College in Barnesville, Georgia, for two years and afterward became a businessman in real estate for eight years in Atlanta. He joined the Marine Corps at nearly 27 years old in January 1909 to become a commissioned officer. He was four to five years older than most who attended the officer's candidate school at Port Royal, South Carolina. Physically fit and determined to succeed, he received his commission. Afterward, he served aboard the *New Jersey* (BB-16) and *North Carolina* (BB-29) between 1909 and 1911 as a member of the Marine detachment, which served aboard ships of the fleet.

His interest in aviation probably began eight years earlier, in 1903, when he went aloft in a balloon flight at age 21. Thus, it probably started his desire to become an aviator while stationed at the Marine Barracks in Philadelphia. He may have become aware of the Army's interest in aviation and of Ellyson, Rodgers, and Towers, who had become certified pilots in 1911. Possibly based upon reading books and periodicals and the exploits of military aviation, he leased a home-built airplane nicknamed "Noisy Nan" for $25, hoping to teach himself how to fly it. The intrepid Marine

Alfred Cunningham beside a Blériot monoplane, circa 1912. Chambers believed Blériot planes were superior to those of American-built aircraft. A Blériot could have become the Navy's first airplane, except for the desire that planes must be built by domestic manufacturers. (Courtesy of the Library of Congress)

may have leased the aircraft after Chambers' suggestion that officers learn how to fly outside the service. Unfortunately, the plane never became airborne, and fellow officers laughed. Still, it taught him the basic principles of aeronautics.

His thirst never ceased as he read books and articles on aviation-related topics. Like Ellyson, he absorbed works on the Wrights and other aviation pioneers. Cunningham had charm and strong interpersonal skills that helped his military career and membership in the Aero Club in Philadelphia, with a penchant for attracting VIPs, including politicians, which may have helped him as well. Commandant of the Marine Corps, General Biddle, pressured by a congressman, detached Cunningham from the naval yard for the Naval Aviation Camp at Annapolis, Maryland. He reported for duty on May 22, 1912, for training as an aviator, which the Marine Corps officially recognizes as the birthday of Marine Corps aviation. The individual destined to become the first marine aviator was 29 years old, a bachelor, and three years older than Ellyson.

He arrived at Annapolis the same day as the wrecks of the Curtiss and Wright planes arrived. Aeronautical experimentation by Glenn Curtiss, Ellyson, Rodgers, and Towers was brutal as they attempted to construct suitable aircraft for naval use. Mechanical issues with the A-1, A-2, and B-1 plagued the program; aerodynamics was in its infancy, and trial-and-error was customary. Infighting between pilots, and disagreements with Chambers, especially with Ellyson, persisted and would ultimately drive the first naval pilot out of aviation. After completing ground training, Cunningham's flight instruction began three days later at the Burgess Aircraft Factory at Marblehead, Massachusetts, since there were no aircraft available at Annapolis.

Cunningham became Marine Aviator No. 1 when he arrived for training on May 22, 1912, but his ACA Seaplane Certification No. 2 is dated May 26, 1913 – the date he completed flight training. It was common practice for the Navy to retroactively certify naval aviators on the day they arrived for flight training.[6] In July 1912, he visited Greenbury, where he flew with

Towers in the A-2 for additional practice, then to Marblehead, where he soloed on August 1, 1912. After completing only two hours and 40 minutes of instruction, he officially became Marine Aviator No.1 and Naval Aviator No. 5. His ability to take flight and descend upon the water without killing himself in a minimum amount of time met early qualifications.

Flight training would increase to 12 months during World War One. As marine aviation slowly grew during the next four years, Cunningham, joined by a few other far-sighted Marines, continually worked diligently to promote its interests. Cunningham would become one the most outspoken supporters of an independent marine aviation force and became the commanding officer of the First Marine Aviation Force in 1917. In 1916, he wrote about the potential importance of aviation as a significant part of the Advanced Forces concept in the *Marine Corps Gazette* by stating airplanes could provide, "Offshore patrols to prevent surprise raids by enemy light forces. Anti-submarine patrols. Spotting for shore batteries in attacks by enemy ships. Photography, bombing, and torpedoing enemy craft and bases within reach."[7]

The early marine aviators flew the Wright B-1; they had no other aircraft left, since it had all been wrecked and rebuilt several times after heavy use.

Cunningham and his groundcrew prepare the Wright B-1 for flight at an unknown location, possibly Hammondsport. The Wright was one of the three planes purchased by the Navy. (Official USMC Photograph, Digital USMC Archives)

Parts from it were used to reconstruct the plane Alfred Cunningham used. Unfortunately, its performance deteriorated over time, so much so that he reported to Captain Chambers:

> My machine, as I told you and Mr. Towers probably told you, is not in my opinion fit for use. I built it from parts of the Burgess F and Wright B, which are not exactly alike and nothing fitted. I had to cut off and patch up parts and bore additional holes in beams in order to make them fit. The engine bed, made by Burgess, was not exactly square with the front beam, so the engine had to be mounted a little out of true (with reference to the engine bed). I have made over 200 flights in this machine and recently, despite unusual care of myself and men, something seems to vibrate loose or off most of the flights made. One of the propeller shafts is the same one used with the Gyro motor [manufactured by the Gyro Motor Company] in the old machine. It is the only left-hand shaft here. While the engine runs smoothly, it does not deliver nearly as much power as when it was newer, and even then, it did not have enough power to fly safely in any but smooth weather, it is impossible to climb over a few hundred feet with a passenger. The whole machine has just about served its usefulness and & would like very much to have a new machine of the single propeller type… Will you kindly let me know what the prospects are for my getting a new machine.

Canvas hangars at Annapolis during 1913. Several planes, including the Wright B-1, were heavily damaged during a storm at the academy. (COLL/1691 at the Archives Branch, Marine Corps History, official USMC photograph)

Cunningham took charge of the B-1; Herbster took control of the "new" B-2, a twin-engine machine he had built out of spare parts; and Towers took control of the A-2. Cunningham made 400 flights in the Wright B-1 between October 1912 and July 1913 – the aircraft could cover 80 miles with a maximum altitude of 800ft. It would take until February 6, 1914, before the Navy provided them with a second aircraft, the A-1, converted to the OWL (over water and land) plane. The founder of Marine Corps aviation did not actively participate as a pilot for long as events within naval aviation and a personal part of his life began to sway his options. Cunningham and Bernard Smith were the only certified marine aviators between January and April 1913. They diligently worked with their opposites in the Navy. Initially, friction between the two services was not apparent until the Guantanamo fleet exercises during the winter and spring of 1913.[8]

First Lieutenant Bernard "Barny" L. Smith became the second marine aviator on September 18, 1912, when he reported for instruction at

Bernard "Barney" L. Smith, USMC, here on March 25, 1918, became the Marine Corps' second aviator and sixth naval aviator when he reported for aviation training on September 18, 1912. (Courtesy of the US Naval History and Heritage Command, NH 44942)

William M. McIlvain became the third Marine Corps pilot and was designated Naval Aviator No. 12 on March 10, 1915. During World War One, he was assigned to temporary duty with 217 Squadron 217 RAF and then as CO of Squadron B of the Northern Bombing Group, Day Wing. (Official USMC photograph, USMC Archives)

the naval aviation camp. Smith was born in Richmond, Virginia, on June 19, 1886. He attended Virginia Polytechnic for three years, studying mechanical engineering before receiving his commission in the Marine Corps as a second lieutenant on January 22, 1909. He was big and husky with broad shoulders, and, like most pilots, had a penchant for partying and women. His first sea duty was aboard USS *Louisiana* as part of the Marine detachment, and he would become instrumental in developing the concept of naval close air support and aerial reconnaissance.[9] He transferred from the Annapolis aviation training to the aviation camp at Guantanamo, Cuba, where he received certification as the second Marine officer assigned to flight training.[10] Towers began instructing him in the A-2, and the student proved to be an apt and enthusiastic individual, taking every opportunity to fly with Ellyson and Towers. He was designated as Marine Aviator No. 2/Naval Aviator No. 6. He, like Cunningham, was not a Naval Academy graduate and this may have contributed to Ellyson's dislike of some marine aviators. Smith, during the next few years, would go on to

Francis "Khaki" Evans, Naval Aviator No. 26 and Marine Aviator No. 4, became the CO of the first overseas Marine Corps aviation detachment stationed in the Azores. (Author's collection)

participate in the Tampico Affair in Mexico, conduct aerial bomb testing, and become a special attaché in Paris.

The growth of Marine Corps aviation did not advance as quickly as its naval counterpart. After Lieutenant Smith, the number of Marines appointed as aviators was considerably smaller, with only two additional certifications occurring between 1913 and 1916 due to budget constraints. Two years after Cunningham's certification, Lieutenant William Maitland "Mac" McIlvain was appointed Marine Aviator No. 3 on March 10, 1915. He graduated from high school in Indianapolis, Indiana, and, at 21, enrolled in the officer candidate school in 1909 and served aboard USS *Connecticut* (BB-18) and *North Dakota* as part of the Marine detachments before attending flight school. He was one of the few without a college degree. McIlvain would become a squadron commander in France during World War One. First Lieutenant Francis T. "Khaki" Evans became Marine Aviator No. 4 on March 31, 1916.

He graduated from Ohio Wesleyan University and became an infantry officer upon graduating from officer candidate school in 1909. He served aboard the *Mississippi* and *North Dakota*. Evans would become the commanding officer of the First Aeronautical Company during World War One. Sixteen months would pass until First Lieutenant Roy Stanley Geiger became Marine Aviator No. 5 in June 1917, two months after the United States declared war on Germany. He would serve 40 continuous years in the Corps.

By Geiger's certification, the Navy had grown to 48 qualified aviators – 38 of them designated before the US entered World War One. Those four Marines formed the nucleus of the Marine Corps early air service. Many in the Navy associated with naval aviation may have seen USMC pilots as redundant, and funding and aircraft were nearly non-existent for the Corps through 1916. However, Cunningham and individuals like Smith

Lieutenants McIlvain and Smith of the Marine Corps tested a hydroplane, probably the Wright B-1, at Annapolis in 1913. The Wright B-1 was known for being underpowered, with design flaws that caused numerous accidents. (Official USMC photograph, Digital USMC Archives)

continuously fought for every plane and budget dollar to develop marine aviation into an effective fighting force. It would be a fight that would last through World War One and beyond.

Cunningham's and Smith's participation in exercises off Cuba in 1913 would open up a schism between them and Ellyson. John Towers, by 1913, had acquired friends within the Marine Corps and defended them from accusations. Ellyson remained skeptical of marine aviation abilities and usefulness. It may have been clashing egos between Ellyson and Cunningham. It appears Captain Chambers saw no practical benefit in Marine Aviation and was no fan of Cunningham. Chambers warned Ellyson about the senior Marine aviator: "In regard to the Marines, we must be diplomatic, but the first serious indication that Cunningham exhibits of big head, or lack of willingness to cooperate and I will ask for his detachment."

Additionally, Chambers, it appears, held some form of resentment about Cunningham and maybe Smith. It may have been that Marine

The Navy's Curtiss experimental OWL boat (A-2) on the ramp at Hammondsport. Lieutenant Holden C. Richardson is adjusting the horizontal stabilizer; Lieutenant Patrick Bellinger is in the center of the three, and Lieutenant Bernard L. Smith is in the cockpit. The A-2 became the Marine Corps' first plane. (Courtesy of the US Naval History and Heritage Command, UA 41.01.34)

officers took precious resources, such as slots for naval student aviators. For some reason, the de facto head of naval aviation influenced Ellyson's behavior toward marine aviators. Towers held a different viewpoint toward Cunningham and the Marines as a whole. As head of the Guantanamo detachment, Towers could have sabotaged and ended Marine Corps aviation. All he needed was any infraction perpetuated by Cunningham, Chevalier, or Smith, However, he stated: "Towers was pleased that the Marine Cunningham had not been uncooperative . . . he had not only worked with Towers and performed well but also helped him [Towers] court Marines in the fleet for interest in aviation."[11]

Yet, at his own request on August 11, 1913, Cunningham resigned from aviation duties due to his fiancée, Miss Josephine Jefferies' plea that he either leave aviation or she would not marry him. Love won out. Why Ellyson appeared to dislike the Marine is unknown as his biography, *Anchors in the Sky,* has no entry on the matter, and Cunningham is only mentioned once in the book.

On April 29, 1913, Cunningham officially detached from naval aviation as an active pilot.[12] However, his passion for aviation continued as he transferred to Headquarters Marine Corps, Washington, DC, which allowed him to be actively engaged in the administrative aspects of aviation. His charisma, interpersonal skills, and ties to significant individuals were instrumental in building a marine aviation force and he was called to assist in drawing up a comprehensive plan for the organization of a Naval Aeronautic Service. In February 1914, he assisted Naval Constructor Holden Richardson, Naval Aviator No. 13, in flying the new D-2 flying boat. The war in Europe would find him expanding the role of Marine Corps Aviation, including establishing a marine landplane unit. Lieutenant Bernard Smith became the senior Marine Corps aviation officer while Jack Towers led the Navy. Like Cunningham, he possessed both charisma and interpersonal skills. Afterward, he became a test pilot at Hammondsport. During World War One, he acted as an assistant attaché in Paris, flew several intelligence missions with the French Armée de l'Air, and would command a Marine Corps land-based air wing.

The Birth of Marine Corps Aviation

Above: Cunningham at the controls of a Curtiss hydroplane, circa 1914. Note the dual controls, which could be turned over to a student pilot or passenger. (Courtesy of the National Archives, RG-127-GR-42, 532292)

Right: Roy Geiger, Marine Aviator No.5, standing next to the Aviation Training School Office, circa 1915, when he was a student aviator at Pensacola. He became the Director of Marine Corps Aviation and Commander of the 3rd Amphibious Corps in the recapture of Guam in 1944. (Official USMC photograph, Digital USMC Archives)

Smith led himself as the senior aviator until William McIlvain qualified for his seaplane certificate on December 22, 1913. Another 20 naval officers would become aviators before a third marine officer arrived for duty as a pilot. The reasoning behind training so few marine aviators came down to budget issues and politics. Why train Marines for the same flying duty as naval pilots? As before, future marine aviators needed their independent mission; if there were none, why teach them? Naval students trained to operate seaplanes as scouts for the fleet. The majority of scarce funds allocated to the Navy was for training naval aviation students, not so much the Corps, which held no defined mission in aviation. By the early 1920s, two of the first five Marine Corps pilots – Cunningham and Geiger – would remain active in aviation duties, and continued to build Marine Corps aviation.

Husky Bernard Smith standing next to C-3 with a USMC tag on the tail. The C-3 originally had the designation AB-3. The lettering is white and the plane appears to be painted overall light gray or bare unpainted canvas. (Courtesy of the Marine Corps Digital Archives)

Smith (center) standing by the nose of plane A-2 and a maintenance crew preparing for an amphibian water test, circa 1914. Note the designator A-2 and "USN" painted on the nose. (Courtesy of the Marine Corps Digital Archives)

A hydroplane at Culebra, Puerto Rico with Lieutenant McIlvain, USMC Aviator No. 3, seated in the boat with an unknown individual standing on the plane. Note the pennant attached in front. (Courtesy of the Marine Corps Digital Archives)

Preparing for a water test with the Curtiss A-2, possibly at Hammondsport. Smith is sitting on the left with Richardson on the right, circa 1914. (Courtesy of the Bernard Smith Collection [COLL/1691] at the Archives Branch, Marine Corps History Division)

Lieutenant Smith aboard an AB flying boat with the Pensacola camp mascot, circa 1914. The AB series was redesignated the C series. (Courtesy of the Bernard Smith Collection [COLL/1691] at the Archives Branch, Marine Corps History Division)

Chapter 5

Fleet Operations (1913–14)

As the only Marine in the aviation group, before resigning from aviation duties, Cunningham remained quiet – listening and learning by following the advice of Chambers and the senior naval men without question. His steadfast attitude would help him during World War One. Meanwhile, Captain Chambers named Spuds Ellyson as the lead naval aviator, by intention or design, placing him over the senior-ranked Rodgers. Ellyson and Towers were the most serious of the four naval aviators and were bachelors living dangerously. Each time they took to the air could be their last. As the number two naval aviator, Ellyson was characterized as being reserved, or even bashful, but he knew how to lead and loved to fly. When Ellyson was on the ground, he worked to solve problems with the A-1 and -2 aircraft. Yet, he loved riding motorcycles and drinking; some would say he was a boozer, and some called him erratic, but his consumption of alcohol never seemed to interfere with his flying.

Ellyson wrote to Chambers regarding the skills of Towers and himself: "I do not think there are two safer 'safer and sane' pilots than Towers and myself… Towers and I have confidence in each other."[1] Once again, the aviators began to see Chambers as a hindrance to advancing aviation because the captain had no concept of flying except for the mechanical side of it, and even then, he saw pusher-type planes as the future of aviation. The pilots probably did not understand the political basketball involved for Chambers to gain appropriations while different bureaus continued infighting about which bureau would control aviation. His naval pilots came from another generation, not merely pilots controlling an airplane

The Wright B-2 aircraft in the Severn River, near Greenbury Point, Annapolis, in 1912. Lieutenant Herbster rebuilt the B-1, and it was redesignated as the B-2. William Billingsley was killed while flying this plane. (Courtesy of the US Naval History and Heritage Command, NH 44375)

but also in their schooling. Towers, for example, majored in engineering in college and saw potential advancements in aviation through physics.

The pilots, once again, clashed among themselves, primarily regarding who trained them – the Wrights or Curtiss. There appeared two opposing camps, which built animosity regarding lawsuits against Curtiss by the Wrights. Rodgers and Herbster were trained by the Wrights, while Ellyson and Towers were Curtiss men. Orville had so much hate toward Curtiss that he would not accept Curtiss-trained pilots, such as Towers, as trained aviators. Two decades later he admitted that Towers "had one of the finest minds in the service." Chambers brushed it off as simple jealousy among the pilots and desired that the aviators assist each other to learn to fly both Curtiss and Wright planes, since each had different control systems. The captain had no hint that his aircraft, with rear-mounted engines, would become one of the standard aircraft designs for the Navy over the next decade.

Fleet Operations (1913–14)

At the time, he said, "In my opinion, the Wright control must be very tiresome to the arms in fluky winds, aside from its unnatural features, but… I am extremely anxious to settle upon a standard control [meaning his own] for the Navy…"[2]

Ellyson remained an active flyer for the rest of 1912. Still, disagreements with Chambers intensified. Spuds became angrier at the captain after Ellyson broke his foot in January 1913 after falling down a flight of stairs. He could not fly and became agitated; the captain ignored his ideas. Ellyson became Chambers' assistant while his foot healed; Spuds hated it. His boss' attitude never seemed to waver, although his subordinate jumped the chain of command. The captain wrote, "I never lost faith in Ellyson, notwithstanding the fact that he lost his head far enough one day to go to the Chief of the Bureau and state that he did not agree with my policies, without ever mentioning to me the points wherein he differed…"[3]

Lieutenant Bellinger seated at the controls of an early Curtis A-type seaplane, A-1 to A-3, at an unknown location, possibly off Annapolis, circa 1911. (Courtesy of the US Naval History and Heritage Command, NH 56143)

Spuds still loved to fly; he just hated the bureaucracy. His days were numbered. He wrote to his wife Helen:

> … I have decided to quit flying for good and all, that is never to get in a machine again for any reason. Things have come to such a pass here that I had to decide, either to go to Annapolis and take charge of the camp or quit for good. I have not told anyone yet of my decision, nor will I for the present. I cannot do the job half way… I hope you approve.[4]

Winter at Annapolis forced the fledgling naval air service to look for better weather. In January 1913, the fleet began exercises off Cuba, and the aviation detachment at Annapolis wanted to participate. Naval aviation at the time consisted of five certified officers and one student, Bernard Smith; pilots Godfrey "Chevy" de Chevalier, William Billingsley, and Patrick N. L. Bellinger would join the detachment between January and June in the 18-week maneuvers.

Bellinger, as another southerner, like most of the first ten naval aviators, grew up in Cheraw, Georgia, and attended Clemson College for two years before being appointed to the Naval Academy for four years, passing the physical despite weighing only 106lb. To gain weight and muscle, he became a boxer. Upon graduating from the Academy, class of 1907, he proceeded to serve aboard the *Vermont* (BB-20) and *Wisconsin* (BB-9). He then went in to submarine duty, commanding the C-4. Bellinger's entry into aviation proved cumbersome as several months passed following his application for aviation duty. He asked Towers to check the status and was informed his slot had gone to William Billingsley due to a clerk's spelling error with their names.

On November 26, 1912, after waiting more than a year, he was detached from the C-4 for aviation duty. He completed flight training and was issued ACA certification Certificate No. 4 on May 3, 1913, and Naval Aviator No. 9 on June 1, 1914. He would become certified as a seaplane pilot while participating in the Guantanamo exercises.[5]

The air detachment's purpose in Cuba was to participate in and market aviation during fleet maneuvers off Cuba beginning on January 6. Ellyson was conducting experiments at Hammondsport during that time so did not join the detachment, and thus Towers became the senior aviator. Towers loved to fly, and by the summer of 1912, he had accumulated 202 flights and 2,035 miles to Ellyson's 200 and 2,227, so it was logical to appoint Towers

Photographed circa January–March 1913, during naval aviation's first fleet deployment to Guantanamo Bay. The two left hangars appear to contain the Wright B-1 and B-2 aircraft. Ships of the Atlantic fleet are in the distance, with USS *San Francisco* (CM-2) in the right center. (Collection of Commander T. G. Ellyson; courtesy of the US Naval History and Heritage Command, NH 95635)

Camp personnel, circa January–March 1913, during Naval aviation's first fleet deployment. Officers (left to right): Lieutenant (jg) Patrick Bellinger, USN; First Lieutenant Bernard Smith, USMC; First Lieutenant Alfred Cunningham, USMC; Lieutenant John Towers, USN; Ensign Victor Herbster, USN; Ensign William Billingsley, USN; Ensign Godfrey Chevalier, USN. Note the goat and dog mascots and canvas hangar with a Curtiss A-type airplane inside. (Naval Historical Foundation; Collection of Commander Theodore G. Ellyson; courtesy of the US Naval History and Heritage Command, NH 95636)

over Rodgers. Herbster, however, was considered a problem. Towers and others classified him as jealous of nearly everyone. A troublemaker and anxious to excel, as some described him, he hated to share the Wright B-2 he'd built from scratch. He appeared to hate Jack Towers as well. He complained to Chambers that his superiors would not allocate additional funds for the Wright machines since Towers was pro-Curtiss.[6]

Meanwhile, the aviation detachment set up an aviation camp on Fisherman's Point, Guantanamo Bay, Cuba, for aircraft flying, scouting missions, spotting mines, and detecting submerged submarines. Aircraft were still primitive pusher-types that lacked speed and agility. Once again, the higher naval echelon saw planes as experimental, but their use during maneuvers swayed some military personnel. Some 100 sailors and Marines were taken up for flights to arouse interest. At Guantanamo, naval and marine pilots took senior officers for rides in their airplanes, hoping to show how valuable aviation could be for the fleet. One officer taken on a flight was Commander William A. Moffett, the executive officer of the battleship *Arkansas* (BB-33). He attempted to talk Towers out of aviation but failed to persuade the aviator.

An AH-type plane, either AH-2 or AH-3, over Guantanamo Bay in 1913. Both types suffered from mechanical issues during the fleet exercise, limiting their use during the exercises. (Courtesy of the US Naval History and Heritage Command, NH 112925)

Fleet Operations (1913–14)

Lieutenants Smith and Cunningham at Guantanamo Bay, Cuba, in 1913. Smith was earning his ACA certification at the time and would become USMC Aviator No. 2. (Courtesy of the Bernard Smith Collection [COLL/1691] Marine Corps History Division)

Lieutenant Ellyson and possibly his maintenance crew during the Guantanamo exercises in 1913. All aircraft participating in Cuba suffered mechanical failures. (Courtesy of the Alfred Cunningham Collection, Marine Corps Archives)

Early Naval Aviators at Guantanamo Bay, Cuba: Smith, Bellinger, Cunningham, Billingsley, Herbster, and Chevalier, sometime before June 1913. (Courtesy of the US Navy History and Heritage Command, 80-G-426948)

Post-Guantanamo fleet exercises set milestones, including the first death of a naval aviator. Bellinger broke the world's seaplane record on June 13, 1913, by ascending to 6,200ft in 45 minutes, flying the Curtiss AH-3. A week later, on June 20, Towers hitched a ride with Billingsley on the B-2, now fitted with pontoons. Herbster was initially assigned for the flight but missed it; a mechanic initially took his place but was replaced by Towers. Finally, at 9.23am that Wednesday, the plane shoved off.

The route was to St. Michaels, Maryland, and back, a round-trip distance of about 40 miles, with Billingsley as pilot and Towers as a passenger. The pilot reversed his course at St. Michaels and was at about 3,000ft when the machine crossed Kent Island Neck about 10.00am. Then, losing altitude slowly while passing around the edge of a rain squall, turbulent air lifted both men out of their seats. Towers managed to wrap himself around the forward wing strut on his starboard side. Billingsley was pitched forward onto the control yoke, throwing the machine into a steep dive. At about 1,200ft, Billingsley fell clear of the machine with his arms spread out and into the Chesapeake Bay – the first naval aviator fatality.[7]

According to Towers' report:

> The machine seemed to take quick darts, shifts of direction, now and then. I don't know how I ever held on… After the machine turned upside down it shot down at least 400 feet, not straight but at an angle of about 50 degrees… I was still holding on with my left hand, unable to get a better grip. The machine was still upside down…Then came the crash.[8]

Towers managed to hold on even as the plane struck the water in an inverted glide. He was in shock and bruised over his entire body, but he survived. A search party found Billingsley's body a week later. The B-2 was a total

On June 13, 1913, Ensign William "De Votie" Billingsley, Naval Aviator No. 9, was piloting. Suddenly, the plane hit severe turbulence 1,600ft above Chesapeake Bay. Without warning, Billingsley was hurled out of his seat and fell to his death into the water far below. This tragically made Billingsley the first navy pilot to make the supreme sacrifice. Incredibly, John Towers, the passenger, was able to catch and cling to a wing strut and ride the plummeting unpiloted plane down, miraculously surviving the crash. After that incident, he ordered safety belts for all the Navy planes. (Courtesy of the US Naval History and Heritage, NH 56176)

wreck. Billingsley's death would lead to the installation of safety straps and seat belts in the Wright machines and Curtiss planes. The death did not impede the advancement of naval aviation, but Herbster had to defend the airworthiness of the B-2; he could not explain its constant mechanical problems, but those were not to blame – the absence of a seatbelt/harness caused Billingsley's death.[9]

Despite the death of Billingsley, aviation was becoming popular, and by the spring of 1913, Navy Secretary Josephus Daniels made a brief flight with Lieutenant Towers during an inspection tour of the academy while Assistant Secretary of the Navy Franklin Roosevelt flew as a passenger with Ensign Herbster at the controls. The formal establishment of naval aviation as a separate division of the Navy materialized on October 7, 1913, with the creation of the Chambers' Board of Aeronautics, appointed by Secretary Daniels and named after senior member Captain Chambers. The primary purpose was to create a comprehensive plan for organizing the Naval Aeronautic Service. The

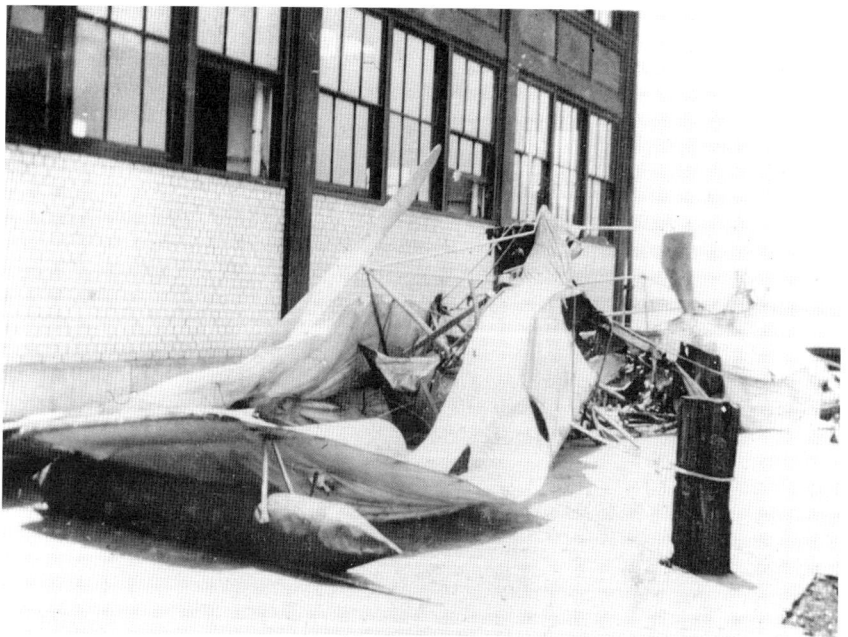

The Naval engineering experiment station, Annapolis, Maryland. The aircraft wreckage on the station grounds is probably the Wright B-2 following its fatal crash on June 20, 1913. (Courtesy of the US Naval History and Heritage Command, NH 43902)

board members included Commander Carlo B. Brittain, Commander Samuel S. Robison, Lieutenant Manley H. Simons, Lieutenant Towers, Assistant Naval Constructor Lieutenant Holden C. Richardson, and First Lieutenant Cunningham. Following 12 days of deliberation, the board submitted a report emphasizing the need for expansion and the integration of aviation within the fleet. This report established the first comprehensive program for the orderly development of naval aviation.

The board's recommendations included setting up an aeronautic center at Pensacola for:

Establishing flight and ground training
Study of advanced aeronautical engineering
Creating a central aviation office under the secretary to co-ordinate the aviation work of the bureaus
Assigning a ship for training in operations at sea
To make practical tests of equipment necessary for such operations, and assigning one aircraft to every major combatant ship.

The aircraft originally designated A-2 seen here as the C-2 at Pensacola, with black USN lettering and possibly painted light gray in the aft section and had natural varnished wood on the bow. (Courtesy of the Naval History and Heritage Command)

Accordingly, the board approved the recommendation to establish an aviation station at Pensacola in January 1914. Apparently, it seriously considered establishing an independent Marine Aviation section according to the following memorandum.

Op-MLB 6 January, 1914
TO: Lieutenant J. H. Towers USN. (Thru Superintendent, Naval Academy
Subject: Marine Section of Navy Aviation Camp
Reference: (a) Dept's letter N-13Z, 12/27/13

1. Reference (a) is hereby cancelled.
2. Fist Lieut. B. L. Smith USMC and 2d Lieut. W. M. McIlvaine USMC will go by USS *Hancock* from Philadelphia, Pa., direct to Culebra with the Advance Base outfit, including Navy Flying Boat C-3, Navy O.W. L. Boat E-1, two hangar tents, spare parts, and other equipment as requested by 1st Lieut. Smith.3. This outfit is to be regarded as a Marine Section of the Navy Flying School to be established at the aeronautic station under your charge.[10]

For days after the memorandum's release, Lieutenant Towers led the aviation unit from Annapolis, consisting of nine officers, 23 enlisted men, seven aircraft, and gear. Portable hangars arrived at the former Navy Yard in Pensacola aboard the aeronautic training ship *Mississippi* under Commander Henry "Rum" Mustin. Naval Aviator No. 11 took command of the station. A native of Philadelphia, Pennsylvania, Mustin was born on February 6, 1874, and graduated from the Naval Academy in 1896. Like most, if not all, naval men who entered aviation, he was characterized as an adventurous individual with fierce determination and athletic abilities. Upon graduating from the academy, he participated in the Philippine independence movement in 1899 as commanding officer of the gunboat USS *Samar* (PG-41*)*. He earned his aviation seaplane license at 29 and would become the commanding officer of aviation activities in Mexico during the Tampico Affair. He was outspoken in supporting naval aviation, including developing high-speed aircraft. Possibly because of his demeanor, he acquired a few enemies within the service who saw aviation as a non-contributing factor in overall naval operations.[11]

Marine Corps aviators continued to organize and advertise the importance of aviation to their fellow Marines, especially the concept of the Air-Ground Task Force. On January 3, 1914, Lieutenants Smith and McIlvain, with mechanics and a flying boat, boarded the USS *Hancock* and sailed for Culebra, Puerto Rico, for fleet exercises. They established a seaplane base from where Smith and McIlvain flew reconnaissance and scouting missions. It was the first time the Corps utilized combined air and ground power together.[12]

Chambers, as before, suggested the creation of an Office of Aeronautics. However, some within the Navy were unimpressed with Chambers' position in aviation administration. Admiral Fiske wanted to replace him before organizing aviation and desired a sizable naval aviation force, not be in charge of a half dozen airplanes. In late October 1913, Captain Bristol, a non-aviator, replaced Chambers as the head of aviation. His previous ill fame came from grounding his ship off the Chinese coast, so he needed a new command, or future promotions may not be offered. His firm administrator skills sealed the deal and Chambers' future. On January 8, 1914, he officially took command of the aeronautic section under the Bureau of Navigation. Chambers meanwhile continued serving throughout World War One until he was relieved of active duty on November 8, 1919, after serving 43 years in the Navy.

In early 1914, three more Curtiss boats were also delivered along with the Burgess-Dunne (the last recommended by Naval Constructor Lieutenant Richardson). The latter aircraft consisted of a long narrow hull and tandem seats. This seaplane, named DH-8, had wings arranged in V form and no tail surfaces. Finally, in the fall of 1914, Curtiss delivered two single-float seaplanes. Those had larger wing surfaces than the earlier types and much larger floats. Another Burgess design, the D-1, later redesignated the AB-6, became a test bed at Pensacola for future Burgess designs. Unfortunately, Lieutenant James M. Murray, Naval Aviator No. 10, was killed flying this aircraft when it stalled at 200ft and crashed into Pensacola Bay.[13]

An early Curtiss F-5 flying boat, possibly one of the five (C-1 to C-5) that were redesignated AB-1 through AB-5. The F-boat series was by far superior to the early A/AH-designated aircraft. (Author's collection)

The first operational test for the Navy's air arm arrived in April 1914 while participating in America's military intervention in the Mexican Revolution and subsequent occupation of Veracruz. By 1914, the US had established a long history of military intervention in the internal affairs of Latin America, exerting a handful of political and military actions before the Mexican War of 1846–48, including counterinsurgency operations between 1833 and 1936 in the newly independent countries of Argentina and Peru. Interventions continued throughout the years leading to the American Civil War, with naval forces engaged in protecting American interests in Argentina (1852–53), Uruguay (1855), Nicaragua (1855–57), Columbia (1856–60), and Paraguay (1859). The initial intervention in Nicaragua was an egregious misuse of military assets with a naval bombardment of San Juan del Norte, Nicaragua (July 9–15, 1854), and subsequent burning of the city by a marine landing party as retribution for insulting the American Minister to Nicaragua. Successive American administrations continued aggressive diplomatic and military pressure in the decades leading to the United States becoming a world military power after the Spanish–American War of 1898. Independence movements

Fleet Operations (1913–14)

Possibly one of the earliest photographs of the Atlantic fleet at Veracruz, Mexico, in April 1914 during the Tampico Crisis. (Courtesy of the US Naval History and Heritage Command, Bernard Smith Collection, Archives Branch, Marine Corps History Division)

within Columbia's Panamanian region (1865–66, 1873, 1885, and 1895) – with revolutionary upheavals in Nicaragua (1867, 1894, 1896, 1898), Uruguay (1868), Haiti (1888, 1891), and Argentina (1890) – cemented American permanence in protecting economic interests in the Americas and the Caribbean.

A century of foreign policies on Latin America coalesced around a central theme of protecting business interests in Latin America, including preventing or overthrowing revolutionary movements the United States viewed as countering the quid pro quo of those interests. As a result, Mexico became a focal point in the Wilson administration's efforts to maintain political and economic stability, especially in the oil-rich regions, where it accounted for 38.5 percent of total American investments.

Diplomatic relations between the US and Mexico became tenuous after General Victoriano Huerta conducted a successful coup in February 1913, resulting in the resignation and assassination of President Francisco I. Madero. President Woodrow Wilson refused to recognize the legitimacy of Huerta's government, amplifying his stance by establishing an arms embargo. That was followed in October by stationing elements of the

Third Squadron, US Atlantic Fleet, off Tampico, Mexico – an oil boomtown 300 miles south of Brownsville, Texas, in the Gulf of Mexico.

The United States was deeply concerned that revolutionary movements could spread across Central and South America, which determined such movements must be eliminated. Mexico would be pivotal in stopping such potential revolutions. Accordingly, the American naval presence off Mexico increased as the Fifth Division of the US Atlantic Fleet, composed of the battleships *Connecticut* (BB-18) and *Minnesota* (BB-22), with cruisers *Chester* (CL-1) and *De Moines* (CL-17), arrived off Tampico under the command of Admiral Henry T. Mayo. His orders were to protect the lives of US citizens and American economic interests tied to Mexico's oil industry in the region.

By early April, Constitutionalist forces had Tampico under siege and in control of oil facilities at Doña Cecilia and Arbol Grande. Clashes between rebel forces and federal forces commanded by General Ignacio Zaragoza intensified, causing the city's US consul to request help to

View on the ship's afterdeck while it was carrying the Navy's first combat air group to Veracruz, Mexico, in April 1914. Planes visible include a Curtiss AB-type flying boat (on deck at left), and a Curtiss AH-type floatplane (on the rear of the 12/45-gun turret). Note the boom rigged to the battleship's superstructure, left, for hoisting the planes on and off the ship. (Official US Navy photograph, now in the collections of the National Archives, NHHC, 80-G-0461428)

evacuate Americans. On April 9, Captain Ralph Earle, commanding the gunboat *Dolphin* (PG-24), sent a whaleboat with unarmed sailors to secure drummed gasoline from a German merchant. Instead, a squad of Zaragoza's men detained the Americans at the dock and marched them to the Mexican headquarters in what became known as the Tampico Affair.

Captain Earle and Consul Clarence Miller met with Zaragoza, who apologized and released the two captured sailors. The general's actions should have been enough to satisfy the Americans. Still, Admiral Mayo saw the incident as a hostile act and sent a letter demanding that the officer in charge of detaining the sailors be severely punished. In addition, he ordered the Mexicans to hoist a US flag prominently ashore and give a 21-gun salute. Although General Zaragoza released the sailors, personally apologized, and arrested the officer in charge of their detainment, Mayo's reaction created a diplomatic crisis. Huerta refused to allow the US flag to be hoisted or saluted on Mexican soil, seeing such acts as humiliating to national sovereignty.

Five days after the Tampico Affair began, President Wilson demanded the Mexicans hoist the American flag and render a 21-gun salute by ordering Rear Admiral Charles Badger's Atlantic Fleet into Mexican waters in preparation for occupying the port of Veracruz. However, the situation rapidly deteriorated as Wilson received news that a German-registered cargo ship carrying weapons for Huerta's forces would arrive at the port of Veracruz in violation of the US arms embargo. Under Rear Admiral Frank F. Fletcher, the Fourth Division arrived in Mexican waters on April 21, with orders from Wilson to occupy Veracruz. Naval and marine forces landed before noon, securing the city the following morning after brief but intense skirmishes with Mexican armed forces.

The Tampico Affair and subsequent occupation of Veracruz brought the first operational use of naval aircraft, resulting in the first time any US naval plane became the target of enemy ground fire. Accordingly, Marine Corps aviation detachment First Section – equipped with three aircraft, an AH-2 hydroplane and flying boats AB-4 and AB-5 – embarked upon the cruiser *Birmingham* (CS-2) from Pensacola on April 20 to join the Atlantic Fleet operating in Mexican waters. Lieutenant John Towers, in command, led First Lieutenant Smith, Ensign Chevalier, 12 enlisted men, and spare parts. Lieutenant (jg) Patrick Bellinger, commanded the Second Section, with student pilots Lieutenant (jg) Richard C. Saufley, Ensign Melvin L. Stoltz, and Ensign Walter D. LaMont. They followed on April 21, embarking on the *Mississippi* with two aircraft: a hydroaeroplane AH-3 and a flying boat AB-3.[14]

Heavy swells did not deter the lowering of flying boat AB-3 from the ship and the first reconnaissance flight of a naval aircraft on April 25. Bellinger took flight in search of a purported mine in Veracruz harbor. The 28-minute flight failed to locate the device, as did a second with Bellinger and Ensign Stolz. Hazardous swells canceled further flights until April 28 when naval aviation scored another first when Bellinger and LaMont, aboard AB-3, flying some 200ft over Veracruz, took the first aerial photograph of a US task force.

On May 3, Bellinger and LaMont went aloft again, operating hydroplane AH-3 in support of US ground forces near Tejar, Mexico, receiving enemy

Lowering a Curtiss hydroplane into the water before conducting the first reconnaissance mission at Veracruz in April 1914 during the Tampico Crisis. (Courtesy of the National Archives via the U.S. Marine Corps Archives)

fire – another first for naval aviation. Still, the plane and its occupants escaped without injury. However, during the morning of the sixth, enemy rifle fire hit AH-3, flown by Bellenger with Lieutenant (jg) Saufley, as the observer while investigating a report of 100 Mexican soldiers encamped near Punta Gorda, a mile north of Veracruz. They found the Mexican force who, possibly stunned at seeing the flying machine, fired several rifle shots toward AH-3. A couple of rounds punctured the thin-skinned airplane, and Bellinger returned to the ship where he reported the engagement. Thus, the encounter became the first combat mission of a US naval plane where it suffered damage from enemy fire.[15]

By late May, the scouting services of the aviation section diminished as the Tampico crisis settled with the exile of General Huerta. The First Section, aboard *Birmingham*, arrived at Veracruz on May 24; after scouting flights at Tampico, the *Mississippi* began its voyage back to Pensacola on June 12, 1914. The deployment of naval aircraft proved the significant importance of stationing aircraft as advance scouts when the future of naval aviation was in doubt. Still, in the months to come, a war in Europe would prove the importance of aviation as a tool of war.[16]

First flight of a Navy plane on the warlike mission at Veracruz, Mexico, piloted by Lieutenant Bellinger, April 1914. (Courtesy of the National Archives, 80-G-410394a from the Marine Corps Archives)

Contact!: Early US Naval and Marine Corps Aviation, 1911–18

The second flight on a warlike mission at Veracruz, Mexico, April 1914. The pilot was Lieutenant R. C. Saufley. The plane is a Curtiss AH type, and the ship is probably the *Mississippi*. (Courtesy of the National Archives, 80-G-39198 from the Marine Corps Archives)

US Navy aviation camp on the beach at Veracruz, Mexico, 1914. Planes on the shore include a Curtiss AH-type pusher and a Curtiss F-type flying boat. (Courtesy of the US Naval History and Heritage Command, NH 73778)

Left to right: Ensign W. D. Lamont (unknown Naval Aviator No.), Commander Mustin, Lieutenant Saufley, and Lieutenant Bellinger (seated) at the aviation camp, Veracruz. (Author's collection, official Navy photograph)

Austria's invasion of Serbia on July 28, 1914, quickly grew from a regional war into a world war as Germany crossed the border into Luxembourg and Belgium on August 4. Prewar military alliances remained strong as Britain, France, and Russia declared war against Germany and the Austro-Hungarian Empire. Neither President Wilson nor the American people desired to become embroiled in the European war, except for the industrialists of a free-market economy. Therefore, the United States declared neutrality on August 4; although merchant ships continued to sail from US ports to Europe, their cargo holds, courtesy of domestic manufacturers, having a slight bias in supplying the warring nations, were filled with metaphorical "guns and butter." Neutrality became a valuable tool for the US military as the warring factions allowed access to the mechanisms of war, enabling military advisors to inspect the military industries of the warring nations. This idea was not lost on the advocates of

Planes and personnel at the Veracruz naval aviation camp. On the right is Lieutenant Bellinger. Planes are Curtiss AH (right) and AB (left) types. According to *Wings for the Fleet*, page 108, the AH behind Bellinger was the first Navy plane to be hit by enemy fire. (Courtesy of the National Archives, 80-G-391984 from the Marine Corps Archives)

Mechanics, possibly Lieutenant Barney Smith's, at Veracruz sometime between April and May 1914 during the Tampico Crisis. (Courtesy of the National Archives from the Bernard Smith Marine Corps Archives)

Fleet Operations (1913–14)

A Curtiss pusher seaplane used at Veracruz. The landing gear was built for installation while en route to Mexico on board the *Mississippi*. This plane was used by Lieutenant Bellinger. (Courtesy of the National Archives, 902874 from the Marine Corps Archives)

Marine artist Henry Reuterdahl is carried ashore after a flight over Veracruz, circa April–June 1914. The plane is a Curtiss AB pusher type. (Courtesy of the National Archives, 80-G-391983 from the Marine Corps Archives)

The US aviation camp at Veracruz circa April–May 1914. Note the landing gear in place of the pontoon(s). (Courtesy of the Alfred Cunningham Collection, Marine Corps Archives)

The launching of a hydroplane at the US aviation camp, Veracruz, in either April or May 1914. The planes were fitted with pontoons or landing gear. (Courtesy of the US Naval History and Heritage Command)

naval aviation as it allowed them entry as observers to British, French, and German aircraft factories and aerodromes (airfields). However, in terms of personnel and aircraft, the growth of naval aviation remained stagnant during the prewar years of 1914–16.

The few aviators continued to experiment with the practicalities of flight primarily by setting endurance and distance records. Organizationally, naval aviation was enhanced with the establishment of an official Office of Aeronautics on July 1, 1914, which Chambers had pushed for, and which Secretary of the Navy Daniels lauded by stating to journalists: "The science of aerial navigation has reached a point where aircraft must form a large part of our naval for offensive and defensive operations…aircraft will take their place with the fleet."

By November of that year, naval aviation consisted of only 12 planes in service. The secretary designated a director of naval aeronautics on November 23, 1914, to become the officer in charge of naval aviation. Captain Mark L. Bristol, already serving in that capacity, officially reported to the Secretary of the Navy under the new title. Interestingly, he provided very little funding for the newly established Office of Naval Aviation. [17]

America invented the airplane, yet funding for military aeronautics was minuscule compared to major European nations. Japan was much more foresighted, as seen by the aviation expenditures of those countries in 1912. France was spending $7,500,000, Russia budgeted $5,000,000, while Germany, Italy, and Great Britain allocated $2,000,000. Even Japan spent $600,000 a year. Nevertheless, the United States Congress and the US Army felt that $140,000 was enough to fund military aeronautics.[18]

The Navy Board requested $1,297,700 to implement the aviation program. Captain Chambers, and later Bristol, struggled with an unresponsive Congress in appropriating monies for naval aviation and from obstructionists among the dreadnaught mindset of naval officials. Finally, Congress authorized the $10,000 for aviation in its second year and approved $55,000 more from amounts initially appropriated for other purposes. The skeptical admirals did not divert all the money, however. In the same year, Congress authorized $100,000 for Army aviation.

The appropriations and growth of Army and Navy aeronautics fell behind that of European counterparts, falling to 14th in the world by 1914. This was less than two years after the Navy formed an independent aviation program – six years after the Army's Signal Corps purchased its first aircraft in 1909. From then onward, supporters of naval aviation would see the Army taking the lead in American military aviation as Congress authorized far more money to the Army between 1912 and 1916. In the 1911 fiscal year, Congress appropriated $125,000 for Army aviation compared to $10,000 for the Navy. By 1912, the Army Signal Corps had six Wright aircraft in its inventory.

Congress passed an appropriation bill of over $300,000 for Army aeronautics for the fiscal year 1916 (September 1915–August 1916), while naval aeronautics received $200,000 over five years. By the fiscal year 1917, the Army's inventory had grown to 224 aircraft – all obsolete compared to their European counterparts. By 1917, the US Army's air establishment consisted of 131 officers, who were practically all pilots and student pilots (11 were reservists on active duty), and 1,087 enlisted men.

Total Military Aeronautical Expenditures 1912–17

Presidential Administration	Fiscal Year	Amount Allocated
Taft	1912	$24,532
Taft	1913	$56,032
Wilson	1914	$194,492
Wilson	1915	$219,429
Wilson	1916	$884,679
Wilson	1917	$3,920,000

Chapter 6

The United States Naval Reserve Flying Corps

The Naval Appropriations Act, passed on March 3, 1915, expanded the number of naval personnel assigned to aviation to 48 officers and 96 enlisted, with 12 officers and 24 enlisted for the Marine Corps. Bristol requested 80 planes for 1916 with pilots and crews, but Secretary Daniels and Rear Admiral Benson turned him down. President Wilson requested that Congress keep naval aviation funding at the 1915 level. When Wilson discovered the cost of one airplane for the Navy, he asked, "Why can't the Navy buy just one aeroplane and let them all take turns flying it?"

A year later, on July 10, 1915, General Order No. 153 recommended the naval militia establish its aeronautic force not exceeding six officers and 38 enlisted personnel. By 1916, supporters of national defense took a more aggressive tone for increased spending on aeronautics, as Alexander Graham Bell stated to the National Convention of the Navy League in April 1916: "Navies do not protect against aerial attack. This also we know that heavier-than-air flying machines of the aeroplane type have crossed right over the heads of armies, millions of men, armed with the most modern weapons of destruction, and have raided places in the rear. Armies do not protect against aerial war."[1]

Malaise was the constant companion of the average American held together by a political system in which the country remained divorced from international matters, with military affairs centered on the defense of the continental United States. The Army argued that air defense should

President Wilson questioned the Navy's need for planes but supported Army aviation. He asked whether one plane would satisfy the Navy's needs. Even at the time, there were few supporters within the Navy to endorse allocating money to aviation. (Courtesy of the Library of Congress)

become part of that service's mission, while the Navy continued to hold on to its traditional role of protecting the seas. Such groups as the ACA, the National Security League, the American Defense Society, and the Navy League wanted the Navy to allocate more significant money to aviation. However, the ACA became the spotlight for American defense when it established the National Aeroplane Fund to train and equip airmen for state militias. Moreover, Theodore Roosevelt became the foremost speaker on American preparedness, and supported the creation of the First Yale Unit for aviation training. Roosevelt spoke on naval aviation during one of his preparedness speeches: "We might conceivably supply ourselves with seaplanes, but where would we get the pilots to operate them and the observers capable of rendering them of value? It takes six months to turn out a first-class operator, and competent observers could hardly be trained in less time."

At the National Convention of the Navy League in April 1916, Alexander Graham Bell cited the lack of trained pilots as evidence of America's poor readiness to defend itself. He said, "But there is one element concerning the flying machine that we are not producing, that we cannot produce in an emergency, and that is the men. We can produce machines, but not aviators. That takes time." He went on, "Where are we to get the men, and where are we to train them?"[2]

Passing the National Defense Act of June 3, 1916, unleashed the mobilization process. Congress finally bowed to pressure from the preparedness forces, whose calls for action reached a crescendo when Germany unleashed an unrestricted submarine campaign. The National Defense Act placed the country on a wartime footing. It modestly increased the strength of the regular Army and expanded and federalized the National Guard. Nevertheless, America was unprepared for the war regarding military personnel and materiel, as noted in the following quote by Lieutenant Commander W. Atlee Edwards, an early supporter of naval aviation, on the status of prewar US airpower:

> In common with all the nations involved in the Great War, save perhaps Germany, America was unprepared for using aircraft as a tool of war. There was some excuse for this in the case of Great Britain and France. Aeronautics was hardly beyond its beginnings in 1914, but this does not explain America's lack of attention to air preparedness. Nor is it an excuse to say that we could not foresee our participation in the general world upheaval, for events proved that anything was possible, and a reasonable amount of foresight in preparation would have been of incalculable value during 1917. Indeed, it is more than strange that Americans should have noted the enormous expansion of aerial activities in Europe, read the accounts of results obtained by the air squadrons on land and sea, and yet remained so inert in demanding at least a nucleus of an air force. In fact, before 1916, no appropriations, save small ones for experimental purposes, had been made for aviation, the first appropriation of any consequence, $1,000,000, being made in 1916.[3]

The Navy had acquired its first aircraft six years earlier. Its first pilots trained piecemeal and had nothing resembling a formally organized

USS *North Carolina* (CA-12) became the Navy's first official seaplane tender. It was used to send the most experienced naval aviators to France in 1914. (Courtesy of the Naval History and Heritage Command, NH 60278)

aviation force – with not one aircraft designed for combat. The Navy did acquire N-9 seaplanes in late 1916, and the first dedicated seaplane tender, *North Carolina* (ACR-12), was placed into commission. Outside the Navy, civilian aviation organizations existed, such as the naval militia, the National Naval Volunteers, and university student groups that raised money to purchase aircraft and hire mechanics.

A standard organization prescribed by General Order No. 153 on July 10, 1915, became the first to provide for an aeronautic force within the naval militia. Its composition, paralleling that of other forces established simultaneously, consisted of sections not exceeding six officers and 28 enlisted men, with two branches forming a division. Officers served in the "aeronautics duty only" category, with the highest rank provided as lieutenant commander at the division level. The Navy's enlisted structure meant that personnel holding regular rates as machinist mates and electricians were to perform duties as aeronautic machinists, while carpenter mates were to

Admiral William S. Sims, Commander, US Naval Forces Operating in European Waters. Sims supported enlarging the Navy's aviation branch in France during World War One. (Courtesy of the US Naval History and Heritage Command Photograph UA 48.02)

perform duties as aviation mechanics. While the warring powers expanded their air forces, the US Navy continued to plug along without adequate funding. Lieutenant Commander Edwards pointed out,

> That our outlook in [naval] aviation at the moment of our entry into the war was gloomy, to say the least, is obvious; we were not only unprepared but we had very little idea of how to prepare for aerial warfare, as is evidenced by the following cablegram from the Secretary of the Navy to Admiral Sims under date of 20 April, 1917: Immediate and full information is desired by the Navy Department as to the present development by the British of their naval aeronautics. What style of aircraft is most used, and what is most successful over the water? What is the method of launching at sea when [the] carrier vessel [seaplane tender] is underway? For coastal patrol and submarine searching, what are the types of aircraft used?[4]

Contact!: Early US Naval and Marine Corps Aviation, 1911–18

Rear Admiral Robert E. Peary, circa 1919. He died on February 20, 1920, in Washington, DC. He supported the creation of a naval reserve flying corps. (Courtesy of the US Naval History and Heritage Command, NH 47447)

Rear Admiral Robert E. Peary directed the creation of the National Aerial Coast Patrol Commission in 1916 to provide trained Aerial Coast Patrol units and aircraft to patrol the coasts of the United States against potential enemy activity. Aerial Coast Patrol units were recruited primarily from students studying at Yale, Harvard, Princeton, and Columbia Universities, termed the Yale Units. Most of the recruits came from that university, as will be discussed later. The members, mostly in their late teens and early twenties, were recruited into the US Naval Reserve Force (USNRF) Class 5 (Aviation) under the 1916 Naval Appropriations Bill. Several hundred young men were recruited and trained by the Aerial Coast Patrol, initially named the Naval Reserve Flying Corps (NRFC).

A memorandum dated October 25, 1916, from Captain Bristol to Rear Admiral Victor Blue, Chief of the Bureau of Navigation, provided details on the composition of the NRFC for

The United States Naval Reserve Flying Corps

Above: Burgess-Dunn AH-7 operated by the New York naval militia. State aerial militias were established in 1916 to patrol offshore off the United States. The militias began to disappear once the United States declared war, and many in the militia became naval aviators. (Author's collection)

Right: Josephus Daniels served as Secretary of the Navy during Woodrow Wilson's presidency. He was in office from March 5, 1913, to March 5, 1921. On January 10, 1914, he stated that aircraft must be an integral part of the Navy. (Courtesy of the US Navy History and Heritage Command Photograph, NH 2336)

commissioned officers aged 20 to 28 and enlisted men aged 22 to 35. The USNRF would consist of:

(1) Officers of the Line of the Navy and the Marine Corps, detailed as student aviators for the Courses of Instruction as laid down in the Bureau of Navigation's Circular of January 26, 1916.
(2) Enlisted men of the Navy detailed as student airmen for the Courses of Instruction as laid down in the aforesaid Circular.
(3) Enlisted men transferred to and rated as members of the Naval Flying Corps in accordance with the requirements herein laid down. Those are mechanics with knowledge of gas engines and machine tools.
(4) Enlisted men and civilians enlisted in the Naval Flying Corps as herein recommended. [The qualifications went on to state they had to be recommended by their commanding officer and shown to be particularly capable, trustworthy, and sober after one year of enlistment.]
(5) Acting Ensigns, Naval Flying Corps, as prescribed by Congress and under regulations prescribed by the Bureau of Navigation.
(6) Student Flyers appointed as required by the law passed by Congress and the regulations prescribed by the Bureau of Navigation.
(7) Line officers for administration (Airplane), Navy Air Pilots (Dirigible), Naval Aviators, airmen, and mechanicians detailed to duty in aircraft as may be necessary to operate aircraft of the Navy.
(8) Acting Ensigns and student flyers appointed and enlisted for the Naval Flying Corps should be required to take the Courses of Instruction as laid down in the Bureau of Navigation's Circular of 26 January 1916 and, in addition, courses of instruction to suit them for naval duties. These courses are to be specially prepared to meet this particular condition.[5]

Those individuals who joined came from the Aerial Coast Patrol, various state naval militias, the Yale Units, and some were experienced civilian pilots. The urgency for training and equipping aerial coastal patrols became apparent as, on October 16, 1916, the German submarine U-53 entered the harbor at the naval base at Newport Beach. It was a clear signal by

German authorities to deter the United States from entering the war and supplying the Allies. The vessel's appearance additionally displayed the vulnerability of the base and that of the entire eastern seaboard. Within 24 hours, U-53 sank five merchant ships off the eastern shoreline of the United States.

However, the money appropriated in 1916 for naval and Marine Corps aviation sections was significantly behind the Army's Aviation Section of the Signal Corps, which consisted of 35 pilots, 1,987 enlisted men, and 55 training airplanes. In comparison, naval and Marine Corps aviation combined comprised only 48 officer pilots, 239 enlisted men, 54 aircraft, one airship, three balloons, and one air station (Pensacola).

By 1916, general supervision of naval aviation fell to Captain Josiah S. McKean, an aide for materials with Lieutenant Towers, who had direct control of naval aviation activities until Captain Noble Irwin relieved him. Captain Irwin continued being an assistant for aviation under the aide for materials until March 7, 1918, when the Secretary of the Navy issued Navy General Order No. 375, creating the office of the Director of Naval Aviation, and Captain Irwin became the first director. This order made the Director of Naval Aviation directly responsible to the Chief of Naval Operations.

Naval aviation suffered a severe setback in training future aviators when the aviation ship *North Carolina*, with most of the aviation service's personnel on board, was sent to Europe to evacuate Americans. The ship stayed in European waters until the summer of 1915. Consequently, very little training transpired at Pensacola due to sending the best and most experienced naval aviators to Europe. Lieutenant Towers became assistant naval attaché in London. At the same time, on August 21, 1914, Lieutenant Commander Mustin, with Lieutenant (jg) Patrick Bellinger and the Marine Corps' second aviator, First Lieutenant Smith, arrived in Paris, France, to tour aircraft factories and aerodromes as neutral observers. Those junkets followed the inspection of German aircraft facilities and bases, since the Allies and Germans wanted to curry favor with the Americans. Nevertheless, sending Smith and Towers to Europe was invaluable as it created a working

Above left: Captain Noble Edwin Irwin, Director of Naval Aviation, was wounded during the Spanish–American War. He pushed for additional allocations for aviation and was awarded the Navy Cross for his command of naval aviation. (Courtesy of the US Naval History and Heritage, NH 1091)

Above right: Vice Admiral Josiah S. McKean, USN, aboard the flagship USS *Wyoming* at the time he served as commanding officer of the Scouting Fleet. He graduated from Annapolis in 1884 and was awarded the Distinguished Service Medal as acting Chief of Naval Operation. (Courtesy of the US Naval History and Heritage Command Photograph, NH 47985)

relationship and collaboration between naval and Marine Corps aviation. In 1917, the American naval attaché in Paris, Commander William R. Sayles, reported on Lieutenant Smith: "Under practically war conditions, [he] had as much knowledge of the theory and practice of aviation as any officer in the world and that he would be invaluable to the country on aviation duty."[6]

A positive relationship between the two was vital in obtaining appropriations to expand Marine Corps aviation. Meanwhile, as naval officers investigated the capabilities and use of aircraft in Europe, the service's fledgling air arm remained at a standstill throughout the

Above: The first catapult plane (AB-2) launched from USS *North Carolina* on November 5, 1915, probably at Pensacola; Lieutenant Mustin was the pilot. (Courtesy of the US Naval History and Heritage Command Photograph, UA 462.04)

Right: Lieutenant Commander Mustin, USN, 1914. His attitude toward safety made friends and enemies within the naval establishment. (Courtesy of the US Naval History and Heritage Command Photograph, NH 361)

remainder of 1914 but picked up again as the *North Carolina* returned to Pensacola. By 1915, naval aviation continued to evolve in organization and capabilities while slowly gaining trained personnel and aircraft.[7]

While Smith was away in Europe, McIlvain became the senior Marine Corps aviator. His forward thinking on the role of Marine Corps aviation became instrumental in World War One and beyond. He saw that land flying would become an essential aspect of aviation, as was seen by the Army's landplane operations. As a result, he requested a temporary assignment to the Army Aviation School in San Diego, California: "My reason for requesting this, is that I think Marine officers doing any flying, should be able to pilot either over land or over water machines, so that in case of an expedition, they would be of some use to the Marine Corps on land, as well as the Navy at sea."[8]

The Navy denied his request, but it later paved the way for Alfred Cunningham to request a Marine Corps landplane unit during World War One. McIlvain's interest in the Corps having a dual role of seaplane and landplane duties may have been instrumental in Cunningham's return to aviation. He said, "My reason for making this request is my interest in and knowledge of this work and my good record while engaged in it as shown by my efficiency reports." In the spring of 1916, Cunningham requested assignment to the Army school for land flying, becoming the first Marine aviator to attend the course. There, he learned the skills that would be utilized in France when he formed the First Marine Aviation Force.[9] His pursuit of acquiring additional skills and pushing for Cunningham's training may have led the Secretary of the Navy, Daniels, to write a request to the Secretary of the War, Newton Baker: "It is desired to train a limited number of naval aviators to fly land machines, in order to provide for Advanced Base Operation of the Navy, and to have officers of the Marine Corps so trained that they will be available when the Marines are acting with the Army."[10]

By the dawn of 1916, Europe's war was nearly two years old and had become a quagmire consisting of fortifications, tunnels, and trenches stretching across the French and Belgian countryside for hundreds of miles. Tens of thousands of men were sacrificed in useless battles to gain not miles but feet and yards. Neutrality still held firm in the United States, but some believed America would one day join the fray, and thus the country would need to be prepared for such an eventuality of war. The sinking of the passenger ship *Lusitania*, the deaths of over 100 Americans aboard the ship, the Zimmerman Telegram, in which the Germans requested and urged Mexico to enter the war against the US, and the issuance of unrestricted submarine warfare by the Germans, moved the United States closer to join the Allies. By 1916 it became evident to many knowledgeable individuals that war was closing in.

The motto "He has kept us out of the war" aided in Wilson's reelection in 1916. However, in April 1917, a month after his inauguration, the statement was no longer valid as President Wilson asked Congress to declare war. Nevertheless, the country was not militarily ready to engage

The Curtiss AB-2 (C-2) aircraft catapulted from *Coal Barge 214* during catapult experiments at Pensacola, in April 1915. Such testing was conducted before attempting to launch from ships. (Courtesy of the US Naval History and Heritage Command, NH 43905)

the Central Powers. The strength of the Army was less than 135,000, but the Navy was more extensive, with over 194,000 men and some 44 ships. Yet, naval aviation was seriously understrength.

An inventory of naval aviation effects in the spring of 1917 showed that it had practically nothing in the way of materiel and very few personnel. "Would our intervention be sufficiently prompt to ensure success?" asked Admiral Sims. He continued:

> The outlook in aviation of the United States' entry into the war was gloomy, to say the least, and is unmistakable. The Navy was not only unprepared, but it also had a minimal idea of how to prepare for aerial warfare, as is evidenced by the following cablegram from the Secretary of the Navy to Admiral Sims on the date of 20 April 1917.
>
> We deduced our mission: (a) To make our primary air effort a continuous bombing offensive against enemy naval objectives. (b) To make our secondary air effort a patrol of those areas frequented by enemy submarines in readiness for a tactical offensive. (c) Troop and merchant convoy escort duty. This general policy was endorsed by Admiral Sims and agreed to, in principle, by the Navy Department.[11]

Admiral Bradley Allen Fiske, a supporter of aeronautics, voiced his opinion before the House Naval Committee on March 24, 1916:

> I became convinced and I am still convinced that the thing in which we are more backward than any other thing is aeronautics… No matter how fine and strong you are, if you have a weak point you want to out for that, and in aeronautics I think we are weaker than we are in anything else… we need a competent aeronautical corps and we need it right off.[12]

The bill created the means to create and expand naval aviation support, but growth in personnel and aircraft remained stagnant. By authorizing the establishment of the National Aerial Coast Patrol Commission and the NRFC, along with authorizing aircraft purchases, including providing ten planes for the naval militia, a somewhat diluted gesture was made in expanding naval aviation. Fiske understood the Navy was woefully unprepared for war, not just in aviation but in manpower, stating the service was short of battlecruisers and nearly 17,000 men. Three months after speaking to the committee, he retired, at the mandatory retirement age of 62.

The Naval Appropriation Act of 1916 established the NRFC to enlist able-bodied men, preferably college educated, for aviation training. The first of these groups was the First Yale Unit, which flew privately purchased early pusher-type Curtiss flying boats at Peacock Point, Long Island, during the summer of 1916.[13]

The authority for the first nucleus of a Naval Air Reserve, first identified as an aeronautic reserve, to the naval militia in the various states, was proposed and adopted by the Navy Department in 1915. At this point, it was entirely a volunteer organization operating on donated funds. By 1916, a total of ten state-run militia units had commenced operations, primarily

F. Trubee Davison established the First Yale Unit in 1916. His desire to become a naval aviator was crushed when he suffered injuries in a plane crash. (Courtesy of the F. Trubee Davison Papers, Manuscripts, and Archives. Yale University Library)

to satisfy the desire for adventure and flight time among naval-oriented aviation enthusiasts. Official federal status was first achieved on August 29, 1916, with the passage of the annual Naval Appropriations Act, which contained a rider providing for establishing an NRFC in that year. Naval Aviation had only commenced five short years before and was still considered unneeded. In 1916, total aviation appropriations were limited to less than $1m. Personnel was limited to 48 officers and 96 enlisted men, plus 12 Marine officers and 24 enlisted men.[14]

In addition, several state naval militias, notably Massachusetts and New York, established aviation units that trained at Squantum, Massachusetts, and Bay Shore, Long Island, New York, respectively.

Peary raised money through individual subscriptions to form the commission. Its first unit, Aerial Coast Patrol No. 1, consisting primarily of Yale students, increased the number of fully or partially trained pilots

The photograph shows men who came to train at the aviation school at Port Washington, Long Island, New York, to become a unit of the Aerial Coast Patrol. Pictured: Robert Lovett, David H. McCulloch (sometimes misspelled McCullough), Albert Dillon Sturtevant (1894–1918) was killed in action, John Martin Vorys, Erl Clinton Barker Gould, Frederick Trubee Davison, Artemus Lamb Gates, John V. Farwell III, and Allan Wallace Ames. (Courtesy of the Library of Congress. Source: Bain News Service, publisher)

The photograph shows Erl Clinton Barker Gould, Frederick Trubee Davison, Artemus Lamb Gates, and others who went to train at the aviation school at Port Washington, and became a unit of the Aerial Coast Patrol. (Courtesy of the F. Trubee Davison Papers, Manuscripts, and Archives. Yale University Library)

outside the Navy. The "Unit," as members called it, comprised affluent young students of the university.

Yet, at first, the unit had no official support from the Navy. Thus, the 18 to 20-year-old sons of early 20th-century American aristocracy enamored with aviation formed an aero club that evolved into the United States NRFC, the first unit of reserve pilots in the Navy. This first group of 29 men, led by the bespectacled Yale sophomore student F. Trubee Davison, enrolled in the program. Davison possessed strong leadership, management, and interpersonal skills along with possibly a notebook filled with family connections to the rich and powerful. His skills created the Yale Unit, and he did not have a problem with recruiting like-minded young men. The group trained at Palm Beach, Florida, equipped with privately purchased seaplanes at their own expense. A second group trained at Newport, and a third at Buffalo.

They were the sons of the millionaire elite. They formed the unit out of patriotism and probably an urge for adventure to pass the time outside of

Yale Unit members Gould, Davison, and Gates, possibly at Port Washington. Gould, Naval Aviator No. 68, became the youngest commanding officer of a naval air station, serving as the CO of NAS Key West at the age of 22. (Courtesy of the Library of Congress)

the day-to-day activities of the highly wealthy, such as traveling, playing polo and tennis, and participating in galas that typified such individuals' lives. Author Marc Wortman named them in his book, *The Millionaires' Unit*. Reading about gallant British and French Air Service pilots flying and battling above the Western Front against German foes gave them the sense of being metaphorical medieval knights. They were not mounted on horses but on fabric-covered flying machines – "knights of the air," such men were named. Many young men across every economic and social class dreamed of becoming pilots. However, what set those men of Yale apart from many others is that they had the influence and financial means to form their private aviation training program. The sons of the privileged formed the framework of the NRFC, and they were young. This private venture had access to private funding, and the young men had the determination.

In June 1916, war with Mexico appeared imminent as President Wilson sent additional Army troops to the Mexican border. F. T. Davison, the 20-year-old son of Henry Pomeroy, a senior partner of JP Morgan & Company, wanted a part in it. Accordingly, Davison gathered the following

Aviation training camp at Port Washington. One of the Yale Unit's seaplanes can be seen in the water. The unit then moved to West Palm Beach, Florida. (Courtesy of the Library of Congress)

Yale undergraduates: Allan Ames, class of '18; Henry P. Davison, Jr., his brother, '20; John Farwell III, '18; Artemus L. Gates. '18; Erl Gould, '18; Robert A. Lovett, '18, Albert Sturtevant, '16; John Vorys, '18; and Yale graduate C. D. Wiman, '15. In addition, two non-Yale men, Wellesley Laud-Brown and Albert Ditman, rounded out the first dozen of the Yale First Unit.[15]

Davison enlisted the aid of John Hayes Hammond, Jr., the governor of the ACA. The latter, in turn, guided him to Henry Woodhouse, an Aero Club member and ardent supporter of military aviation. The famous Arctic explorer Admiral Peary, the chairman of the National Aerial Coast Patrol Commission, envisioned the establishment of air stations along the eastern seaboard as a defense line against invasion. The Yale Unit would be the foundation for establishing such an operation, albeit far away from the problems with Mexico and without the official support of the Navy.[16]

The First Yale Unit's instructor David McCulloch (McCullough). He was awarded the Congressional Medal of Honor during the Tampico Crisis in 1914. He would later serve in France during World War One. (Courtesy of the Library of Congress)

Members of the First Yale Unit in 1917 at West Palm Beach. Back row (left to right): John M. Vorys, Artemus L. Gates, Albert J. Ditman, Allen Ames, instructor David McCullough, F. Trubee Davison, Robert Lovett, Erl Gould. Front row (left to right): Wells Laud-Brown and Harry P. Davison, Jr. John Vorys, Naval Aviator No. 73, served with the British as a patrol plane pilot. Artemus "Di" Gates, Naval Aviator No. 65, was recommended for the Medal of Honor for rescuing the British crew of a Handley Page bomber that crashed at sea but received the Distinguished Service Medal. Albert "Dit" Ditman, Naval Aviator No. 108, became a test pilot in the US. Allen "Alphy" Ames, Naval Aviator No. 67, was assigned to operations and intelligence duties in London. Henry "Harry" Davison, Jr., Naval Aviator No. 72, was assigned to the Northern Bombing Group (NBG) and conducted one of the first ferry flights of a Caproni bomber across the Alps. (Courtesy of the F. Trubee Davison Papers, Manuscripts, and Archives. Yale University Library)

He met Rodman Wanamaker, a New York and Philadelphia merchant, through his new connections and that of his father. Wanamaker, by chance, operated a flying school at Port Washington on Long Island and offered a Curtiss flying boat. One instructor, 26-year-old Pennsylvania native David McCulloch, was an interesting character with prior service as a Brazilian and Italian air services pilot and the Curtiss Aviation School's chief instructor. The Navy would later commission him as a lieutenant with the newly formed NRFC along with the Yale students he instructed. After the war, in May 1919, he co-piloted the NC-3 flying boat on a transatlantic flight.

The unit began learning to maintain aircraft and flight instruction during the summer of 1916 at Locust Valley, New York. According to Davidson, "If it had not been for the interest and enthusiasm of the pupils and their desire to labor in any way that could facilitate instruction, it would have been impossible to accomplish what we did that summer."[17]

The backing of such men as Woodhouse and Peary was quite influential when procuring aircraft and instructors to teach college students to fly. Davison's connections included John Towers, who provided him with moral support and advice when the young man tracked down the aviator in New York City; he suggested the men join the Naval Reserve and follow their plan to train in Palm Beach. Funding of their burgeoning enterprise seemed no issue as some $200,000 came from JP Morgan & Company, which provided half; $25,000 came from millionaire sportsman Lewis Thompson, and businessmen Payne Whitney and George Baker provided another $25,000 each, while other donors contributed the rest.[18]

As with other fledgling pilots of the time, the young men immersed themselves in the principles of aeronautics and in maintaining their one craft. Affluence and influence paid off when the unit received two seaplanes from friends and family. By the end of the summer, McCulloch had trained four of them to solo; they became members of the Aerial Coast Patrol and, in turn, took part in naval maneuvers off Sandy Point, New York. Davison pointed out aircraft were valuable scouting platforms, and the men from Yale were not only interested in developing the aviation branch of naval warfare but were also devoting their own time, money, and energy to meet that end.[19]

More Yale men joined in the fall of 1916 and spring of 1917 as war with Germany seemed inevitable. They included Yale men Charles Beach, '18; Graham Brush, '17; Reginald Coombe, '18; David Ingalls, '20; Robert Ireland, '18; Francis Lynch, '18; Kenneth MacLeish, '19; Archibald McIlwaine, '18; Curtis Read, '18; Russell Read, '20; William A. Rockefeller, '18; Kenneth Smith, '18; W. P. Thompson, '18; C. M. Stewart, '17; and Samuel Walker, '17.[20]

In March 1917, the unit transferred to West Palm Beach for better flying weather and to possibly enjoy the finer things in life that, even at

Right: Bob Lovett, Naval Aviator No. 66, at West Palm Beach. He flew with the RNAS and RAF in France and was instrumental in creating the NBG. (Courtesy of the F. Trubee Davison Papers, Manuscripts, and Archives. Yale University Library)

Below: Gould, Naval Aviator No. 68; Read, Naval Aviator No. 83; Gates, Naval Aviator No. 65, and John Farwell III, Naval Aviator No. 76, preparing to be sent to France. Farwell III served as an armaments officer at NAS Saint-Trojan, France. (Courtesy of the F. Trubee Davison Papers, Manuscripts, and Archives. Yale University Library)

that time, Palm Beach offered – pleasurable fun for the wealthy and well connected. By March 24, 1917, 29 members had enlisted in the Navy with Lieutenant Edward Orrick McDonnell, Annapolis '12, Naval Aviator No. 18, in command. However, Davidson did not join Yale's growing list of naval pilots as he suffered severe injuries during his final solo flight; he did remain in the Navy as a member of the Committee on Aeronautics. Some members would become instructors while others performed patrol duties along the eastern seaboard or went to France and Britain.[21]

The Second Yale Unit centered on training for duty with seaplanes and operating such aircraft from bases along the eastern seaboard of the United States. This was due to massive losses of Allied shipping in the North Atlantic by German submarines. Admirals Peary and Fiske presented a speech to a small group of Yale students, describing the submarine menace and how valuable naval aviation would be to counter this threat. They would become the eyes of the Navy.

Curt Read of the First Yale Unit, possibly taken at West Palm Beach. He was killed while flying a Donner-Denhaut flying boat off the French coast. (Courtesy of the F. Trubee Davison Papers, Manuscripts, and Archives. Yale University Library)

Three individuals from the First Yale Unit are shown here. Two are unknown, with the nicknames of "Sully" and "Big Boots," and Fred Golder. (Courtesy of the F. Trubee Davison Papers, Manuscripts, and Archives. Yale University Library)

The "Wag" crew shown here consisted of Bob Lovett, Sam Walker, Charlie Stewart, Reg Coombe, "Snort" Brush, and "Hen" Landon. Sam Walker, Naval Aviator No. 86, became an anti-submarine pilot. Charlie Stewart (no information). Reginald "Reg" Coombe, Naval Aviator No. 92, became a patrol plane pilot in France. Graham "Snort" Brush, Naval Aviator No. 79, became a "trouble shooter" to investigate delays in the assembly and use of new aircraft. Henry "Hen" Landon, Naval Aviator No. 93, became an anti-submarine pilot in France. (Courtesy of the F. Trubee Davison Papers, Manuscripts, and Archives. Yale University Library)

The entire complement of the First Yale Unit at West Palm Beach was taken in 1916. The sons of wealthy fathers had good times in West Palm Beach after completing a day of flying. (Courtesy of the F. Trubee Davison Papers, Manuscripts, and Archives. Yale University Library)

In April 1917, just days after the declaration of war, the Second Yale Unit was officially organized, consisting of 12 men who began training at their own expense in Buffalo, New York, learning to operate seaplanes from bases along the eastern seaboard. Ganson Goodyear-Depew became the group's leader. The unit named itself Aerial Coast Patrol No. 2, following the example set by Davison in 1916 when forming the first Aerial Coast Patrol. The men lived in tents behind a rented seaplane hangar on the shore of Lake Erie; the location was protected by a breakwater, enabling smooth take-offs and landings. Flight training began using a flight-worn Curtiss F boat on May 30, 1917, with students taking test hops with flight instructor

Fred Zimmer. The fifth flight ended in tragedy when the plane crashed, killing Zimmer and causing severe injuries to his student, Seymour Knox, permanently putting an end to Knox's training.

The Navy seriously considered abolishing the program and sending the remaining students to the Massachusetts Institute of Technology (MIT) ground school, possibly because Knox was the son of Seymour H. Knox – philanthropist and co-founder of the Woolworth chain of stores. Fortunately, Depew obtained the services of civilian pilot Harold Katner, who had 1,500 hours of flying time to his credit and had acquired a new flying boat. His resume and the purchase of a new plane without government funds convinced Admiral Benson, Chief of Naval Operations, to allow the program to continue. The remaining members completed training in October 1917 and were commissioned as ensigns in the United States Naval Air Force (USNAF), formerly the NRFC.

A Curtiss twin-engine flying boat taxiing while operating with probably the Second Yale Unit, Port Washington, New York, 1917. (Courtesy of the Naval History and Heritage Command, NH 44234)

Chapter 7

Pushers Versus Tractors

Admiral Fiske noted the poor state of naval aviation at the time but continued to be a vocal supporter of it, noting its unpreparedness for war. He saw a future where the Navy would have hundreds of planes in service and ready for war. However, when the United States entered World War One, the reality was an organization with fewer than two dozen planes, few fit for combat operations, with 38 qualified pilots and approximately 160 enlisted men. On March 24, 1916, Fiske spoke before the House Naval Committee and understood the poor state of naval aviation. He said:

> When I was Aide for Operations I became convinced and I am still convinced that the thing in which we are more backward than in any other thing is aeronautics; and I think it is a matter of common sense that in any large problem which is composed of a great many factors, we should look out for the weak point you want to look out for that, and in aeronautics I think we are weaker than we are in anything else…we need a competent aeronautical corps and we need it right off… If we get one thousand aeroplanes together and had them well organized to meet an attacking force, we would have aircraft that could drop large bombs and launch torpedoes and it would help a great deal. You see, we could probably get ready to do that in a year.[1]

He additionally noted: "Without the advent of practical aircraft, command of the air becomes just as important as command of the sea, to be for land and sealike operations."

His advice went unheeded as the Navy and Congress saw no need to expand naval aviation as they truly believed the Unites States would not be drawn into the war.² Placed on a total war setting by 1916, the Navy would not have produced the results it wanted, nor was naval aviation close to being ready for war by April 1917. Neither Congress nor the Navy saw a need to fund naval aviation in what both saw as a wasteless endeavor. At Pensacola, safer and more reliable planes were not on the offing. Those within Congress and those of the naval bureaucracy inhibited the growth and advancement of naval aviation, which became a significant issue as the Navy tended not to replace older aircraft.

As a result, the Navy was seriously short in the number of planes procured between 1911 and 1915, with approximately 21 aircraft purchased from

A backdrop of the first two permanent hangars built at the Naval Aeronautic Station at Pensacola. At the rear left, the Navy's AB-2 flying boat, previously designated C-2, taxies through the waters of Pensacola Bay in the fall of 1915. Lieutenant Commander Mustin is probably at the controls. The bureau number on the tail is A-2332, indicating the new designation system adopted in 1914. (Author's collection, US Navy photograph)

Curtiss. Burgess-Dunne, and Wright companies. The approximate number of aircraft purchased by the Navy for each year is shown in the table below:

Year	Number of Aircraft Purchased
1911	3
1912	2
1913	4
1914	6
1915	6
	Total = 21

The lack of better-designed planes and poor training caused the deaths of several pilots between 1913 and 1916. There had been two fatalities in naval aviation by 1915: William Billingsley, who fell to his death over the Chesapeake Bay while piloting the Wright B-2 on June 20, 1913, and Lieutenant (jg) James Murray, killed on February 16, 1914, while operating the Burgess K model when it crashed into Pensacola Bay. Both planes were pusher-types which, by then, the Army Air Service had designated as "man-killers" and were moving onto the tractor-type, with the pilot and crew stationed aft of the engine and radiator. Meanwhile, Captain Chambers, followed by his successor Captain Mark L. Bristol, as Director of Aeronautics, supported the pusher as the Navy's scouting aerial platform for the fleet. Non-aviator administrative chiefs, like Chambers and Bristol, believed the pushers, with the pilot and observer in front with an unobstructed view, were superior to the tractor with the propeller and engine in the front of the plane. The argument continued through the deaths of the two aviators and a student pilot between 1915 and 1916.

In late February 1915, Wadleigh Capehart, Naval Aviator No. 19, was lucky when he nearly fell out of a Curtiss hydroplane when it experienced a "bump" (turbulence) that knocked him out of his seat; he climbed back in and landed. Afterward, Lieutenant Commander Mustin ordered waist straps on all planes. By spring 1915, Mustin had become alarmed and

Lieutenant (jg) James Murray, Naval Aviator No. 10, was killed on February 16, 1914, while operating the Burgess D-1 (Model K) flying boat when it crashed into Pensacola Bay. (Author's collection, official US Navy photograph)

requested safer airplanes and engines. Still, Captain Bristol, the aeronautics chief, scoffed that the aircraft was at fault and would not allow Constructor Richardson to design any new planes. The new aeronautics chief was a firm and decisive administrator. However, he was unpleasant and left behind a trail of bitterness among some of the flyers. Two of those were Bellinger and Mustin, who had both returned from special attaché duty in Europe investigating British, French, and German aircraft manufacturing.[3]

Bristol's major problem was his belief, shared by Chambers and in opposition to flyers, that pusher-type planes were superior planes to the tractor. Bristol wrote in April 1915: "Tractor planes are probably through for military use."[4] His viewpoint was the extreme opposite to that of the warring Europeans who utilized tractors as pursuit, bombing, and reconnaissance aircraft. Perhaps, he meant that type of plane would not be successful for sea duty. The argument continued as he and Richardson were named to the National Advisory Committee on Aeronautics, making them experts but voicing two conflicting views, as Richardson was a certified aviator and Bristol was not. Richardson, meanwhile, expressed his opinion that

Lieutenant Commander Mustin photographed here, probably at Pensacola, in 1914. The Navy seaplane C-3 (redesignated AB-3 in March 1914) is in the background, with a 13-star boat flag flying from its port forward wing strut. This photograph was mounted on Mustin's certificate as US Navy Air Pilot No. 3, issued in January 1915 with a June 1, 1914, date of precedence. (Courtesy of the US Naval History and Heritage Command Photograph, NH 105934-A-KN)

naval aircraft should move toward tractor-type planes. The Navy ignored it. It would take the deaths of two pilots before the Secretary of the Navy and the Chief of Naval Operations took a serious look at the design flaws of pushers and considered purchasing tractors to replace or supplement them.

The first fatality since the death of James Murray was Lieutenant (jg) Mel L. Stolz, who loved flying and was sick of standing deck watches on the *North Carolina*. He obtained orders in January 1915, returning him to Pensacola and aviation; he had not flown in nine months. On May 8, Saufley tested Stolz's ability by letting him fly a Curtiss AH pusher, primarily used as a training aircraft. He took it out, slowly climbed to around 100ft, and made a slight turn before nosing over and crashing into the bay. Ensign Clarence King Bronson landed his seaplane close to where Stolz had crashed and dove into the water but could not free the pilot. A crash boat arrived, and two men joined Bronson in releasing Stolz. They were successful and freed the trapped pilot. However, they found the engine had crushed his head. A subsequent investigation ruled that the plane stalling was the cause of the crash.[5]

Rear Admiral Mark Lambert Bristol, USN, here in 1920, initially resisted the move from pusher to tractor planes. He would later become a proponent of tractors. (Courtesy of the Naval History and Heritage Command NH 56254)

The investigation board of Stolz's crash also concluded: "... the pusher-type planes, with the pilot in front of all the weights, should be abandoned in favor of a tractor-type with the personnel in a fuselage aft of the concentrated masses." Meaning the pilot was more likely to be crushed by the engine breaking loose.[6]

Once again, Commander Mustin and others pursued using tractor planes, but the non-flyer administrators ignored their suggestions. Bristol told him the Navy was short of aircraft and continued to purchase pushers, blaming Stolz's limited experience as the cause of the crash. Bristol attempted to satisfy the pilots in July by purchasing two Thomas Tractors, but pilots wrecked both during testing; Bristol bought six Curtiss pushers in their place. Mustin kept requesting tractors, but it took the deaths of two more naval officers and a near mutiny before his requests were answered. The first was Lieutenant James V. Rockwell, a Navy engineer who volunteered for flight instruction in early 1916, accumulating 35 hours of solo time. On May 24, 1916, he took out a Curtiss pusher; an hour into the flight, witnesses saw the plane spiraling out of control before crashing into the

Above left: Midshipman Clarence King Bronson, Naval Aviator No. 15, USNA class of 1910, was killed in an explosion while attempting to release a bomb from his aircraft at Indian Head, Maryland, on November 8, 1916. (Courtesy of the Naval History and Heritage Command, NH 56256)

Above right: Lieutenant Commander Mustin, USN, battled with Rear Admiral Bristol and Captain Benson over pusher versus tractor planes regarding pilot safety. (Courtesy of the Naval History and Heritage Command)

bay. Lieutenant Kenneth Whiting dove into the water, freed the pilot from the seat, and pulled him out to a waiting crash boat.[7] Rockwell's head, as with Stolz's, had suffered skull fractures.

An investigation blamed the crash on a stall or a broken bamboo tail section – Curtiss' planes were still being engineered using bamboo and had not changed much in design. Bristol again blamed the incident on pilot error and disagreed with purchasing other aircraft models that others deemed safer. The two deaths were obviously due to inadequate training, lack of instructors, the small number of operational planes, and pushers with bamboo tail sections. However, six naval pilots survived training with pushers in 1916 and were certified. Still, it would take the death of a celebrated aviator for the naval hierarchy to change their minds about purchasing new planes. The death of Lieutenant Richard Saufley followed in 1917.

Saufley was a Kentuckian and a veteran of the Tampico Affair. He had previously broken the American altitude record for a hydroplane by reaching 11,975ft in the Curtiss AH-14 on December 3, 1915, surpassing his record. On March 29, 1916, Saufley broke his record with a flight of 16,010ft and again, on April 2, by flying 16,072ft. By March 1915, he worked to rebuild the AH-9 after Lieutenant (jg) Stolz's death. Saufley, flying the AH-8 on June 9, exceeded the previous endurance record by being in the air for eight hours and 51 minutes. There is some confusion as to whether Bellinger warned Bristol that Saufley's "stunts" were getting more dangerous and said, "If you don't put a check on Saufley is going to kill himself."[8]

The captain ignored Bellinger's concern. At 1pm, witnesses saw the plane nosedive from some 700ft above Pensacola Bay, crashing into the

Commissioned officers of the Aviation Corps USN, left to right: Lieutenant Herbster, Lieutenant McMvain, Lieutenant Bellinger, Lieutenant Saufley, Lieutenant Towers, Lieutenant Commander Mustin, Lieutenant Smith, Ensign de Chevalier, and Ensign Stolz. Two men in this photograph were killed in flying accidents: Saufley and Stolz. (Author's collection)

water, instantly killing the pilot. The investigation that followed blamed the structural error of the plane's tail surfaces. The investigation board consisted of Bellinger, Earl Winfield "Duke" Spencer, and Whiting; all were close friends of Saufley. They concurred that pushers were weak in construction and dangerous to fly. Captain Bristol disagreed and said there was no supporting evidence that such planes were to blame. He believed Rockwell and Stolz were killed due to inexperience, while Saufley was dead because of his poor workmanship on the aircraft. Bristol's belief in the inferiority of the tractor-type plane would change upon the advice of his aide, Lieutenant John Towers.[9]

By June 1916, three of naval aviation's earliest pioneers were dead: Billingsley (Naval Aviator No. 9), Murray (No. 10), and Saufley (No. 14), along with pilot Stolz and student Rockwell.[10] The investigation committees found the planes at fault for all the crashes, while Captain Bristol blamed pilot error. Bellinger could no longer tolerate the deaths of individuals he knew well and informed his commanding officer (CO), Mustin, he was willing to make a written statement that he would never operate

Lieutenant Saufley, circa 1914, was killed when his plane crashed into Pensacola Bay during a flight endurance record in June 1916. Some fellow officer called him foolhardy for attempting such flights. (Official USMC photograph)

a pusher again. His CO told him not to make such a hasty decision as all his complaint did was raise "perfect Hell." Mustin held a conference with the pilots at Pensacola, and they all agreed with Bellinger. A mutiny appeared in the offing until Admiral Benson provided Mustin with all the investigative committees' records and examined how to fix responsibility for future plane safety. As CO of NAS Pensacola, Mustin knew the problem was primarily with the lack of aircraft, the pusher's design, and insufficient instructors to train students. But, unfortunately, the Secretary of the Navy refused to acknowledge the findings of Whiting's board along with Mustin's concurrence regarding Stolz, Murray, Rockwell, and Saufley's deaths.

The admiral supported the board's findings and grounded the pushers, leaving Pensacola with only four operational planes by July 1916 – a month after Saufley's death. Unfortunately, that action left student pilots and instructors idle for months, creating an atmosphere of partying and

Captain, later Rear Admiral, William Benson, gutted naval aviation at one point, leaving the section with only four operational planes. He later became Chief of Naval Operations. (Author's collection, US Navy photograph)

drinking, and the skills students had learned were mainly lost. Benson looked to Chief Constructor D. W. Taylor to quickly find suitable planes. The Bureau of Construction and Repair turned to Glenn Curtiss' land biplane – the JN, nicknamed the "Jenny" – and Constructor Richardson to develop a rugged pontoon for the land-based plane. This plane became the model N-9, the standard training aircraft with the engine, gas tank, and radiator in the front. Behind them were the instructor's front cockpit and the student's rear cockpit. The Navy received the first deliveries of the plane in November 1916 for evaluation, five months before America entered the war. Yet, pushers remained part of the Navy's inventory beyond the end of World War One. The lack of safety harnesses, the inability to recover from spins, and the early construction methods of Curtiss pushers may have been the primary factors causing the deaths of aviators. However, accidents involving other types of planes, such as the N-9 and R-6 trainers, occurred due to various causes throughout the war.[11]

Mustin's outspokenness during the investigations made enemies within the naval establishment, and it seemed there was a concerted effort to drum him out of the service. A letter signed by Daniels, but probably prepared by Benson, accused Mustin of being responsible for Rockwell's and Saufley's deaths due to insufficient flying instructions. They asked for a response. His strong-willed character provided a rebuttal that "the real responsibility for those deaths was primarily the Navy Department, secondary Bristol."[12]

The Navy took no action on his rebuttal, but soon he received poor fitness reports, detrimental to future promotion. He wrote to his wife Corrine: "After the selection board had met, I suddenly get those unfavorable reports of Bristol's and as I am advised to return them immediately…" Mustin remained a thorn in the side of the naval hierarchy. Meanwhile, Mustin continued requesting tractor planes to replace pushers and argued for an independent naval aeronautics director who was "a qualified aviator." The Navy followed up by revoking his aviator designation on January 30, 1917. He was initially passed over for captain but remained in the Navy despite the accusations hurled at him. He became the executive commander of the battleship *North Dakota* (BB-29) a month after losing his

Pushers Versus Tractors

John Towers supported using tractor-type planes and helped persuade Captain Bristol to purchase such aircraft. (Courtesy of the Navy History and Heritage Command 7.9 NH 119270)

aviator designation. Afterward, he worked on matters related to aviation, eventually reaching the rank of captain before retiring.[13]

Bristol's negative attitude toward Mustin never seemed to waver, but his views on naval aviation had evolved by 1916, as had aerial warfare in Europe. Bristol came to the same conclusion as Mustin regarding tractor-type planes when he asked John Towers in July 1915 about the practical placement of the engine(s) on seaplanes. Towers had a positive working relationship with his superior (unlike Benson whom he blamed for gutting naval aviation). Towers rejected pusher-type planes in favor of the tractor while on an intelligence-gathering trip to Britain. He suggested an aircraft like the British Sopwith for scouts, and large flying boats for anti-submarine duties. Bristol was pleased with Towers' thoughts and pushed for larger appropriations for naval aviation. By late 1916, Bristol and Benson would become significant naval aviation supporters.

Prior to Mustin's battle with Bristol over pushers, senior aviation personnel – Bellinger, Herbster, Mustin, Smith, and Towers – were detached from other duties to Europe upon the beginning of the war in 1914, leaving few qualified instructors at Pensacola. In August 1914, Bristol ordered Towers to inspect British and French planes the Navy were considering buying, but it would encompass a broader mission. He would remain in England for two years as Bristol wanted men such as Towers there as they understood the intricacies of aviation and would wisely report the status of European aviation compared to the United States.

On August 13, 1914, while aboard the *Tennessee* heading to England, Towers, a proponent of aerial scouts aboard warships, was asked about the current state of naval aviation. He emphasized that each battleship and cruiser should have two to four seaplanes and be able to launch them from catapults for scouting duty. In addition, he suggested that each plane carry Elmer Sperry's course indicator and automatic stabilizer. At the same time, research continued to find a suitable air-to-ground (sea) radio system.

The Curtiss AH-13 aircraft is equipped with double pontoons. The pilot is Lieutenant Bellinger. The AH series, beginning with the A-1 to A-4, was redesignated AH-1 to AH-4, along with the block series AH-5 to AH-18, which were constructed between 1915 and 1918. (Courtesy of the Naval History and Heritage Command, NH 74076)

Mustin, Bellinger, and Smith followed Towers and traveled to Paris to investigate the status of French planes that were, as Mustin wrote, "so far ahead of us… that it looks like an impossibility ever to catch up." It took only two weeks for Towers, in England, to conclude, upon inspecting British aircraft production and visiting aerodromes, "that the [US] Navy Air Department was not prepared for war." Such reports sent by senior naval aviators proved how poorly equipped the United States was in aviation compared to Europe.[14]

The reports went unheeded except by individuals such as Admirals Bristol and Fiske. Both understood the importance of aviation, especially Bristol, in scouting, observation, and anti-submarine operations. The warring powers in Europe initially utilized planes for scouting and observation of troop movements and spotting artillery positions, but they were now being used as bombing and pursuit aircraft as well. On October 21, 1916, in a letter to the Secretary of the Naval War College, Bristol outlined the importance of planes in future warfare as scouts for the fleet. He saw them as scouts for the Navy in which strategy and tactics should be modified to include aircraft use and then taught at the War College. Regarding tactical requirements, he wrote, "It is my opinion that is decidedly the province of the War College to study the requirements of airplanes and prescribe the same and therefore determine the effect upon strategy." He understood the limitations of planes in design and construction for naval use while acknowledging their current use by the warring nations.[15]

Bristol viewed the launching of planes from a catapult system, invented in 1912, as revolutionary and voiced his opinion that battleships and cruisers fitted with such devices would have the capability to launch up to three aircraft, enabling the fleet to spot, identify, and fix the location of enemy ships. Again, the need for sturdy construction and design was paramount for success, and he pointed out that current machines should have radio systems capable of contacting friendly ships. Bristol pinpointed the blame for current problems with aircraft on the Navy and manufacturers. He voiced his concerns by stating:

> … Thus far, the Navy has done very little to develop the design of airplanes and airplane engines. The main dependence in this country has been placed

upon private manufacturers who have not been scientific engineers except for very few cases. The principle results have been obtained by "cut and try" methods, which cannot be dependent upon such a complex and complicated problem as the design of airplanes.

Bristol maintained two significant causes for such problems: those who exaggerated the accomplishments of aircraft and those with a pessimistic view who saw no practical application of them, such as Admiral Benson. He equivocated that there existed a third party who represented views between the two extremes: "They are attempting to develop to the full capacity the capabilities of those aircraft that are being designed and can be constructed and are studying every lesson of the present war in order to apply it to future development."

Nevertheless, he voiced criticism and downplayed the accomplishments of airplanes in the current war in Europe, despite journalists and officers

The Curtiss F-boat (AB-2) being hoisted aboard USS *North Carolina* (CA-12), alongside a dock at Pensacola in November 1915, prior to catapult trials. Lieutenant Commander Mustin performed such trials during the argument regarding the safety of pusher planes. (Courtesy of the Naval Heritage Command of the NH 83909)

The first plane catapult was launched from the *North Carolina* at Pensacola on November 5, 1915. Lieutenant Commander Mustin piloted the Curtiss AB-2 seaplane. (Courtesy of the Naval History and Heritage Command, NH 44886)

within the armed services enthusiastically reporting on the aircraft's contribution to the war effort. He noted one War College officer who gave a glowing review: "Why haven't [sic] we airplanes for the Navy? I thought we had a million dollars for them?"

"Because there are none to be had," Bristol replied.[16]

Now the captain completely understood the problems facing the acquisition of naval aircraft: funding issues and detractors who saw very little or no valuable purpose for planes. Indeed, he acknowledged that current machines in service were dangerous to fly, and it took the pilots' skill, determination, and courage to operate them. Bristol remained singularly focused on the development and use of seaplanes based aboard ships and not land planes, since the latter was in the interest of the Army. He pointed out that Europe was primarily engaged in a land war, and the use of aircraft in support of such a war was well known, while the opposite was true of seaplanes. Intelligence reported that the primary use of seaplanes was providing coastal patrols, anti-submarine duties, air-sea rescue, and, on occasion, participating in bombing missions against German targets along the Belgian coast.

Bristol did compare and recognize that the warring powers did not initially possess large numbers of seaplanes compared to land planes. Britain relied on United States manufacturers, such as the Curtiss type H series flying boats. In September 1914, Commander Mustin reported the Royal Navy Air Service (RNAS) consisted of 200 men. By October 1916, the RNAS had grown to 2,000 officers and 25,000 enlisted men. That is how quickly the naval air operations advanced in England in such a short time. The British knew the importance of a large naval air service at a time when the maritime air service of the United States Navy was barely surviving,

A close-up view of the engine in the Curtiss flying boat from the front right. The radiator and engine would prove deadly for some pilots. (Courtesy of the Naval History and Heritage Command, UA 41.01.39)

The Curtiss AH-13 fitted with triple pontoons just before taking off. Mustin and others thought such pusher airplanes were inherently dangerous to fly. (Courtesy of the US Naval History and Heritage Command, NH 74078)

Curtiss AH-12 seaplane in the hoist of USS *Sterett* (Destroyer #27), circa 1916. Note the steering chain running along the *Sterett*'s deck. (Courtesy of the US Naval History and Heritage Command, NH 2246)

with officers having to purchase fuel from their own pockets. Towers' and Mustin's reports would assist in developing seaplanes and flying boats, increasing personnel within the air service, and creating a concise training syllabus.[17]

United States naval aviation barely covered tactics and strategy but centered on experimentation and setting aerial records. In contrast, aerial gunnery and bombing practice were practically non-existent during the prewar years. Moreover, military aircraft construction lagged so much that the British, French, and Italians had to arm the Americans with their pursuit, scout, and bombing aircraft upon the declaration of war. To meet this challenge, the Council of National Defense created the Aircraft Production Board on the recommendation of the National Advisory Committee on Aeronautics. The board was later transferred to the Secretary of the Navy by an act of Congress on October 1, 1917. The Navy Department emphasized providing seaplanes for its aviation branch.

Hydroplanes docked at Pensacola in January 1914 before Lieutenant Commander Mustin began complaining about the suitability and danger of hydroplanes. (Bernard Smith Collection [COLL/1691] at the Archives Branch, Marine Corps History Division).

The Burgess-Dunne AH-7, a tailless seaplane at Pensacola in 1916, was developed from the D.8. The aircraft's wingspan was 46ft and it was nearly 46ft long. It was powered by a Curtiss OX eight-cylinder 100hp engine. Only two were built. (Courtesy of the US Naval History and Heritage Command, NH 74080)

Glenn Curtiss experimented with tractor-type planes. This is an early Curtiss seaplane version with floats, circa 1914. (Courtesy of the Naval History and Heritage Command)

Military allocations for naval aircraft between 1911 and 1915 were minuscule, with some 37 planes purchased by 1916. The number of aircraft procured by the Navy considerably increased by the beginning of 1917, with some 60 planes on hand, and practically all had improved engine performance, but it was still a small number compared to what the British, French, and Germans were building. Various United States manufacturers produced similar types of naval aircraft as the possibility of war grew. One of the most crucial developments in aeronautics was the production of a tractor-type airplane, discussed earlier, with the Thomas Tractor being one of the earliest – its engine placed forward instead of behind the pilot as in a pusher-type. In 1916, the Navy placed its first production order with the Curtiss Company for 30 type N-9 trainers to replace inferior pusher planes. American-manufactured pusher-type seaplanes remained in service as trainers and observation aircraft in the

A Thomas tractor seaplane taken circa 1915–16 at NAS Pensacola. Note the tail of the Curtiss AH-12 pusher seaplane on the left and the destroyer docked in the background. (Courtesy of the Naval History and Heritage Command, NH 83914)

Curtiss N-9 Training Plane at USN Aeronautic Station, Pensacola, November 1916. The model became one of the Navy's primary trainers during World War One. (Courtesy of the Navy History and Heritage Command, 76000)

United States and Europe. By late 1916, the number of aircraft purchased by the Navy had nearly tripled. The number of planes previously received by the Navy between 1911 and early 1914 was approximately 14, all pusher-types – the Curtiss C-1 to C-5 and AH-11 through the AH-18 series – were purchased between 1914 and early 1917.

Chapter 8

Naval Aviation Training (1915–18)

The earliest naval aviators first earned pilot certification from the ACA before being formally recognized by the Navy as aviators on March 4, 1913, by the Navy Appropriations Act for the fiscal year 1914. This act increased pay and allowances by 35 percent for officers detailed to duty as flyers of heavier-than-air craft. The performance standards for becoming a naval flyer solidified on April 10, 1913, when Secretary of the Navy Meyer approved Captain Chambers' recommendations on April 4 for the requirements in becoming a Navy Air Pilot (seaplane). The Bureau of Navigation was initially responsible for administering the Navy Air Pilot Certification. A commissioned officer had to pass the advanced training course and an examination board of qualified air pilots. Up to April 22, 1914, the Bureau of Navigation approved courses in in-flight instruction for flyers and aviation mechanics.

However, there did not exist a formal and qualified examination board to test student pilots, as pointed out by Admiral Fiske, on January 9, 1915, to the Bureau of Navigation. It, therefore, appointed the first seven qualified pilots to that board: Ellyson, Towers, Mustin, Bellinger, Herbster, Smith, and Chevalier. Afterward, the service pinned the first seven as Navy Air Pilots 1 through 7. In March and April 1915, the five additional and just-minted air pilots joined the others on the board. They were appointed as Navy Air Pilots 8 through 12: Richard C. Saufley, USN, as Naval Air Pilot No. 8 dated March 6; William M, McIlvain, USMC, No. 9 on March 10; Clarence K. Bronson, USN, No. 10 on April 6; Kenneth Whiting, Naval Aviator No.16 on April 10; and Holden C. Richardson, USN, Naval Aviator No. 13 on April 12, 1915.

Naval Aviation Training (1915–18)

Lieutenant Earl W. Spencer under way in the Burgess-Dunne "Skimmer" taxiing trainer in June 1916. The plane appears to be a Curtiss A-type aircraft, with the tail and most of the wings removed to instruct students on taxiing. (Courtesy of the US Naval History and Heritage Command, NH 74079)

Tent hangars at the Pensacola flying school, photographed from the watch tower, fall 1915. The planes in the foreground are the Curtiss C-1 type. Other planes appear to be Curtiss A types. (Courtesy of the US Naval History and Heritage Command, NH 74082)

Naval and Marine aviators pose with a Curtiss AB-type airplane, probably at Pensacola, circa late 1914. Seated (left to right): Lieutenant (jg) Robert G. Saufley, USN; Lieutenant (jg) Patrick N. L. Bellinger, USN; Lieutenant Kenneth Whitling, USN; Lieutenant Commander Henry C. Mustin, USN; Lieutenant Albert C. Read, USN; Lieutenant Earle F. Johnson, USN; First Lieutenant Alfred A. Cunningham, USMC; Second Lieutenant Francis T. Evans, USMC; and Lieutenant (jg) Walter A. Haas, USN. Standing (left to right): Lieutenant (jg) Robert R. Paunack, USN; Lieutenant (jg) Earl W. Spencer, USN; Lieutenant (jg) Harold T. Bartlett, USN; Lieutenant (jg) Walter A. Edwards, USN; Lieutenant Clarence K. Bronson, USN; Lieutenant Joseph P. Norfleet, USN; Lieutenant (jg) Edward O. McDonnell, USN; Ensign Harold W. Scofield; and one man, possibly the last, is unidentified. (Author's collection)

On March 3, 1915, Congress authorized the term "naval aviator" for those authorized to receive flight pay defined in the Navy Appropriation Act of 1914. The Secretary of the Navy officially directed commanding officers of the Navy and Marine Corps on May 21, 1915, to issue orders detailing officers of the Navy and Marine Corps to duty as naval aviators

Above: Lieutenant (jg) Marc A. "Pete" Mitscher, USN, in a Curtiss type-A seaplane, at NAS Pensacola, circa 1916. After completing flight school that year, the Navy designated him Naval Aviator No. 33. (Official US Navy photograph, now in the collections of the National Archives, 80-G-433310)

Right: Roy S. Geiger, Naval Aviator No. 49/USMC No. 5, at the controls, circa 1917. He became squadron commander with the NBG in France, earning the Navy Cross twice during combat operations. (Official USMC photograph from the Marine Corps Archives)

A Navy Burgess N-9H trainer with bureau number 2504, with the gunner/observer equipped with a single Lewis machine gun. It sports the numbers painted white, black spade, and overall gray. The photograph was probably taken at Pensacola, circa 1918. Note the missing pilot. (Courtesy of the Emil Buehler Naval Library, NAS Pensacola)

or student naval aviators when required to operate aircraft. Yet, confusion regarding an official designation for flyers continued until the Bureau of Navigation formally issued its syllabus of instruction and qualifications in January 1916, using the terms student naval aviator, naval aviator, navy air pilot and military aviator.

Between 1911, when Spuds Ellyson became the first naval aviator, and 1916, only 35 had earned their wings; the lack of funding inhibited the growth of naval aviation. Four Marines were trained as aviators between 1911 and 1916, since available allocations were considerably smaller than the Navy's. Early aviators earned seaplane certification and were granted the title "Naval Aviator." The table below shows those who earned the title "Naval Aviator (Navy Air Pilot)" between 1911 and 1916 (Marine Corps aviator numbers are in parenthesis):

Navy Aviator No.	Name	Branch of Service
1	Ellyson, Theodore G.	USN
2	Rodgers, John	USN
3	Towers, John H.	USN
4	Herbster, Victor D.	USN
5 (1)	Cunningham, Alfred A.	USMC

Naval Aviation Training (1915–18)

Navy Aviator No.	Name	Branch of Service
6 (2)	Smith, Bernard L.	USMC
7	Chevalier, Godfrey de C.	USN
8	Bellinger, Patrick N. L.	USN
9	Billingsley, William D.	USN
10	Murray, James M.	USN
11	Mustin, Henry C.	USN
12 (3)	McIlvain, William M.	USMC
13	Richardson, Holden C.	USN
14	Saufley, Richard C.	USN
15	Bronson, Clarence K.	USN
16	Whiting, Kenneth	USN
17	Maxfield, Louis H.	USN
18	McDonnell, Edward O.	USN
19	Capehart, Wadleigh	USN
20	Spencer, Earl W., Jr.	USN
21	Bartelet, Harold T.	USN
22	Murray, George D.	USN
23	Corry, William M.	USN
24	Read, Albert C.	USN
25	Johnson, Earle F.	USN
26 (4)	Evans, Francis T.	USMC
27	Paunack, Robert R.	USN
28	Scofield, Harold W.	USN
29	Child, Warren G.	USN
30	Dichman, Grattan C.	USN
31	Young, Robert T.	USN
32	Gillespie, George S.	USN
33	Mitscher, Marc A.	USN
34	Strickland, Glenn B.	USN
35	Monfort, James C.	USN

By 1917, the aviator course became considerably more complex, and the number of student pilots had grown significantly with the declaration of war. Per the department's order of April 10, 1917, upon successful completion of the examination, the naval aviator (seaplane) was issued a certificate numbered according to his standing in the class with which he qualified as a "Navy Air Pilot (seaplane)." A revised course of instruction published on January 1, 1918, used the term "Navy Air Pilot." Officers and enlisted men detailed for pilot duty were classified as student naval aviators and naval aviators – seaplane or dirigible. Captain Alfred Cunningham, in 1916, elaborated on what it takes to become a Navy flyer:

(a) Executing spirals, (b) High altitude flying, (c) Rough weather flying, (d) Courses by compass, (e) Endurance flights. An apt and careful student may satisfy his instructors in three months as to his progress in elementary flying and is then allowed to begin his advanced flying course. This consists of:

(a) Being launched from the deck of a ship underway by the catapult.
(b) Landing in deep sea waves and being hoisted aboard ship.
(c) Scouting flights out of sight of land.
(d) Air navigation.
(e) Flying in formation.
(f) Sending and receiving radio messages from the air.

When the student has passed all his practical and theoretical examinations and his flying instruction, he can take his test for a Naval Aviator's certificate. The test comprises the following:

(a) Climb to an altitude of 10,000 feet as shown by the recording barograph and glide to a normal landing, without porpoising, within 200 feet of a mark previously designated by the Board; horizontal flight may be resumed twice during the descent but not within 1,000 feet, where the motor shall be cut off
(b) Make a spiral glide from an altitude of 3,000 feet as shown by recording barograph and land without porpoising within 200 feet of a given mark previously designated by the Board.
(c) Make a landing in a seaway where the height of waves is at least four feet without damage to any part of the aeroplane.

Naval Aviation Training (1915–18)

(d) Make a straight course and return between two objects not less than five miles apart in a wind not less than 25 miles per hour and not more than four points forward or abaft the beam to demonstrate the ability to maintain a given course.

(e) Make a scouting flight over the open sea to a vessel stationed at a designated bearing at a distance of 100 miles and return to the starting point.

(f) Demonstrate to the satisfaction of the Board's ability to fly in terrible weather.

(g) Start a flight from the catapult after personally making all adjustments for its operation.

Pilots: 1. Edwards, 2. Bronson, 3. Chevalier, 4. McIlvaine, 5. Whiting. Edwards may have been an enlisted pilot as his name was not in the commissioned pilots registry when this photograph was taken. (Courtesy of the Naval History and Heritage Command, NH 119469)

Before 1916, there was no formal grouping of students to form classes; instead, training can be defined as sporadic, lacking in standard curriculum, with students assigned individually. For example, a ground school for prospective pilots stressed the technical aspects of aviation but, because most of the students were Annapolis graduates, omitted entirely such subjects as navigation and seamanship fundamentals. The Navy later added those courses for potential officers recruited from the civilian pool.

Training and organization of aviation personnel evolved, with ground officers attending a primary school at the Great Lakes Naval Training Station, Great Lakes, Illinois. Afterward, officers were divided among the following classifications and schools for advanced training: ordnance (Bureau of Ordnance), navigation and administration (Pensacola), communication (Hampton Roads), and aerography (Blue Hills Observatory, Boston). In addition, prospective aviation mechanics

Tent hangars at the Pensacola flying school, photographed from the watch tower, fall 1915. The planes in the foreground are of a Curtiss C type. The third plane in the background appears to have bureau number 55A or 59A, which dates the photograph possibly later than 1915. (Courtesy of the US Naval History and Heritage Command, NH 74082)

Naval Aviation Training (1915–18)

attended elementary trade schools nationwide, with advanced training at Great Lakes. Finally, naval aviator designations evolved between 1911 and 1918, with Captain Chambers, as the first Director of Aeronautics, setting the exact requirements as prescribed by the ACA (the American chapter of the FAI).

As described earlier, training did not go smoothly at Pensacola between 1914 and 1916, according to Lieutenant Edward O. McDonnell. There were only 11 planes in the Navy during that period; three were demolished quickly by student pilots, leaving only one or two aircraft available at any given time.[1]

By 1917, upon the United States' entry into World War One, there needed to be an established formal wartime training syllabus. On May 1, the Navy

Student naval aviator class pictured at Pensacola October 1915 aboard the *North Carolina* (ACR-12), which was used for experimental aviation launches. Standing (left to right): Ensign Louis R. Ford, USN; Ensign James C. Monfort, USN, Naval Aviator No. 35; and Ensign Marc A. Mitscher, USN, Naval Aviator No. 33; Instructors seated in a Curtiss AH pusher plane: Ensign Edward O. McDonnell, USN, Naval Aviator No. 18; and Ensign Earl W. Spencer, USN, Naval Aviator No. 20. Standing (left to right): Ensign Glenn B. Strickland, USN, Naval Aviator No. 34; Ensign George S. Gillespie, USN, Naval Aviator No. 32; Ensign Robert T. Young, USN, Naval Aviator No. 31; and Lieutenant (jg) Grattan C. Dichman, USN, Naval Aviator No. 30 Additional identification of aviators for this photograph was obtained by Mr. Charles Striebig, May 1999. Collection of Commander Grattan C. Dichman, USN. (Courtesy of the US Naval History and Heritage Command, NH 104884)

Above: Students outside the flying school office, by a sign (left) with the name of Lieutenant (jg) Clarence K. Bronson. Both station staff and student aviators are present. Most are identified below (as annotated on the print). Standing (left to right): Ensign Harold W. Scofield, USN; Assistant Surgeon Charles L. Beeching, USN; Lieutenant (jg) Clarence K. Bronson, USN; Lieutenant (jg) William M. Corry, Jr., USN; Lieutenant (jg) Joseph P. Norfleet, USN; and Lieutenant Albert C. Read, USN. Seated (left to right): Unidentified lieutenant (jg); Lieutenant (jg) Earl W. Spencer, Jr., USN; Lieutenant (jg) Walter A. Edwards, USN; Lieutenant (jg) Robert R. Paunack, USN; Lieutenant Earle F. Johnson, USN; Lieutenant (jg) George D. Murray, USN. Photograph from the photo album of Vice Admiral T. T. Craven. (Courtesy of Lieutenant Rodman DeKay, Jr., USNR (Ret.), 1979; US Naval History and Heritage Command)

specified a new course of instruction with student classifications of student aviator, naval aviator, and navy air pilot, the latter for dirigibles. Completing the student naval aviator (seaplane) course of instruction enabled students to attend the advanced phase of elementary and solo flying, followed by the examination board.

An expansion of the training program was approved, calling for the assignment of new classes every three months and establishing an 18-month window to qualify officers as pilots of either seaplanes or dirigibles. The program also trained enlisted men as aviation mechanics and selected a few for pilot training and qualification as quartermasters. However, the Navy soon abandoned this curriculum for being impractical in conducting both types of training at Pensacola and the Curtiss Exhibition Company at Newport News, Virginia. Therefore, heavier-than-air activity remained at Pensacola while the Goodyear Company completed balloon and dirigible training at Akron, Ohio.

At the outbreak of hostilities, the number of trained aviators or persons familiar with naval aviation was relatively small. The early training of pilots and mechanics covered only aircraft flying, without particular attention

Below: US Navy student aviators of Company 19, at MIT, June 4, 1918. MIT was the naval aviation ground school during World War One. (Courtesy of the US Naval History and Heritage Command, UA 571.31)

to the requirements of aerial combat or other warlike operations. For war purposes, it immediately became necessary to obtain numerous trained crews composed of pilots, machine gunners, and observers, to successfully operate the bombs, machine guns, and radio equipment. In addition, a considerable force of trained ground personnel needed training. The enrollment and training of the tremendous numbers of officers and enlisted men needed was a task of astonishing magnitude. The strength of naval aviation personnel on April 17, 1917, is shown in the following table:

Officers	April 6, 1917
Naval aviators	38
Student naval aviators	0
Ground	0
Total officer personnel	38
Enlisted Men	—
Aviation ratings	163
General ratings	—
Assigned to aviation	0
Total enlisted personnel	163
Total personnel	201

By contrast, Britain's Royal Flying Corps (RFC) consisted of 3,300 pilots and more than 3,500 planes divided between frontline and training aircraft. Captain Bristol, in a communique dated October 25, 1916 to Rear Admiral Victor Blue, Chief, Bureau of Navigation, formally addressed how the Naval Flying Corps would be composed as stated in a circular dated January 26, 1916. In the circular, the captain identified which officers and enlisted personnel would qualify to enter the Naval Flying Corps. Qualifications for admission were laid out in the October 25 communique, followed by course prerequisites. The qualifications for entering corps aviation included men between the ages of 20 and 28 with high character and capability. Finally, he elaborated on the type of individuals needed for the Flying Corps and its importance:

> Flying an aircraft is no mysterious art, though it requires courage and nerve for the pioneers to master it… the same sort of officers who have done so much in developing the art are still required. Still the development of an Air Service composed of officers, men, and vessels, trained in the necessary new tactics and strategy of the air is a bigger problem than the art of flying.

On May 1, 1917, the Director of Naval Aviation presented a new course and an updated revision of the course syllabus dated January 26, 1916. Completing the course of instruction for Student Naval Aviator (seaplane) qualified the student for elementary and solo flying advancement. Upon completion of that stage, the student took the exam for Naval Aviator (seaplane) and was then eligible for what appears to be the advanced course. For this course, the instruction stated: "Upon successful completion of the examination, the Naval Aviator (seaplane) will be designated Navy Air Pilot (seaplane) and issued a certificate numbered according to his standing in the class with which he qualified as a Navy Air Pilot (seaplane)." On January 1, 1918, the Director of Aviation issued a revision of the May 1917 course of instruction. In this revision, officers and men detailed for pilot duty were classed as student naval aviators and naval aviators, seaplane, or dirigible.[2]

The Navy established the Office of Aviation Operations under Lieutenant Earle F. Johnson, Naval Aviator No. 25. He supervised training and directed the movement of personnel with the supervisor of the Navy Reserve Flying Corps, Lieutenant Commander John Towers. The multiple activities connected with these tasks made the training section one of the most significant parts of the Aviation Division at the war's end. The National Advisory Committee for Aeronautics (NACA) meeting in Washington, DC on April 23, 1917, discussed the problem of training thousands of men. This meeting led directly to the Navy establishing coursework at six national scientific schools. Training consisted of three phases: ground school, elementary flight training, and advanced ground school. On July 23, 1917, the first 50 men arrived in Cambridge on the MIT campus from the First Naval District headquarters in Boston.

They were the first of over 4,000 to receive their introduction to naval aviation. By the summer of 1918, the Navy had established additional ground schools at the University of Washington in Seattle, Washington, and Dunwoody Institute in Minneapolis, Minnesota.[3]

The six-week ground school was followed by preliminary flight training to bring the student through five to ten hours of solo work. Primary flight training occurred at Bay Shore, New York, Miami, Key West, and San Diego, while Pensacola was the site of advanced training. In addition, student naval aviators were taught gunnery, bombing, navigation, and seaplane flying at Pensacola. In the final stage, advanced flight training, the student would qualify as a naval aviator and receive his commission in the NRFC.

Collision of a Curtiss N-9H, bureau number 2489, and a dirigible, possibly the D-1, at Pensacola, NAS, circa 1918. Accidents were common during advanced flight training. (Author's collection)

As stated earlier, naval aviation was small, fragmented, and its personnel were untrained in aerial warfare. At the outbreak of hostilities, the number of trained aviators or persons familiar with naval aviation consisted of 48 officers and 239 enlisted personnel. Marine Corps Aviation comprised five pilots and 30 enlisted men based at the US Aeronautical Station Pensacola, later NAS Pensacola. That number paled compared to the Army, which had 131 officers and 1,087 enlisted men. The number of planes operated by Marine aviators at Pensacola, Florida, on April 6, 1917, was four AH Curtiss seaplanes.

Crashes of naval training planes by student pilots often resulted in severe injuries or death. At Pensacola, some 36 instructors and student pilots were killed in flying accidents between 1917 and 1918. (Author's collection)

Before the Navy's training program became fully functional, it accepted an offer from the Canadian government to train pilot applicants at the School of Military Aeronautics, RFC, in Toronto. In July 1917, 24 candidates reported for duty. All but one of the detachments were Ivy League graduates, most from Princeton, Yale, and Dartmouth. Training took approximately four months, consisting of two months of ground instruction and two months of advanced flying camps.

J. Sterling Halstead, who would become Naval Aviator No. 160, recalled, "We were told to take notes on everything so that we could bring back to the US Navy complete information on the subjects taught, the equipment, and the methods used."[4] Another student, Thomas H. Chapman, related a tradition at that Canadian airbase:

> The plane I was using was one of the veterans of CTS 85, as was evident from the right paw of the Black Cat painted on either side of the fuselage. We were the Black Cat Squadron, and after each crash, the upraised right paw of the cat was marked with a white stripe. My plane had eight of those white stripes already and one more would finish the proverb.[5]

There were a few minor injuries but no fatalities among the American contingent. All candidates finished the course in October or November 1917, receiving orders to Bay Shore and Hampton Roads Naval Air Stations to qualify in seaplanes and flying boats. Afterward, the new pilots were scattered across the US, England, and France. By May 18, 1918, the Chief of Naval Operations scheduled training goals that called for 124 pilots and 62 gunners trained in night bombers by July 1, and 552 pilots with 156 engineers trained in operating the H-16 and HS-1 patrol planes by August 1. Therefore, the Navy formed approximately six elementary training squadrons to meet that goal, two at Key West and four at Miami.

On January 6, 1916, the first class of enlisted men from the Navy and Marine Corps were selected as potential pilots for training at Pensacola. The purpose: to increase the number of qualified naval and marine aviators and begin issuing "certificates of qualification as airman" to enlisted

Naval Aviation Training (1915–18)

NAS Pensacola during November 1918. In the foreground is an H-12, bureau number 778, received by the Navy in April 1918; in the middle is H-16, bureau number 3537; in the background is an H-12, bureau number 767. (Author's collection)

personnel meeting the requirements set up by the Bureau of Navigation for flight training. From a handwritten logbook maintained at Pensacola, aviator certificates were numbered, beginning with one and ending at 358. The Number 1 Certificate of Qualification as Airman was issued to CMM (Chief Machinist Mate) Harry E. Adams on December 15, 1916, with a course completion date of November 27, 1916. Enlisted personnel followed the same course syllabus as officers.

This airman certificate should not be confused with the enlisted qualifications for a pilot; there is no connection between the two designations. The issuance of a certificate of qualification from the Aeronautic School at Pensacola for Airman was discontinued on October 1, 1917. It is believed Pensacola discontinued the enlisted certificate program because of the changes in the "Course of Instructions," the addition of other training stations, and the influx of a large number of enlisted men during World War One. However, the name "airman" continued to be applied to enlisted personnel in the aviation field unless they rated commissioned status.

Upon qualifying, they received commissions as second lieutenants in the Marine Corps Reserve Flying Corps. Marine flying candidates were all enlisted Marines of physical superiority, weighing from 135lb to 165lb and with at least two years of college or university study to their credit. The age limits were 19 to 39 years. The Marine Corps section of the naval school for mechanics went to Great Lakes and trained mechanics, riggers, and armorers for eight weeks. North Island in San Diego established a similar school for aviation mechanics. In addition, the first Marine lighter-than-air section (LTAS), composed of two officers and ten enlisted personnel, attended Army balloon schools beginning in December 1917, located at St. Louis, Missouri and Omaha, Nebraska.

On January 1, 1916, a class of ten enlisted men was formed and placed under flying instruction. These men were selected from the "bluejackets" and Marines already on duty at the station or aboard *North Carolina*: P. J. Dunleavy, F. Grompe, A. A. Bressman, L. A. Welty, A. Hayes, A. P. Bauer, J. Makolin, W. E. McCaughtry, A. F. Dietrich, and Walter D. Bonner. A second class began flight training on May 15, 1916: C. L. Allen, J. Sunderman, W. Diercks, J. Salsman, A. Ward, T. H. Murphy, and G. Varini.

In the fall of 1917, the Chief of Naval Operations released a memorandum stating the end of flight training for enlisted personnel by saying, "It is desired to train no more enlisted personnel as pilots." It appears the last class ended during the fall of 1917. The following individuals attending the last class were A. F. Dietrich, J. T. Sunderman, G. Enos, John H. Bunt, James A. Whitted, A. Feher, Carlton D. Palmer, George W. Stone, and Robert H. Kerr. A. F. Dietrich, J. T. Sunderman appear in both classes for an unknown reason.[6]

Those promoted later as commissioned officers were provided separate naval aviator numbers. Those were:

Walter D. Bonner, Naval Aviator No. 50
Alexander "Gus" Bressman, Naval Aviator No. 44
John H. Bunt, Naval Aviator No. 1301
Arthur F. Dietrich, Naval Aviator No. 115
George Enos, Naval Aviator No. 61

Clarence A. "Jim" Hawkins, Naval Aviator No. 63
Alfred Hayes, Naval Aviator No. 609
Robert H. Kerr, Naval Aviator No. 178/630
Oliver Pierce "Ollie" Kilmer, Naval Aviator No. 70
Walter E. McCaughtry (Marine Corps), Naval Aviator No. 1310
Guy McLaughlin, Naval Aviator No. 90
Thomas Henry Murphy, Naval Aviator No. 51
Carlton D. Palmer, Naval Aviator No. 116
James Salsman, Naval Aviator No. 52 ½
George W. Stone, Naval Aviator No. 111
Allen J. Sunderman, Naval Aviator No. 55 ½
George W. Stone, Naval Aviator No. 111
Peter "Pete" Talbot, Naval Aviator No. 71
Guy Adler Walker, Naval Aviator No. 69
James A. Whitted, Naval Aviator No. 179
Giochino "Count" Varini, Naval Aviator No. 62.[7]

Naval Aviation

Officers	April 6, 1917	November 11, 1918
Naval aviators	38	1,650
Student naval aviators	0	288
Ground officers	0	891
Student aviators under training for commission	0	3,881

Enlisted	April 6, 1917	November 11, 1918
Aviation ratings	163	21,951
General ratings assigned to aviation	0	8,742
Total enlisted personnel	163	30,693

At the time of the entrance of the United States into the war, there were only four commissioned Marine pilots: Cunningham, Smith, McIlvain, and Evans. Three additional aviators joined the group during 1917: Lieutenant

The first class of enlisted aviation students at Pensacola. Standing (left to right): Charles L. Allen, Naval Aviator No. 110 1/2; Walter D. Bonner, Naval Aviator No. 50; George Enos, Naval Aviator No. 61; Augustus A. Bressman, Naval Aviator No. 44; Oliver P. Kilmer, Naval Aviator No. 70; Alfred Hayes, Naval Aviator No. 609. Seated (left to right): Thomas H. Murphy, Naval Aviator No. 51; John T. Sunderman, Naval Aviator No. 55 1/2; Guy McLaughlin, Naval Aviator No. 90; Giochino Varini, Naval Aviator No. 62. (Courtesy of the US Naval History and Heritage Command, 47997)

Roy Stanley Geiger in June; Lieutenant David Lukens Shoemaker Brewster, nicknamed "Big Dave," followed in July; and Warrant Officer Pilot Walter E. "Mac" McCaughtry. The Marine Corps, during the war, selected and trained its pilots and mechanics and possessed its aviation field and equipment but nothing in terms of an established organized flight school until the spring of 1918. At MIT in Boston, enlisted Marines, selected as promising pilots and given the rank of gunnery sergeant, took a ten-week course in groundwork. About 80 men a month graduated. After graduation from ground school, they did their actual flying. This course embraced preliminary, acrobatic and formation flying; bombing; gunnery; and reconnaissance work, including aerial photography.

The strength of commissioned officers and enlisted personnel assigned to aviation duty on April 6, 1917, and the same data as of November 11, 1918, appears in the following table:

Marine Corps Aviation	April 6, 1917	November 11, 1918
Officers	4	250
Warrant Officers	1	32
Enlisted Men	30	2,180

When the Board of Aeronautics chose Pensacola as the primary location for naval aviation in 1914, it assessed other potential sites. However, with the US declaring war against Germany, plans for those sites were

Burgess N-9H Seaplane, bureau number A-2558, undergoing tests before a flight at NAS Pensacola, 1917. (A. E. Wells, photographer; Courtesy of the US Naval History and Heritage Command, NH 60877)

Above: US NAS Cape May, New Jersey, with HS-2L, bureau number 1920, in the foreground, and a Lowe-Willard-Fowler HS-1L, bureau number 1210, in the background. (Courtesy of the Naval History and Heritage Command, NH 113048)

dusted off and implemented and additional air stations were established or transferred from state militias. At the time of the Armistice, some two dozen air stations and training schools were in operation in the Continental United States, Canada, Panama, and the Azores. See Appendix C.

Above: NAS Miami, Florida, with F- and R-type planes on the beach on May 3, 1918. Miami was an advanced training base along with Pensacola and Key West, Florida. (Courtesy of the National Archives, 80-G-426941)

Below: Burgess N-9 trainers, bureau numbers 2379, 2375, 2374, 2364, and 2371, visible in this photograph, located at US NAS San Diego, California, in 1918. Note the difference in the wing insignias on 2364 and 2371. (Courtesy of the Library of Congress)

PART TWO

NAVAL AND MARINE CORPS AVIATION AT WAR

Chapter 9

Wartime Aircraft Production (1917–18)

P rewar naval aircraft primarily consisted of the original F-type flying boats and the AH series. In the early months of 1917, before the United States' entry into World War One, 11 planes were purchased by the Navy; among them were the Curtiss R-3 tractor seaplane with twin floats, and the H-12 flying boat. Upon the declaration of war against Germany on April 6, 1917, it became essential to build planes to suppress potential enemy submarine activity off the eastern seashore. For offensive operations against submarines, planes with long endurance and large carrying capacity were immediately necessary. However, the Navy's first requirement was acquiring training machines. Therefore, the Navy ordered 64 N-9s and 76 of the larger type designated R-6 from the Curtiss Company. These orders filled the available capacity of the Curtiss Company, which at that time had large orders for training airplanes from the US Army and the British government.

The N-9 was a single-seat naval trainer powered by a 150hp Hispano-Suiza engine, while the R-6 had a larger wingspan than the N-9 and a Curtiss V-2-3 engine.

General N-9 Specifications:
Wingspan: 53ft (16.0m)
Length: 30ft 10in (9.4m)
Height: 10ft 9in (3.3m)

Empty weight: 2,140lb (973kg)
Gross weight: 2,765lb (1,257kg)
Maximum speed: 78mph (126kph)

The naval air service consisted of 45 seaplanes, six flying boats, three land planes, two kite balloons, and one non-rigid airship, the D-1, in April 1917. Meanwhile, the Army's aviation section had approximately 300 aircraft; however, most were unfit for service in Europe as they were too slow and lacked maneuverability. By contrast, the British RFC inventory consisted of over 3,500 planes, 846 of which were in France. Nevertheless, building an aviation force began in earnest on August 10, 1916, when the Bureau of Construction and Repair (BuC&R) sent a telegram to Glenn Curtiss requesting him to supply 30 hydroplanes with specific requirements. Specified characteristics included two seats, loading of about 4lb per sq ft, and power loading of about 20lb per horsepower (or a horsepower of approximately 120–150mph.

A Curtiss AH Seaplane, possibly the AH-13, in flight circa 1917. Note the "Circle-Star" insignia applied to American naval aircraft from May 17, 1917, to February 8, 1918. AH-13 made its first appearance in 1916. (Courtesy of the US Naval History and Heritage Command, NH 44378)

A Curtiss F-type boat at Pensacola in 1914. The aircraft began production in 1912 and became one of the standard US Navy trainers throughout World War One. (Courtesy of the US Naval History and Heritage Command, NH 2274)

The telegram concluded, "speed, climb and details of construction to be proposed by you. Rate of delivery is important and must be guaranteed."[1]

The telegram resulted in a contract for 30 N-9 model seaplanes between November 1916 and February 1917. In addition, the Navy emphasized the production of seaplanes to escort Allied merchant ships crossing the

Contact!: Early US Naval and Marine Corps Aviation, 1911–18

Left: A flying boat with an unknown occupant. Note the "fish" nose art. The photograph was possibly taken at NAS Miami in 1918. The bureau number is either 05341 or 14350. Bureau number 05341 was part of a canceled "F" boat order, while 14350 or (1435) without the "0" digit was an HS-1. (Author's collection)

Below: Burgess N-9H seaplane, bureau number 2475, moored after a test flight at NAS Pensacola in 1917. It was a seaplane based on the Curtiss JN-4D trainer. The wingspan had to be increased by 10ft to accommodate the floats. (A.E. Wells, photographer; courtesy of the US Naval History and Heritage Command, NH 60876)

Atlantic to Europe and back. However, they could not patrol more than a few hundred miles off the coast. Furthermore, until September 1917, the Navy did not know whether pilots and observers would be sent to Europe and, if so, what role they would take.

Meanwhile, until early 1918, the Navy saw no discernable use for Marine pilots except for seaplane duty. However, that changed when Captain Cunningham saw the potential use of Marine Corps aviators as part of a strategic bombing force. He began pushing for such a force in 1917, and the fledgling Marine Corps land-based units had to beg and borrow airplanes from the Army, primarily the Curtiss Jenny (JN-4) trainer and the AirCo DH-4 bomber. The latter was the American variant of the British de Havilland DH-4 bomber with a 400hp V-12 Liberty engine.

DH-4 General Specifications:
Length: 30ft 8in (9.35m)
Wingspan: 32.4ft (13.21m)
Height: 11ft (3.35m)
Empty weight: 2,387lb (1,083kg)
Gross weight: 3,472lb (1,575kg)
Maximum speed: 143mph (230kph)

The Secretary of War and the Secretary of the Navy created the Joint Technical Board on Aircraft (Army and Navy) on May 5, 1917. The original members of this board were Major B. F. Foulois, Captain V. E. Clark, and Captain E. S. Gorrell of the Army, Lieutenant. A. K. Atkins, Lieutenant. J. H. Towers, and Lieutenant J. C. Hunsaker (Construction Corps) of the Navy.

As no official name was given to the board by its precepts and to avoid confusion with the Aircraft Production Board and the Joint Army and Navy Airship Board, it decided to call itself the Joint Technical Board on Aircraft, upon its creation. Its function was to advise the War and Navy departments on purchasing types of aircraft and engines. The board also drew up a set of specifications titled "General Specifications for Building Airplanes," which the Navy adopted.

Contact!: Early US Naval and Marine Corps Aviation, 1911–18

De Havilland DH-4, bureau number A-3273, at the United States Marine Corps Flying Field, Miami, Florida, circa 1918. Over 2,500 pilots were trained in the seaplane version of the "Jenny," as it was nicknamed. (Courtesy of the US Naval History and Heritage Command, NH 43437)

Members of the Joint Technical Board. Standing (left to right): Captain E. S. Gorrell, J. C. Hunsaker, Lieutenant J. H. Towers, and Captain V. E. Clark. Sitting: Lieutenant Commander A. K. Atkins and Major B. D. Foulois. (Courtesy of the Library of Congress)

To permit the expansion of the training program, the Navy placed additional orders with other aircraft manufacturers to sample training planes of their designs. Several companies submitted their plans for testing, and the board placed orders for production in the summer of 1917 as follows: Burgess Company of Marblehead, Massachusetts, 12 planes of Burgess design, plus 30 Curtiss N-9s; Boeing Company of Seattle, 50 planes of Boeing C-1 design; Aeromarine Company of Keyport, New Jersey, 39 A/Bs and 40 F, N9/R6 and HS planes from the Willard Company design; Curtiss Company of Buffalo, 15 Curtiss Model Fs and 122 Curtiss R-6s. The Navy received those orders at a reasonable rate, allowing the training of some 2,000 pilots during the war.

On May 23, 1917, the Joint Technical Board on Aircraft recommended the initial production program to equip the Navy with aircraft necessary for war. It consisted of 300 trainers, 200 seaplanes, 100-speed scouts, and 100 large seaplanes or flying boats. The Aircraft Production Board approved the Curtiss N-9 and R-6 seaplanes, both single engine, as the most satisfactory for training but inadequate as frontline anti-submarine platforms. Nevertheless, Curtiss continued to build the first production "F" boat as the standard naval trainer, with models designated "F," "L," or "MF." This series is not to be confused with the Curtiss class "C" H-12/16 models.

On May 29, 1917, the board authorized the construction of five prototype models of 8- and 12-cylinder Liberty engines; the design, based on conservative engineering practices, allowed the motor to be mass produced. Another significant accomplishment of the board that greatly benefited the Navy was the creation and production of the engine. E. A. Deeds of the Aircraft Board selected engineers to develop the Liberty engine, with the automobile industry working under the control of the Aircraft Board. Lieutenant Harold Emmons, United States Naval Reserve Force (formerly of the Ford Motor Company, Detroit), was assigned to the War Department. He took charge of the production of Liberty engines. The engine's complete success was vital in making the Navy aircraft program possible as every flying boat for overseas, whether single or twin engine, was designed for the Liberty.

In the summer of 1917, the Aircraft Production Board went to Europe as the expert committee to study the aeronautical situation overseas. The board's purpose was to arrange with the British and French the necessary design and production data for such foreign aircraft and engines as the United States should build. This commission was commonly known as the Bolling Commission. The head of the commission was R. C. Bolling (an attorney for the United States Steel Corporation), other members were Captain V. E. Clark and Captain E. S. Gorrell of the Army; Naval Constructor G. C. Westervelt and Lieutenant W. S. Child of the Navy; Howard Marmon of the Nordyke-Marmon Company; and Herbert Hughes of the Packard Company.

Perhaps the most significant accomplishment of the commission was the Bolling Agreement with the British, French, and Italian governments. Specifically, the agreement allowed any country to produce any aircraft, aircraft engine, or accessory found in any other country. Furthermore, their government would address the compensation for any national on account of patent infringement, royalties, etc.

To further meet the demand for naval aircraft, the Navy established its aircraft factory, officially called the Naval Aircraft Factory, to assist in the problem of aircraft supply. But, again, the issue was the fundamental law of supply and demand. The Army's requirements for an enormous quantity of planes created a lack of interest among domestic aircraft manufacturers. They had no interest in supplying the relatively small number of aircraft required by the Navy; therefore, the Navy chose to build an aircraft factory to meet its requirements. The Navy went into business building its planes with the aid of such aviation pioneers as Glenn Curtiss.

In June 1917, the Navy Department directed Lieutenant Commander Coburn of the Construction Corps to survey constructing a naval aircraft factory that could produce 1,000 training seaplanes a year. He recommended using vacant land at the Philadelphia Navy Yard as a site, and constructing the main building for the factory with three auxiliary installations for a dry kiln, dry lumber storehouse, and boiler house. The Navy estimated the cost at $1m, with a completion timescale of 100 days.

Wartime Aircraft Production (1917–18)

On July 27, 1917, the Secretary of the Navy approved the project. The first power-driven machinery went into operation on October 16, and the entire plant was completed by November 28, 1917 – 110 days after breaking ground. Commander Coburn, as detailed as the first manager of the Naval Aircraft Factory, reported to the Philadelphia Navy Yard for duty on August 27, 1917. Initially, the decision to build training planes took precedence. Still, the training plane program was well in hand in other airplane factories by October. The greatest need for patrol planes was anti-submarine warfare, so the Naval Aircraft Factory switched to producing seaplanes and flying boats.

By December 1917, the Navy Department practically quadrupled its flying-boat program to take care of additional responsibilities that the Navy assumed for patrol and convoy work in European waters. However, the plant was not yet fully operational. Thus, a search began to locate idle manufacturing facilities since the Army refused to allow the Navy to use

Curtiss R-6, bureau number A-327, anchored at NAS Cape May on August 1, 1918. A Curtiss V-2-3 engine powered this two-seat floatplane. The Navy ordered 76 of them. (Courtesy of the US Naval History and Heritage Command, NH 60785)

those that the Aircraft Board had assigned to the Army. On February 9, 1918, the Secretary of the Navy acquired the idle facilities and enlarged the Philadelphia yard.[2]

In the early months of 1917, 11 planes were purchased by the Navy, among which were the Curtiss R-3 seaplane with twin floats, and the H-12 flying boat equipped with two V-2 Curtiss motors developing about 200hp. It became essential to build such aircraft for warfare. The need to suppress the submarine menace meant planes with long endurance and large bomb-carrying capacity were immediately necessary.

In July 1917, a board of officers traveled to England, France, and Italy to obtain firsthand information on suitable aircraft. On their return, on September 1, 1917, the board reported there was no wholly satisfactory foreign seaplane ideal for coastal patrol – those American types equipped with the new Liberty engine would be superior to any operated by the Allies.

The Naval Aircraft Factory, Philadelphia, Pennsylvania. This aerial view was photographed from an F-5L aircraft on November 14, 1918. The factory was used to manufacture the H-series of flying boats. (Courtesy of the US Naval History and Heritage Command, NH 2664)

Wartime Aircraft Production (1917–18)

A Curtiss HS-1L, bureau number A-1735, preparing for a flight at NAS Pensacola in 1917. Note the patriotic top hat on the forward hull. (A.E. Wells, photographer; courtesy of the US Naval History and Heritage Command, NH 60878)

A Thomas-Morse S-5 seaplane, bureau number A752, at NAS Miami on May 28, 1918. The US Navy used Thomas-Morse SH-4bs and four SH-4cs for fighter pilot training, which were also used primarily for camera-gun use. The Navy purchased approximately 20 of them as advanced trainers. (Courtesy of the US Naval History and Heritage Command, NH 60989)

Above: Frontal view of an Aeromarine 39-B. The Aeromarine was used as a training plane for an advanced trainer. It was a two-seat aircraft manufactured by the Aeromarine-Plane and Motor Company. The Navy purchased 50 of the original A-type. (Courtesy of the Naval Heritage and History Command, 44283.)

Left: Boeing Model "C" training aircraft with a Curtiss engine, photographed November 8, 1918. This aircraft may be the C-1F, bureau number A-4347. When the Curtiss Company failed to fill orders, several manufacturers, including Canadian Aeroplanes Ltd, were pressed into service to manufacture the aircraft. (Courtesy of the US Naval History and Heritage Command, NH 44105)

Wartime Aircraft Production (1917–18)

Curtiss R-6, bureau number A190, misidentified in the original caption as an A-963 seaplane at NAS Hampton Roads, August 17, 1918. (Courtesy of the US Naval History and Heritage Command, NH 60783)

According to acceptance records markings, the Curtiss R-3 with a Curtiss VXX 200 HP engine plant indicates this picture was taken in 1917. The aircraft's color seems to be overall darkish gray. (Courtesy of the US Naval History and Heritage Photograph Collection, NH 61147)

The joint Army and Navy Technical Board, acting upon this information and knowing that the United States Navy would operate 15 coastal air stations abroad, prepared a building program approved by the Secretary of the Navy in October 1917. This initial program provided for 1,185 single Liberty engine flying boats, known as the HS-1, and 235 twin Liberty engine flying boats, known as the H-16. Provision of the single-engine HS series simplified production and maintenance. On November 6, 1917, the Aircraft Production Board adopted a resolution that all measures be taken to defend the eastern seaboard from submarine attacks, which gave the Navy priority in obtaining materials to create a fleet of flying boats and manufacturing the Liberty engines. One such series was the Curtiss H flying boat.

The Curtiss HS-1 flying boat was developed from a Curtiss design known as H-14, brought out in the summer of 1917. It was a typical Curtiss flying boat with a length of 38ft and a wingspan of 62ft. The gross weight of the standard HS-1/2 series in the air was 5,900lb, including a crew of two men, one machine gun, and two 180lb bombs. Its maximum speed of 82mph, powered by a Liberty L-12 engine, could be maintained for four hours in the air. However, after production had gotten well under way, the Curtiss Company obtained information that the standard 180lb-bomb carried by the HS series was ineffective against submarines. Thus, they needed to carry a heavier bomb load. It was necessary to increase the wing area to permit the carrying of this extra load by designing a 6ft wing panel inserted outboard of the engine section on each side. This change resulted in an increased span to 74ft and an increase in total weight to 6,500lb. A larger rudder was also provided for the planes thus modified, and these modified planes were designated model HS-2.

The other type adopted for production by the joint Army and Navy Technical Board was the Curtiss H-16 flying boat equipped with twin Liberty engines of 360hp each. This type was developed between 1915 and 1916 by the Curtiss Company and the British Admiralty. Curtiss then designed the H-12, a larger aircraft on the same lines, fitted in England by the Admiralty with twin Rolls-Royce engines. The Admiralty redesigned

Wartime Aircraft Production (1917–18)

Rear Admiral David W. Taylor, chief of the Bureau of Construction and Repair, with Josephus Daniels, Secretary of the Navy; Lieutenant Commander Frederic C. Coburn, USN, manager of the Naval Aircraft Factory; and Rear Admiral J. M. Helm, USN, commandant of the Philadelphia Navy Yard, and others in the high shop at the Naval Aircraft Factory, May 2, 1918. (Courtesy of the US Naval History and Heritage Command, NH 56901)

A Curtiss HS-1 being built at an unknown location, but probably at the Naval Aircraft Factory in Philadelphia, circa 1918. The model had a bow cockpit with a Scarff ring to mount a Lewis machine gun or Davis gun. It could carry two racks of 180lb bombs. (Courtesy of the National Archives via Alan C. Carey Collection)

A Curtiss H-16 patrol seaplane, bureau number 845, at NAS Killingholme, England, on July 3, 1918. It was used for scouting and anti-submarine duties. (Courtesy of the US Naval History and Heritage Command, NH 74089)

the hull of the H-12 to provide greater strength, and introduced, for the first time, the steep Vee bottom with double steps. In early 1917 the Curtiss Company was given a large order for the British redesigned boat, known in England as the F-3 or "Large America" and in the United States as H-16. This machine was already in production at the Curtiss Company's Buffalo works when the United States declared war, but the design used Rolls-Royce engines, which proved inadequate. It became necessary to redesign the H-16 to accommodate the Liberty engines. This redesign of the H-16 involved extensive changes to the plane. Still, time was too valuable to work out a trial installation. On March 27, 1918, just 228 days after breaking ground for the facility and 151 days from receiving technical drawings, the first H-16 built by the factory was tested. On April 15, 1918, the first and second factory-built H-16 flying boats arrived at Killingholme, England, for assembly.

The H-16 was a biplane flying boat, 46ft in length, spanning 96ft, and equipped with two 360hp Liberty engines. The empty weight was 7,400lb and 10,900lb loaded, including a crew of four, a radio, two 230lb depth bombs, and four machine guns. The maximum speed was 95mph. The endurance was four hours at this speed, with patrols of up to nine hours

Wartime Aircraft Production (1917–18)

Right: An N-1 seaplane showing the Davis gun in position at the Naval Aircraft Factory, Philadelphia, May 22, 1918. (Courtesy of the US Naval History and Heritage Command, NH 123934)

Below: Naval aircraft factory C-1 flying boat (Curtiss H-16 design). Lieutenant Arthur E. J. Male, USNRF, in gunner's bow position, with a Lewis aircraft machine gun, at the Naval Aircraft Factory, Philadelphia on March 25, 1918. (Courtesy of the US Naval History and Heritage Command, NH 43130)

A Thomas Martin "S" seaplane on the catapult of an armored cruiser at Pensacola on June 25, 1917. The Navy operated some 20 of them as advanced trainers. (Courtesy of the US Naval History and Heritage Command, NH 43914)

conducted in areas primarily in the English Channel, Bay of Biscay, and connecting waters. In 1917, the British Admiralty redesigned the H-16 again to produce a boat capable of carrying more depth bombs and having greater endurance. The factory successfully began producing them in the spring of 1918. This plane was designated the model F-5L-series flying boat.

The F-5L had an allowable full load of 1,300lb and could carry four depth bombs against two for the H-16, besides having a cruising endurance of 11 hours against nine for the H-16. The advantages of this flying boat over the H-16 were obvious. Hence, the end of manufacturing contracts for the H-16 triggered the decision to replace them with the F-5L series. However, before production of the F-5L could proceed, it was necessary to redesign the British F-5 at the Naval Aircraft Factory.

Wartime Aircraft Production (1917-18)

HS-2-L seaplanes on the anchorage of US NAS Cape May, New Jersey, 1918, with bureau number 1925 in front and 1210 in the rear. This view was a typical scene during submarine activities. The planes are being prepared for another patrol. (Courtesy of the US Naval Heritage and History Command, NH 2678)

The H-12 flying boat mainly served on anti-submarine patrols off the American coasts and in Britain. Nineteen were built for the US Navy. (Courtesy of the US Naval History and Heritage Command, NH 60768)

An air-to-air view of an HS-2 seaplane 1,000ft over NAS Miami, November 28, 1918. This model had a larger wingspan of 12ft, and the rudder was 33 percent larger than the HS-1L. (Courtesy of the US Naval History and Heritage Command, NH 2872)

Manufacturers chose the Liberty engine instead of the British Rolls-Royce engine, which was initially fitted on the F-5, to adapt it for high-quantity production on the assembly line. Production in appreciable quantities began in April 1918. At that time, single-engine flying boats were being received from manufacturers at the rate of six per week, and twin-engine boats at a rate of three per week. Aircraft production reached its height around September 1, 1918, when the aircraft factory and other manufacturers began delivering 42 single-engine flying boats per week, twin-engine flying boats at a rate of 13 per week, and training planes at a rate of 32 per week.[3]

Wartime Aircraft Production (1917–18)

An F-5L silhouetted against the clouds. This type of flying boat was used extensively in England and France. (Courtesy of the Stephen Polunsky Collection, Library of Congress, S-032.01)

A Naval Aircraft Factory-built F-5L aircraft on exhibit in front of Philadelphia City Hall on the night of October 17, 1918. It was possibly the first of the model built at the Philadelphia factory. (Author's collection)

Chapter 10

Naval Aviation at War

At the outbreak of war, the Army and Navy had little idea of how to prepare for aerial warfare, as evidenced in a cablegram to the Secretary of the Navy from Admiral Sims dated April 20, 1918. Sims pointed out: "Immediate and complete information is desired by the Navy Department regarding the current development of the British of their naval aeronautics. For example, what aircraft style is most used and successful over the water? What is the method of launching at sea when the carrier vessel is underway? For coastal patrol and submarine searching, what aircraft types are used?"[1]

Anti-submarine warfare primarily focused on the waters off the Irish, English, and French coasts. Yet, German U-boats began aggressive operations off the eastern seaboard of the United States starting in the summer of 1918. However, long-range German U-boats visited the neutral United States beginning on October 7, 1916, when U-53 paid a visit to Newport, Rhode Island. The boat's captain showed Germany's capability to cross the Atlantic and the boat's capacity to wage submarine warfare – a reminder for the United States to remain neutral. The arrival of such a vessel gave a clear message that attacks from German submarines off the United States were quite possible.[2]

The Navy Department, on February 1, 1918, appointed a special board to make recommendations as to the methods to be taken to provide for "defense against submarines in home waters." The Chief of Naval Operations approved the board's report with specific alterations on March 6, 1918. Admiral Sims initially concluded that Germany would not operate submarines in US waters. However, later dispatches by April convinced him of the danger and gave necessary information regarding future German submarine activities off the United States. Accordingly, the board recommended that shipping adopt the convoy system for all eastbound shipping and that aircraft, submarine chasers, and destroyers escort such shipping as far as possible.[3]

On May 1, 1918, intelligence from the British Admiralty reported a U-boat (U-151) had left its Belgian base for operations off the American coast. U-151 was one of five cruiser-class submarines with a length of 213ft 3in, a breadth of 29ft 2in, a displacement surface of 1,700 tons, submerged 2,100 tons, and a range of 17,000 miles surfaced. Armament consisted of two 5.9lb and two 2.2lb guns, one machine gun, and six torpedo tubes (four bow and two stern). From May 15 to October 29, 1918, U-boats 117, 140, 151, 155, and 156 operated singularly off the eastern seaboard with impunity.

The submarines caused extensive damage to merchant ships sailing along the eastern seaboard between May and October 1918. Seventy-nine vessels, including 42 American, were sunk by torpedoes, gunfire, or submarine-laid mines. American naval air stations on anti-submarine duty

German Submarine U-151 was one of six that operated in American waters between May and October 1918. The loss of Germany's submarine bases along the Belgian coast ended such operations. (Courtesy of the US Naval History and Heritage Command, NH 111049)

operated the single-engine N-9, HS-1, and HS-2 flying boats, which could cover approximately 1,500 square miles, while the larger H-12, H-16, and F5L flying boats could cover 3,000 square miles. Naval and Coast Guard planes occasionally sighted enemy submarines but conducted unsuccessful attacks primarily due to dud bombs and inadequate techniques to engage such vessels. One example is the unsuccessful attack on U-156 a few miles from the naval air station at Chatham on July 21, 1918. Ensign Eric Lingard, Naval Aviator No. 540, from Chatham NAS, in an HS-1L, and Captain Philip Eaton of the Coast Guard, Naval Aviator No. 60/Coast Guard Aviator No. 6, piloting a Curtiss R-9 attacked the submarine with bombs, which did not explode. Defensive fire from the boat kept the planes high. Eaton reported, "As I bore down upon the submarine, it fired. I zigzagged and dove as it fired again. They were [U-156's crew] getting under way and scrambling down the hatch when I flew over them and dropped my bomb. The bomb missed, and finally, the U-boat submerged and was last observed heading south."[4]

London's American Naval Planning Section for operational and tactical planning for the waters surrounding the British Isles and those

An aerial view of the US naval air station in Chatham, Massachusetts, in 1918, from which two American planes attacked U-156 after the latter attacked an American tugboat. The submarine was attacked unsuccessfully by an HS-1L and an N-9 based at the station. (Courtesy of the US Naval History and Heritage Command, NH 113053)

Coast Guard pilot Captain Philip Eaton of the Coast Guard, Naval Aviator No. 60/Coast Guard Aviator No. 6, piloting a Curtiss R-9, attacked U-151 unsuccessfully. (Courtesy of the US Coast Guard)

of France were still in the developmental stages ten months after the US declaration of war. On February 15, 1918, the American Naval Planning Section stated that the US naval air effort was still in its initial stages, and made numerous objectives and recommendations. Naval air strength during 1917 consisted of small concentrations of men and materiels scattered throughout France undergoing training by Allied forces. Yet plans called for a superior network of air units to be established as quickly as possible:

(1) To make our primary air effort a continuous bombing offensive against enemy naval objectives.
(2) To make our secondary air effort a patrol of those areas frequented by enemy submarines in readiness for a tactical offensive.

(3) Protect troop and merchant convoy escort duty.

(4) To concentrate principal air effort in the Felixstowe–Dunkirk area in sufficient force to get local control of the air.⁵

(5) To direct all air effort in the Adriatic against enemy bases in succession, choosing areas to fit conditions.

(6) To make patrol areas, whether patrol by flying boats or by kite balloons, coincident with the operating areas of our surface vessels, with the greatest effort where shipping is most numerous.

(7) To plan and build our air effort against the Helgoland area.⁶

Tactical considerations relied on the British, French, and Italians furnishing the Americans with instructors, bases, and aircraft since the Americans lacked everything except willing personnel. Moreover, aircraft requirements were general, comprising capabilities that required building bombers, fighters, and kite balloons. The US had no American-built combat aircraft, except for seaplanes; unprepared for aerial warfare, the Army and Navy had to rely on foreign-manufactured planes. Admiral Sims endorsed the policy, and the Navy Department agreed in principle. While the Navy assembled the personnel and the materiel essential to war operations in the United

First Naval Aeronautic Detachment in Tours, France, circa 1917. This detachment was the first US naval aviation unit sent to France. Most, if not all, the personnel had to be trained by French instructors. (Courtesy of the US Naval History and Heritage Command, UA 80.02.03)

States, future sites for air stations were evaluated. Two weeks after the Navy's announcement, Captain Cone relieved Lieutenant Whiting and assumed command of all naval aviation activities in Europe as commander of United States naval aviation forces under the direction of Vice Admiral Sims.[7]

The US Navy, in conjunction with the Royal Navy, established seven air stations in the British Isles: two in England and five in Ireland, with the principal naval objective being for air and surface forces to protect shipping against submarines. From bases in England and Ireland, patrol aircraft conducted the "Spider Web" network, which sectioned the patrol area in a spider web from a fixed point from the base; it kept submarines from performing overall offensive operations. In this, the success of naval patrol aviation is questionable as there is no evidence American patrol aircraft sank or seriously damaged a single German submarine in the 37 attacks conducted from European bases while carrying out 22,000 flights and air coverage of more than 800,000 miles. However, the Navy claimed ten of those attacks inflicted damage.

Anti-submarine operations during the war were primitive since this was before sonar and radar, with observers aboard patrol planes relying on binoculars to locate a surfaced submarine or following oil patches left behind by such a vessel. Studies written during the 1920s and '30s bestow glowing reports such as the following:

> In general, the work of the naval aviation forces in European waters was of inestimable value. They contributed a significant share in the ultimate victory, not only through their own efforts but indirectly through the assistance rendered to other naval and military forces. Still, their significant contribution was guiding destroyers to submarine contacts and reducing German submarines' effectiveness in attacking shipping convoys by forcing them to submerge.[8]

In May 1917, at the request of the French government, the Navy Department authorized the sending of a naval aviation force to France by establishing the First Naval Aviation Force (FNAF). The force's first detachment

Unknown US aviation staff members at Brest, France, in 1918. The station was primarily used as an assembly and repair station. (Courtesy of the US Naval History and Heritage Command, UA 80.02.05)

An aerial view shows part of the hangars and a building at the end of the camp toward Eastleigh, England. (Courtesy of the US Naval History and Heritage Command, NH 113606)

A Curtiss H-16 patrol seaplane at US NAS Killingholme on June 3, 1918. (Courtesy of the US Naval History and Heritage Command, NH 74089)

US NAS Killingholme. Front view of an H-16 fitted with a 520lb bomb. The photograph was taken on October 24, 1918. (Courtesy of the US Naval History and Heritage Command, NH 113556)

represented a large proportion of the total aviation strength of the Navy then in existence. The first organized American military unit to land in Europe after the United States entered the war was the First Aeronautic Detachment consisting of seven officers and 122 enlisted men – 50 student naval aviators, 50 student aviation mechanics, and 22 administrative support personnel under the command of Lieutenant Whiting.

The detachment set sail aboard the colliers USS *Jupiter* (AC-3) and USS *Neptune* (AC-8). After a 12-day crossing, the force landed in Saint-Nazaire, France, on June 8, 1917. However, the American preparation had been so disinterested in this vital element of 20th-century warfare that few aviators were prepared for combat operations. Furthermore, the detachment had no base to operate from and no aircraft or equipment. Between mid-August and September, those joining the FNAF included graduates of the First Yale Unit; Bob Lovett and "Di" Gates arrived in August 1917, followed by John Vorys and Al Sturtevant. In September, a larger Yale Unit contingent consisted of David Ingalls, Freddie Beach, Sam Walker, Ken Smith, Reginald Coombe, "Chip" McIlwaine, Henry Landon, and Ken MacLeish. Young and innocent about warfare, they looked forward to arriving in France.[9]

Lieutenant Whiting departed for Paris on June 12, where he had little guidance in establishing the force. He found himself in charge of a mission with little specification and, by default, engaged in forming a close working relationship liaising with the French regarding establishing air stations; even Admiral Sims seemed oblivious to Whiting's actions. He had written orders for Whiting to proceed with his detachment to France and to advise the naval attaché in Paris of his whereabouts upon arrival. Before leaving the US, Whiting sought further and more detailed information concerning his duties. Still, he could not obtain instructions or advice except that if he wanted to go to the war zone, he had better leave at once before a policy change revoked his orders. Accordingly, upon his arrival in Paris, he entered negotiations with the French Admiralty, during which he agreed, on behalf of the United States, to establish certain naval air stations on the French coast, entirely on his initiative. He spoke about his lone journey:

"… there was practically no understanding as to the arrangements made in the United States whereby this Detachment had been sent to France." However, Whiting wrote that, despite their surprise, "the French expressed their gratitude and bade us welcome in an enthusiastic manner."[10]

The French were conciliatory toward the American naval officer and made recommendations on structuring the First Naval Detachment by agreeing to send American pilots, observers, and mechanics to French training schools. Whiting and French officials decided to send the American pilots to the French army school of instruction at Tours, and the observers to the French navy school at Saint-Raphaël. The continued discussion resulted in the decision to establish "a suitable nucleus for the operation and manning of three air stations and a training school," located at Dunkerque, at the mouths of the Loire River (Saint-Nazaire) and the Gironde estuary (Brest), and at Lake Hourtin in France's Médoc region. The French plans were to establish 50 seaplane bases for operations against German submarines and additional ones for dirigibles. Of these 50, they wanted the Americans to operate 12.

Whiting returned to Brest on June 12 with orders to take the detachment to the French naval air station at Camaret. With these arrangements, Aeronautic Detachment No. 1 began training at the French bases. Preparations to create an American base began at Lacanau on the Bay of Biscay, which soon became home to France's first US naval air station: NAS Le Moutchic. In August 1917, students from the training schools began operating at the station.[11]

Whiting's presence in Europe was unknown to Admiral Sims until someone brought up the establishment of naval patrol stations for discussion at a meeting of the Board of Admiralty. Sims was asked to explain the reason for his secretive policy of concentrating a large air force in France when the most vital areas of the enemy submarine campaign lay in and adjacent to the coasts of England and Ireland. Admiral Sims was obliged to explain that the total commitment was as much of a mystery to him as it was to them. He did not know any officer empowered to represent the United States in France and, admitting to the contention that England

and Ireland offered a much more fruitful field for aerial operations against submarines, he would investigate the matter without delay. Accordingly, Sims summoned the lieutenant from Paris and found that in the absence of any orders or instructions, Whiting had taken it upon himself to order the construction of several naval air stations. Sims stated that, "because of this, his assumption of responsibility and initiative in doing what he did were commendable."[12]

Lieutenant Whiting immediately proceeded to Paris and held a conference with Admiral Le Bon, French Minister of Marine, and Capitaine de Vaisseau Cazenau, chief of the French Naval Air Service. At this conference, they agreed to send a mission of French and American officers to inspect the French coast and locate sites for future United States Navy air stations. Accordingly, Capitaine de Fregate Laborde, Lieutenant Whiting, Paymaster Conger, and Captain Smith (the assistant to the United States naval attaché), were appointed board members. After a careful inspection of the French coast, completed around July 1, they submitted their recommendations in a report. The recommendations formed the basis of an agreement between Lieutenant Whiting and the French Minister of Marine (French Naval Air Service), who forwarded their recommendations to the Navy Department for approval.[13]

However, significant problems persisted well into the spring and summer of 1918, according to Captain Cone, whose official title was Commander of the United States Naval Aviation Forces, Foreign Service. He stated: "Establishing US Naval aviation in Europe has been one of the most challenging undertakings of early American naval operations. Although delays and mistakes in the shipment of aviation material probably caused more trouble than anything else."[14]

The Navy's First Aeronautical Company and the FNAF found very little in air bases or aircraft to operate as an independent force. Instead, Britain and France provided the sites for establishing air stations – some from scratch – for seaplane and flying boat operations. At the same time, some American naval personnel operated from previously established RNAS bases.

British air stations and their counterparts in France first served as training stations for the newly arrived American aviation personnel, as most had flown less than 50 hours and had very little practice in gunnery or bombing while training in the United States. Afterward, pilots and observers went to active stations to conduct anti-submarine and scouting operations. In contrast, others went to serve with British night-bombing squadrons or the Night Wing of the American Northern Bombing Group (NBG). Finally, an even smaller contingent served as fighter pilots with British and French units.

The Navy established two naval air stations in England. Killingholme, located in north Lincolnshire, between the River Humber and River Hull, and Eastleigh in north Hampshire, between Southampton and Winchester. The station served as a patrol station, which was placed in commission on June 30, 1918. This station was initially intended to conduct offensive operations in the Heligoland Bight area of the Belgian coast. Still, due to the limited fuel-carrying capacity of available seaplanes at that time, patrols of this area were not feasible, and convoy coverage became the station's primary duty. From June 30, 1917, until the signing of the Armistice, the Killingholme patrol station convoyed 6,243 Allied vessels and covered around 60,000 miles during 233 patrols. Meanwhile, a considerable number of naval pilots operated under the Royal Navy's air branch at RNAS Felixstowe.

The Eastleigh station's primary operations consisted of the reception, assembly, and overhaul of DH-4 and Caproni bombers for the NBG when they became available beginning in September 1918. For this purpose, it was located only four miles from the port of Southampton, had good rail connections, and was within flying distance of the aerodromes of the Northern Bombing squadrons across the Channel. Initially designed and built as a reception park for the Royal Air Force, US naval forces began operations from there in the middle of June 1918. This station also served as a supply depot for Killingholme and the NBG.

The Irish stations were Queenstown, Wexford, Lough Foyle, Whiddy Island, and Berehaven. In March 1918, construction of those stations, under US Navy civil engineers' supervision, began. Completion of those stations occurred at practically the same time, around the middle

An unknown pilot or co-pilot aboard a Curtiss H-16 flying boat while performing a reconnaissance flight from NAS Killingholme on November 6, 1918. The photograph was taken only five days before the Armistice was signed, ending World War One. Killingholme flying boats conducted convoy coverage and anti-submarine duties. (Courtesy of the US Naval History and Heritage Command, NH 74090)

of September 1917, and operations started immediately. The station at Queenstown (now known as Cobh) was located in the southwestern section of Queenstown Bay. In addition to being a patrol station, it was also an assembly, repair, and supply depot and the headquarters of the US naval air operation commander. This station supplied patrols and convoys from Cape Clear on the west, south into the English Channel, to the sector covered by the aerial patrols from the north coast of France, and southeast and east to the sectors covered by the stations in the southwest of England and at Wexford. The station at Wexford was located on the eastern shore of a wide, shallow bay in the southeastern corner of Ireland. Its purpose was to provide convoy protection and patrols in the sector to the east of Queenstown.

The station at Lough Foyle was located on a long, narrow arm of the sea on the north coast of Ireland, about six miles north of the

American naval mechanics and armed guards stationed at NAS Queenstown, Ireland, posing for a photograph sometime during the fall of 1918. (Courtesy of US Naval History and Heritage Command, 2017.37)

town of Londonderry. This station patrolled the waters in the vicinity of the northern outlet to the Irish Sea. The Whiddy Island station was located on the eastern side of the island of that name in Bantry Bay. This station furnished patrols and convoys for the waters to the southwest of Ireland. Berehaven was a kite balloon station used in conjunction with torpedo-boat destroyers. This station was located on a sound formed within Bantry Bay behind Bere Island, near Castletown. The total number of aircraft in England and Ireland operating from US naval air stations was 43 H-16 flying boats, although there were 124 authorized. Anti-submarine operations and patrolling by US naval personnel would have extended for many miles with the addition of those aircraft. However, the RNAS carried out most of such duties. The individuals responsible for establishing American naval air stations in France were Rear Admiral Henry B. Wilson, commander of all matters regarding naval aviation forces in France, with Captain Thomas T. Craven becoming the aide for the admiral's staff.

Another view of NAS Queenstown, with a Curtiss H-16 flying boat on the ramp with naval personnel hauling it up in 1918 after the plane performed an aerial operation. American and British forces operated the aircraft. (Courtesy of the US Naval History and Heritage Command, NH 2596)

A Curtiss HS-1L flying boat based at NAS Moutchic, France, in 1918. From here, waters off the French coast were protected against German submarines. American naval personnel operated H-series flying boats from this base and were also trained by French instructors. (Courtesy of the National Archives, 80-G-1053802, U.S. Naval Heritage and History Command)

Hangars at the L'Aber Vrach naval air station operated by the US Navy for overwater patrols. Part of the US Naval Aviation French Unit Collection. (Courtesy of the US Naval History and Heritage Command, UA 80.02.26)

Lieutenant Whiting's independence and diplomatic abilities with the French were paramount, even though he exceeded the authority of his rank by establishing air stations in that country. As a result, on September 16, 1917, the Navy Department authorized the establishment of 17 air stations, with 11 commissioned before the Armistice: Dunkerque, L'Aber Vrach, Brest, Île-Tudy, Le Croisic, Paimboeuf, Fromentine, Rochefort, Saint-Trojan-les-Bains, Moutchic, and Pauillac. Six additional stations, primarily for balloons, were established later at Tréguier, Guipavas, La Trinité-sur-Mer, La Pallice, Gujan, and Arcachon.

Moutchic, located on the north shore of Lake Lacanau, four miles from the Atlantic Ocean and 32 miles from Bordeaux, became active in July 1917. At this station, Ensign Robert Lovett made the first flight from the naval air station in seaplane FBA No. 295 on September 27, 1917. Naval Air Station

Trequier was located between the towns of Trequier and Plougiel, about four miles from the coast at the junction of the Guindy and Jaudy rivers, which form the Trequier River at this point. The purpose of this station was to provide aerial patrols into the English Channel, connecting up with the sectors covered by the French seaplane stations east of the Cherbourg Peninsula, and in the northwest with the L'Aber Vrach sector. The first aircraft delivery, consisting of several HS-1 planes, arrived at the station on September 24, 1918.

Naval Air Station L'Aber Vrach, was situated on the rocky island of Ehre in the harbor of Vrach. The station was one and a half miles south of the large Ile Vierge lighthouse, which marks the southern entrance to the English Channel and is 21 miles north of Brest. The patrol area of this station extended over the English Channel to the sectors patrolled by the Irish bases. The first construction work commenced on February 1, 1918. On July 18, 1918, the first seaplane arrived at the station.

By September 2, 1918, ten planes, all HS flying boats, arrived, and regular patrol flights and convoy coverage began. The United States naval air station, Brest, located in the western extremity of the French navy

A Franco–British-built **FBA** flying in the water at Moutchic, circa 1918–19. This station is one of over a dozen American stations that were established as training, repair, and patrol stations. (Courtesy of the US Naval History and Heritage Command, NH 112931)

The Donnet-Donhaut (DD-8) French flying boat at Moutchic, 1917–19. These were used by the US Navy for patrol operations along the coast of France in World War One. (Courtesy of the US Naval History and Heritage Command, NH 60766)

A Franco–British airplane (FBA) flying boat located at NAS Moutchic, France. Note the ramp used to haul a plane into and from the water. (From the scrapbook of John Lansing Callan, donated by the Naval Historical Foundation; courtesy of the US Naval History and Heritage Command, NHF-039-RR.10.01)

yard, consisted of both a seaplane base and a kite balloon station. The first seaplane pilot to report on the station was Lieutenant Commander F. C. "Dyke" Dichman, Naval Aviator No. 30, who arrived on February 13, 1918. The only fatal accident at this station occurred on August 21, 1918, when an HS-1 seaplane – piloted by Ensign Robert F. Clark, Naval Aviator No. 196, with Ensign Arthur L. Boorse, Naval Aviator No. 333, and W. F. Rodman, machinist mate – crashed, killing the crew.

Le Croisic was the first United States naval air station organized in France; it was also the first completed and the first to operate. The station was on two small islands called Les Petit et Grand Joncheres. These islands had previously been used by fishermen as a place to dry their nets and were a part of the village of Le Croisic, situated on the Baie du Croisic, about 18 miles from Saint-Nazaire. The principal objective of having a station at Le Croisic was to provide aerial escorts for the troop convoys coming into the Loire River. The station's building started on July 26, 1917, and on October 6, 1917, the first planes arrived. These were French seaplanes of the Tellier type. On November 13, 1917, the first patrol flight was made, and from that date to the Armistice, patrol and convoy flights regularly operated, weather permitting. During this entire period, there was but one fatal airplane crash. This crash occurred on July 1, 1918, when T. M. Weddell, pilot, and E. C. Kneip, observer, were killed due to one wing of their plane collapsing, which caused the aircraft to fall into a nosedive.[15]

The US NAS Fromentine was located at the southern end of the island of Fromentine in the Vendée region. The island is about 12 miles long, separated from the mainland by a half-mile stretch of water. The sheltered water between the island and the mainland made it an ideal location for a seaplane station. Construction work at this station began on February 23, 1918, and continued until October 26. United States naval personnel carried out the entire construction work using only American materials. On June 29, two HS-1 flying boats arrived at Pauillac, and by the end of July, eight planes had arrived, enabling patrol operations over the French coast.

HS-1 aircraft at NAS Tréguier with T7 and T6 at the left. The American flag is in the back center. (Courtesy of the US Naval History and Heritage Command, UA 80.02.23)

US Navy personnel at NAS Tréguier, circa 1918: Robert S. Waters, left, Naval Aviator No. 932, and possibly Theodore Fisher Dillion, Naval Aviator No. 1635, in the middle. (Robert S. Waters Collection; Courtesy of the US Naval History and Heritage Command S-012.01)

The assembling of an H-16 aircraft at the Brest air station, where the aircraft was assembled before another air station received it for duty. (Courtesy of the US Naval History and Heritage Command, UA 80.02.33)

Captain Hutchinson Cone managed aircraft, parts, and personnel shipments to France. However, shipping aircraft from the United States to England – assembled, tested, and flown to air bases in France – proved to be the most troublesome. So much so that pilots and mechanics operated with the American Army and the British and French aviation units, warranting a close working relationship. This proved problematic, not with the Allies but with General Pershing, commander-in-chief of the American Expeditionary Force, who believed the Navy was not cooperating with the US Air Service. This view came from meetings of Aircraft Production Board representatives in which the Chief of the Army Air Service regarded the Naval Aviation Force as somewhat insignificant in overall war plans except for the creation of the NBG, discussed later in this book. Naval air representatives, in turn, felt slighted during production board meetings as they pressed their needs primarily in acquiring aircraft and supplies. The poor relationship between the naval air service and the American Flying Corps remained throughout the war.

Above: H-16 in the hangar at Brest, which served as a repair, assembling, and patrol station. This plane does not have a bureau number painted on the stabilizer. (Courtesy of the US Naval History and Heritage Command, UA 80.02.32)

Right: Commander J. Callan, USNRF. He understood problematic issues facing US naval air units attempting to organize and establish air stations in France. (Courtesy of the US Naval History and Heritage Command, NH 64337)

Captain Thomas Craven played a significant role in establishing naval aviation in Britain and France during World War One. He became the director of naval aeronautics in 1919. (Courtesy of the National Archives. 80-G-186889, U.S. Naval Heritage and History Command)

A memorandum sent by Lieutenant John L. Callan to Captain Craven details the problematic issues facing US naval air units:

Lieutenant John L. Callan, U.S.N.R.F., To Captain Thomas T. Craven

28 February, 1918

MEMORANDUM

TO: Captain Craven.

The Officer Pilots from Pensacola, who have lately reported for duty in England and France, have only received training on Curtiss type N.91 and R.62 tractor seaplanes. Each one has had on an average only about 25 hours in the air; none of them have been trained on flying boats.

As our present policy calls for the use of only flying boats at our Stations in France and Ireland, it will be necessary to give all of these Pilots and any others who may come in the future, with the same training, another course in flying which will include flying boats.

At present the facilities for this training in France are very limited owing to the fact that the Lake at Moutchic is too small to conduct both a school for pilots and one for bombing instruction. As the school is primarily for bombing and firing, and as practically all of the Lake is needed for that purpose, it will be very difficult to handle the pilotage instruction there.

However, it is suggested that at least four dual control flying boats, Tellier type, be bought immediately and sent to Moutchic to be used for the instruction of those Pilots who have already reported from Pensacola and for the training of those Pilots now in England on patrol work at British Stations, using tractor seaplanes, who will eventually come to France after completing their work there.

It is further suggested that the Department be notified of the limited conditions for training in France and be advised of the necessity for training on flying boats, and be so instructed that in the future all Pilots will know how to fly boats before being sent abroad for active service.[16]

Yet, cooperation between naval representatives with their British and French counterparts appeared to be very supportive, according to memorandums

A Curtiss HS-1L flying boat is taxiing at NAS Brest on September 30, 1918. Note the sea sled powered by an aircraft engine and the rowboats near the seaplane ramp. (Courtesy of the US Naval History and Heritage Command, NH 42455)

sent by the Commander of Naval Aviation Forces to the commander of Naval Forces Operating in European Waters. However, General Pershing believed representatives of the US Naval Aviation Forces were unreasonable for their concerns about the lack of cooperation between the Army and Navy. A memorandum by the commander of US Naval Aviation Forces, dated May 22, 1918, addressed Pershing's misunderstanding of the matter:

> It has been the aim of this organization to cooperate in every way possible with all the different interests with whom we deal. For this reason, the very general statement of General Pershing, that we have failed to cooperate with the U.S. Air Service without stating in what particular, is to be deplored. This organization is put on the defensive much to our disadvantage and it is believed solely because General Pershing has been misinformed.[17]

Based on the following statement, it does appear that the Army Air Service was providing adequate cooperation or support with establishing naval aviation forces in Europe,

Ensign Theodore Dillon (left) and Ensign Robert Waters flying their Curtiss HS-1 flying boat over NAS Tréguier in 1918. (Robert S. Waters Collection; courtesy of the US Naval History and Heritage Command, NH 81569)

No comment nor criticism has ever been received from them [Army Air Service] on any of these plans nor has the U.S. Air Service furnished us with its own program or organization charts, although requested to do so.[18]

The status of establishing, maintaining, and operating US Naval Air Stations in France, even by the summer of 1918, apparently remained problematic according to Assistant Secretary of the Navy, Franklin D. Roosevelt, in a cablegram to the Secretary of the Navy:

The Assistant Secretary Of The Navy Franklin D. Roosevelt To Secretary Of The Navy Josephus Daniels
Sub-Area: <France>
Subject: Inspection of Air Stations.
Source: Asst. Secretary of the Navy.
Date: <8-18-18>

IN-2471

From: Asst. Secretary of the Navy.
To: Secretary of the Navy.
Have inspected Paulliac and other air stations. Not a single American Naval airplane in France can operate offensively. Only 8 can fly. Propellers and gasoline pumps defective. Liberty motors short of parts and reported improperly assembled. 8 starters received for 145 motors. 220 hours work per motor necessary before it is in good condition. Not a single bomb sight or spare part received. Trouble evidently lack of following up and proper factory and shipping inspection. List missing parts in Washington, D.C. Drastic action on part of all bureaus necessary present condition scandalous. Have absolute proof of above. Figures should be given to all concerned.

Astnav.

3:25 PM.   8-18-18[19]

What other air stations did Roosevelt visit during the summer of 1918? It is difficult to conceive that "Not a single American Naval airplane in France can operate offensively," as he stated. Paulliac was an assembly and repair station. Aircraft there would have been in different stages of repair, and maybe the Assistant Secretary of the Navy did not take that into account. Eight naval air stations received aircraft beginning in August 1917. Brest and Moutchic were both assembly and repair stations, and aircraft could have been in those different stages. The other seven operated American, French, and Italian seaplanes between October 1917 and November 1918. There is an indication that those stations were short of operational aircraft compared to the total number of aircraft allocated. By November 1, 1918, three or four months after Roosevelt's visit, the following air stations, except Brest and Moutchic, had the following American and foreign aircraft on hand:

Station	Aircraft on Hand	Number Allocated
Tréguier	8 HS-1L	18 HS-1L
L'Aber Vrach	19 HS-1L	24 HS-1L
Île-Tudy	19 HS-1L	24 HS-1L
	2 Donnet-Denhaut	
Le Croisic	7 Tellier	24 HS-1L
	4 Donnet-Denhaut	
	5 Levy-LePan	
	1 HS-1L	
Fromentine	14 HS-1L	24 H-16
Saint-Trojan	6 HS-1L	24 HS-1L
	2 Levy-LePan	
	1 H-16	
	1 HS-2L	
Arcachon	7 HS-1L	24 HS-1L
	Total on hand = 96	**Total allocated = 162**

There was a plan to replace French and Italian aircraft with the American HS-1L and the H-16. Such an increase could have extended operations in the North Seas, the English Channel, and the Bay of Biscay. Unfortunately, that plan never materialized due to the Armistice. Instead, Brest was dual-purpose: an assembly and repair station.[20]

Lieutenant Ruttan, USNRF, in a circa 1918 photograph taken at NAS Pauillac. The photograph depicts the type of camera used on navy seaplanes to gather information for maps. The camera is probably the French Appareil 13x18-260 Modele 1916. (Courtesy of the US Naval History and Heritage Command, NH 46073)

Chapter 11

Naval Air Operations in Britain and France

Based on official correspondence, the training and certification of American student pilots and mechanics hindered the immediate deployment of such personnel into frontline fighting forces. Consequently, the First Aeronautical Detachment sent all pilots to the French training schools at Tours and all mechanics of the detachment to the French school at Saint-Raphaël. The French and British quickly realized with dismay that the detachment sent students rather than qualified aviators, and few spoke French, which invariably caused a few problems. This language problem created a significant issue as few skilled American naval and marine aviators were available in Europe between April 1917 and mid-1918.

This token aeronautical force, sent in response to a request by the French government to bolster morale, was made up of men only partially trained at Pensacola. However, when training was completed, under the guidance of French instructors, those individuals went to pursuit, scout, and bombing squadrons – being absorbed into British, French, and Italian units. On June 22, 1917, the first enlisted men of the First Aeronautic Detachment began preliminary flight training in Caudron G-3 aircraft under French instructors at the École d'Aviation Militaire in Tours, France. Six days later, Thomas W. Barrett, a detachment member, died in an airplane crash during training; he was the first detachment member killed in France during World War One.

One of the men assigned to the detachment was Joe C. "Koko Nutz" Cline, Naval Aviator No. 1832, who enlisted as a quartermaster (aviation). He

Flying boats on patrol from NAS Le Croisic. Those are French planes operated by US naval personnel. (Courtesy of the US Naval History and Heritage Command, NH 112930)

summarized his service as a trainee: "We flew with the French, the British, and the Italians. Some of us even flew with the United States Marines, but most of us never fired an American machine gun or dropped an American bomb, or even saw an American-made plane until we got back home."

Flight training began, and none of the potential American pilots even had ground school instruction. Moreover, few of them had any idea about the theory of flight, nor did they speak French; few French instructors knew basic English. The French instructors divided the men into small groups of eight to ten students, with an instructor for each group. For each group, Cline said:

> One leather flying coat, one pair of goggles and one crash helmet were issued to each group and these were passed from one student to another as his turn came to fly. The plane used for our primary instruction was the Caudron G-3, a French biplane with warping wings and a two-place cockpit, powered by a 90-hp Anzani or LeRhone engine. The instructor sat in the rear cockpit. After takeoff, he would turn controls over to the student and instructions would begin. If the nose was too high, the instructor would push forward on

your helmet. If it was low, he would pull back on the helmet. If the left wing was down, he'd tap on the right shoulder; right wing down, tap on the left shoulder. A flight lasted about 20 minutes. After each flight, the instructor would pull out a pasteboard card with a line drawn down the center. One side was written in English and the other in French. The instructor would explain all the mistakes you had made while in flight. He gave you hell in French while pointing to the English translation. Perhaps it was just as well we did not understand his words.[1]

Cline believed two-thirds of the 50 students qualified as pilots, with less than five hours of dual instruction before transfer to seaplane training at École d'Aviation Maritime de Hourin on a small lake outside of Bordeaux. There, the Americans were rushed through seaplane training that consisted

Unknown American naval officers with an HS-1 plane in 1918. Identifiable are Ensign Robert S. Waters, Naval Aviator No. 931 (third from left) and Ensign Theodore 'Jack' Dillon, Naval Aviator No. 1625 (fourth from left). (Courtesy of the Robert S. Waters estate, US Naval History and Heritage Command, NH 81571)

of three hops with an instructor before soloing. Afterward, the group was sent to École d'Aviation de Saint-Raphaël, in the south of France, on the Mediterranean. Cline stated, "On 17 October 1917, I received my French Brevet, Number 346. My total flight time was 31 hours and 52 minutes."

The Navy later commissioned Cline as an officer, and those quartermasters and machine mates who did not complete flight training went to aerial gunnery school and trained as observers. Similarly, the British found American naval pilots unfamiliar and untrained to fly the H-16 flying boats, which most anti-submarine and scouting operations relied upon. As a result, through mid-summer 1918, most American pilots and mechanics depended on their allies for training. Potential American naval pilots who arrived were attached to Allied air services just as the German spring offensive began on March 21, 1918, known as the Ludendorff offensive or Kaiserschlacht (Kaiser's Battle). It became one of the deepest drives achieved by German forces since 1914; however, their army would suffer 230,000 casualties.

Those within the FNAF would participate in Allied offensives throughout the spring and fall of 1918, raiding staging areas, rail lines, and storage depots in southern and western Flanders. Naval pilots and observers trained and operated with the RNAS and the RAF's 7, 213, 214, 217, and 218 Squadrons, and the French air service's Escadrille de Saint-Pol. Those identified as serving with the RAF are Lieutenant Commander Edward Orrick McDonnell with No. 7 Squadron; Lieutenant Kenneth MacLeish and David S. Ingalls with 213 Squadron; those assigned to 214 Squadron were Ensigns Leslie Taylor, James Nisbet, Jesse Easterwood, Phillip Frothingham, William Gaston, and Alexander McCormick; McCormick was killed when he walked into a moving propeller. Ensigns Thomas Mickinnon, Sidney Clark, John McMurran, Peter Lawson, Marcus Whitehead, Yeoman Marolon O'Gorman, and Archibald McIlwane, with observers Randall Brown, Irving Shelly, and Sidney Huey, served with 217 Squadron. Lieutenant Charles Freddie Beach and Ensigns Joe Mosley, Charles "Chet" Bassett, and "Babe" Johnson served with No. 218.[2]

Pilots Beach, Moseley, William Cary Van Fleet, and Hugh Gordon Campbell were later assigned to l'Escadrille de Saint-Pol, where they flew SPADs.

Artimus L. "Di" Gates followed soon after. Gates, a former member of the First Yale Unit, was a confident and skilled pilot operating the SPAD. Unfortunately, he was shot down on October 4, 1918, and taken prisoner by the Germans.[3]

American FNAF airmen serving with Allied units found themselves flying a handful of missions or attached with British crews, since planes and materiel promised for establishing US Naval Aviation squadrons were not forthcoming. Nevertheless, those operating with Allied air services were welcomed as brothers-in-arms. Such was the CO of NAS Dunkirk, who flew a SPAD fighter with the French Escadrille de Saint-Pol before being shot down and taken prisoner.[4]

Those assigned to the British RNAS for anti-submarine duty, based at Felixstowe, found such operations quite deadly. Ensign Albert "Al" Sturtevant was another American naval aviator, an original First Yale Unit member, loaned out to the British. He conducted a few unremarkable convoy escort and anti-submarine flights during January and February 1918. By

Lieutenant Commander William M. Corry, Jr., US Naval Academy Class of 1910, Naval Aviator No. 23 (center in darker uniform), and officers at NAS Brest on September 30, 1918. He served as the CO of NAS Brest and died in a plane crash on October 7, 1920. (Courtesy of the US Naval History and Heritage Command, NH 52844)

February, German land and seaplanes had taken on more audacious and aggressive interceptions of Allied seaplanes in the North Sea off Belgium. Unfortunately, enemy aircraft were in the air that day with Sturtevant. The former Yale man and his crew, aboard a Curtiss H-12 Flying Boat on a Spider Web patrol in February 1918, became the focus of enemy aircraft. The North Sea during the late winter is rough, rainy, and cold, and the chances of surviving immersed in the water without immediate assistance are slim to none. Besides Sturtevant aboard, the crew consisted of an engineer, a British second pilot named "Purdy," S. J. Holeridge, and a wireless operator named A. H. Stevenson. The second flying boat in the patrol, operated by a British Commonwealth crew, followed the American-piloted plane. They had been flying ahead of the convoy, about halfway across the North Sea, with Purdy and Sturtevant in advance of the other aircraft – which was about 800 yards behind.

Although US patrol aviation failed to sink a single submarine, those who operated seaplanes and flying boats, such as Sturtevant, covered hundreds of miles, providing escort for Allied convoys sailing from and to European ports. In several instances, they did encounter German aircraft on similar scouting flights looking for Allied shipping convoys and, in doing so,

The First Aeronautic Detachment used the French Caudron plane for training pilots at Tours, France. Those men were the first American naval personnel to arrive in France. (Courtesy of the US Naval History and Heritage Command, UA 80.02.02)

engaged in aerial confrontations with American, British, and French patrol aircraft. Sturtevant became one of the first American naval aviators to be lost to enemy action when an estimated five German Hansa-Brandenburg W.29 mono-wing floatplanes saw the two H12B flying boats and targeted Sturtevant's seaplane, shooting it down in flames. An observer in one of the German aircraft, Lieutenant Fritz Stormer, described the ensuing fight: "We were victorious over the Curtiss flying boats that we encountered over the sea and subsequently engaged in aerial combat. We suffered no casualties and only a few hits during these battles. We were able to demolish one of the craft in a formation of Curtiss flying boats because we had the advantage of speed and maneuverability."[5]

The second aircraft landed safely at the home base, but one German seaplane followed it until it reached the English coast. Sturtevant's father

Naval aviation at an American naval training station. The original caption reads, "Every boy in this photograph is the son of an American Millionaire, but the censor restrains the use of their name." Most of the men are former members of the First Yale Unit. Those identified, in no particular order, are Kenneth Smith, Henry Landon, Samuel Walker, and Reginald Coombe. Most, if not all, served with Allied air services. (Courtesy of the US Naval History and Heritage Command, NH 120186)

received a telegram stating his son was missing in action and presumed dead. He wanted additional information, but it was not forthcoming until the end of the hostilities. An official report provided details of three men standing on the flying boat's wing section. A French destroyer was in the vicinity, but the ship did not see the stranded men, and evidence suggests the crew died from exposure.

Two days before Germany's spring offensive began, the first enemy plane shot down by an American naval aviator occurred on March 19, 1918, by Ensign Stephen Potter, Second Yale Unit, Naval Aviator No. 130. He and several other British and American aircraft conducted a long-distance reconnaissance mission of Heligoland Bight near a large German naval base. Nearing the German coast, a formation of enemy aircraft went in to intercept. Potter brought down one of them, and the rest scattered toward home. Six weeks later, on April 25, Potter lost his life during a similar aerial engagement. While on patrol near Hinder Light with another plane, Potter sighted two German aircraft and dove toward them, firing at close range. However, two more enemy planes appeared overhead and dove toward

Albert Dillon Sturtevant, Naval Aviator No. 77 (1894–1918), who served as an officer in the United States Navy during World War One, was a First Yale Unit graduate. He was killed in action and was awarded the Navy Cross posthumously. (Courtesy of the Library of Congress)

Potter, followed by four more planes. Potter did not have a chance as four of the enemy came in firing their machine guns – and by that time, the American's guns had jammed. Potter turned his plane, zigzagging, trying to escape. Yet, one of the Germans fired a broadside, sending the American plane down in flames. German pilots reported seeing him sitting in his burning plane; whether he was injured or dead is unknown. After the smoke and fire cleared, Potter and his aircraft disappeared.

Lieutenant Commander Edward O. McDonnell was the first American naval pilot to participate in land-based bombing raids over German-occupied Belgium and was previously an instructor for the First Yale Unit. He graduated from the Naval Academy in 1912 and served aboard *New Jersey, Montana, Florida,* and *Montgomery*. In March 1914, he reported to the ship *Prairie* and participated in the intervention at Veracruz, Mexico. On April 21 and 22, 1914, under continual fire and at an exposed post, McDonnell established a signal station to ensure effective communications between troops and ships. For his "extraordinary heroism," he was awarded the Medal of Honor. Following aeronautical instruction at the Wright Company at Dayton, Ohio, and flight training at the Naval Air Station, Pensacola, Florida, he was designated Naval Aviator No. 18 in March 1915, then remained at Pensacola as an aviation instructor. He later served at the Office of the Chief of Naval Operations in Washington, DC. At the end of 1917, he reported to Captain Cone and took part in air campaigns in France and Italy. He participated in three bombing raids against storage facilities and rail yards during the German offensive on March 22, 23, and 26, 1918 while attached to No. 7 Squadron, RAF.

Twenty-five-year-old Charles Fahy was another typical naval aviator assigned to No. 214 Squadron. He was born in Rome, Georgia, one of 11 children, and graduated from Georgetown Law School. He entered the Naval Reserve in 1917 and attended MIT ground school before reporting to Pensacola for advanced training, where he was commissioned as an ensign with the First Naval Reserve Force (FNRF) in January 1918. At Salisbury Plain, near Stonehenge, England, on April 30, 1918, he began training as a pilot for the 0/400-type Handley Page bomber. By early July, he arrived to join the 214 Squadron at Saint-Inglevert,

Naval Air Operations in Britain and France

A 1917 photographic portrait of Lieutenant (jg) Edward McDonnell in full military dress wearing the Medal of Honor he was awarded for his conduct during the Veracruz campaign in 1914. (Official US Navy photograph, now in the collections of the National Archives, 80-G-428100, courtesy of the U.S. Naval Heritage and History Command)

France, 18 miles from Calais. On the evening of July 8, he participated in his first mission serving as an observer, gunner, and bomb aimer in one of seven Handley Pages assigned to bomb German targets at Bruges, Belgium. Enemy searchlights and antiaircraft fire greeted them as they flew over Ostend. A shaft of light caught them at least ten times:

> I thought surely they would pick us up…[two] played on us for 15 seconds. Parachute flares lit wider swaths of sky, and "green onions" [a type of antiaircraft fire that exploded into numerous nets of green flame] came up frequently. At times I was on the lookout for scouts [German planes], my job…Ellison [the pilot] dodged in and out, changing course as lights flared up too close.[6]

Fahy unloaded the bombs – four 250lb, six 112lb, and four small 20lb Cooper bombs – and all seven bombers arrived safely back to base at 4am. He was detached from No. 214 Squadron on August 1 and ordered to join the night unit of the NBG. His new assignment was ferrying Caproni bombers from Italy to France: "I never thought they [Capronis] were equal to the Handley-Page."

Fahy didn't enjoy ferrying bombers over the Italian Alps as several pilots, Army and Navy, were killed during the process: "We undertook to ferry 17 or 18 Capronis from Milan to northern France, but only seven finished the journey."[7]

He participated in the first night bombing mission by the night group on August 15, flying Capronis without mishap. One of the men on the mission recounted: "We made some very good hits on a repair station on the docks: On 22 August, while returning from a mission, his plane's starboard engine quit, and Fahy attempted to land at an emergency airfield; however, German bombers were over the airfield.[8] Fahy signaled the airfield but got no replay. In total darkness towards an invisible beach Taber [the pilot] came down to land regardless, flattened out, and we crashed." Fahy was seriously injured and recalled he "jumped almost simultaneously with the impact and was catapulted some distance." He revived, "huddled up on the beach suffering the most terrible pains in the back." He also suffered a severe knee injury and remained hospitalized through the last week of October. He never flew again.[9]

One notable American naval aviator serving with No. 213 Squadron was Lieutenant David S. Ingalls. He was a 19-year-old graduate of the First Yale Unit who went overseas in September 1917 and was assigned to various training units in Britain. During two weeks in July 1918, he flew with 213 Squadron RAF (then based in England) on bombing missions to Stend, Zeebrugge, and Bruges, but he had no encounters with enemy planes. He was then ordered to France to oversee flying field construction for the NBG. Unhappy with this assignment, on August 9, he succeeded in rejoining 213 Squadron. Stationed with the RAF, he would destroy four enemy aircraft and a kite balloon in the air, becoming the US Navy's first "ace." On August 11, 1918, he scored his first aerial victory flying a British Sopwith Camel; he shot down an Albatros (possibly an Albatros D-VA fighter) during a running fight over German lines. His second occurred a little over a month later, on September 15.

Venturesome and eager for battle, Lieutenant Ingalls lost no time conducting low-level bombing and strafing attacks. On the night of August 13, he flew a low-level night attack on a German airdrome at Varsenare, Belgium, spraying 450 machine gun rounds into the facility and dropping four bombs while

A British Handley Page bomber. Some American naval pilots, gunners, machinists, and observers were sent to British units to operate the Handley Page night bomber. This aircraft has British markings. (Author's collection)

Lieutenant Commander William Corry, Jr., USN (bending over), CO of US NAS Brest, gives a pilot a demonstration before his flight departure. The photograph was taken on September 30, 1918. Note what appears to be a carrier pigeon basket held by the pilot and a Curtiss HS-type aircraft in the background. (US Naval History and Heritage Command, NH 52846)

destroying searchlights trying to find the attacker. Two days later, Ingalls repeated the same low-level strike against the German airdrome at Uytkerke. He conducted a low-level attack out of the clouds, unleashing 400 rounds upon German hangars. Then he swung the Camel up, releasing four bombs among Fokker fighters parked on the field. On his return to base, Ingalls shot down another two-seat Rumpler C.IV, a two-seat reconnaissance biplane, on September 15 with Flight Lieutenant H. C. Smith, RAF. With his English companion, the young American pilot followed the enemy aircraft, flying 6,000ft west of Ostend, flaming the Rumpler, which crashed to the ground. [10]

Getting back to his base was usually a hazardous endeavor. Lieutenant Ingalls described to his parents in a letter regarding his aerial encounters with the enemy. He wrote:

> I turned and dove down to the ground… for when way over the lines and not high enough to be save from "Archie" the stunt is to race along just over the ground about 200 to 300 feet… The only danger in this low flying is from machine guns. The Huns had these scattered all over their country to get aeroplanes in similar predicaments. I knew fairly well where they

US Ace Lieutenant David Ingalls, USNRF, Naval Aviator No. 85, photographed circa 1918. He shot down four German planes and a kite balloon, making him the only American naval ace of World War One. (Courtesy of the US Naval History and Heritage Command, NH 81838)

were thickest and went along for at least five minutes without a shot. Then suddenly, I heard a rat-tat, my motor faltered, gas poured out of the tank below my seat, and clouds of white vapor rose from it… Evidently I had run into a bad place, for I was shot at till I crossed the lines.

Usually, one turns, zooms, etc., when in this predicament but I expected the controls to go any second and even with what I had I could not do any trick flying, so I sat still and by using the rudder kept going as fast as possible in little turns toward home. It was a big relief to get out of range across the lines. Then I had to land… I came in slowly over the trees on the side and, using the motor, managed to land.

The machine was well shot up. One burst of several bullets had perforated the tank under my seat, and all but one strand of wires that cause one to go up were severed, as well as a number of strands in those to go down. One aileron had been hit at the hinge and, of course, there were a few holes in the wings. I got a new machine the next day.[11]

Three days later, on September 18, a kite balloon was sighted at 3,500ft near La Barrière, while Ingalls was in the company of two British-flown Sopwith Camels. The three aircraft attacked the unarmed balloon. The German kite reeled under the plane's rapid fire as it fell, two observers jumped, opening their white parachutes. Describing this attack, Lieutenant Ingalls wrote, "Looking back, I saw a blaze flare up in the bag, and then it crumpled in a great mass of flames and dropped directly on three balloon sheds which promptly caught fire. It was a lovely sight."[12]

Ingalls scored a probable while being part of a pursuit force of Camels escorting a bombing force of British DH-9s heading for Bruges, Belgium, West Flanders on September 20. The formation spotted four enemy planes heading toward the bombers flying at 15,000ft. The Camels immediately attacked one of them, firing 100 rounds of machine-gun fire. The enemy plane, a Fokker, dove vertically, trailing a white smoke stream; it was last seen out of control and descending toward Bruges.

Four days later, on September 20, Ingalls and three British-flown fighters engaged a formation of 12 Fokkers while flying over the front lines at 16,000ft. The famous Canadian "ace" Captain Arthur Roy Brown, credited with shooting down Manfred von Richthofen, piloted one of the three British-flown aircraft. The four aircraft went on the offensive and immediately broke up the enemy formation. Captain Brown swung into and shot down one German plane, sending it crashing into the earth three miles below. Another Fokker was on the tail of one British plane, piercing the latter's gas tank when Ingalls came to the rescue and quickly shot down the German plane. Ingalls followed a third enemy plane flying down to the deck, just feet off the ground, where the American shot it to pieces. The remaining Germans decided that a three-to-one advantage was not enough to stop the Allied planes and abandoned the fight. Ingalls then attacked another Fokker at a range of 25 yards. His machine-gun fire sent the enemy plane on its back, spinning as it dove toward the ground.

On a test flight on September 24, he sighted a Rumpler, a German reconnaissance aircraft, over Nieuport, France, located on the coast of southern Flanders. Ingalls and a British officer he was flying with attacked at 100 yards, firing 200 rounds. They followed the enemy plane as it fell in flames – this was Ingalls' last encounter serving with 213 Squadron after accumulating four enemy aircraft and one kite balloon destroyed.[13]

The British Air Ministry wrote of his exploits in a citation for the Distinguished Flying Cross:

"His keenness, courage, and utter disregard of danger are exceptional and are an example to all."[14]

The United States Navy wrote in a citation for the Distinguished Service Medal, "For exceptionally meritorious service in the duty of great responsibility as a chase pilot operating with R.A. F. Squadron 213, while officially attached to the Northern Bombing Group, Northern France, where, as a result of his brilliant and courageous work he was made an Acting Flight Commander by the British authorities over their own pilots."[15]

His last flight occurred on October 4, 1918, and he returned to the rear the following day. Ingalls graduated from Yale University and became the Assistant Secretary of the Navy (Air) during President Herbert Hoover's administration. He returned to active duty in World War Two, serving as a commander, then a captain, and received the Legion of Merit and the Bronze Star. He retired as a rear admiral in the United States Naval Reserve.

Lieutenant Kenneth MacLeish was a friend of Ingalls and a fellow First Yale Unit graduate, who enlisted in the Naval Reserve as a Navy Electrician Second Class. His brother, Archibald MacLeish, was a Pulitzer Prize-winning poet. Upon completing flight training, MacLeish was promoted to ensign in the NRFC on August 31, 1917. His letters to his fiancée and family commented on the brutal realities of war. One letter written to his family on April 7, 1918, discussed the harshness of flying at altitude without an electric flying suit or oxygen mask. "Today was worse torture than any I have ever read about." He wore three sets of flying gloves. "Yet, I froze two fingers absolutely solid, and my thumb and one finger were frostbitten." Flying at altitude with no oxygen mask, he complained of nausea, a headache, and ringing in his ears. The patrol he was on saw five enemy aircraft, but he saw none. Prophetically he wrote to his fiancée, "Cheer up. One of these days I may see too many." While serving

Ensign Kenneth MacLeish (1894–1918), USNRF, Naval Aviator No. 74, was a graduate of the First Yale Unit. Ensign MacLeish died after engaging German aircraft on October 15, 1918. (Courtesy of the US Naval History and Heritage Command, NH 48042)

with 213 Squadron, replacing Ingalls, enemy fighters shot him down on October 6, 1918. In December, a farmer discovered his body lying outside of a barn. Investigators saw no apparent wounds on the body, and how he died remains a mystery. He was posthumously awarded the Navy Cross for his actions. His citation reads, "The Navy Cross is awarded to Lieutenant Kenneth MacLeish, US Navy, for distinguished and heroic service as a pilot attached to the U. S. Naval Aviation Force in the war zone."[16]

The precious few flying with British and French squadrons sought and found the excitement of engaging with the enemy during dogfights and bombing German-held territory. The duty of flying patrols above the North Sea, the English Channel, and the Bay of Biscay became monotonous for many. They wanted excitement, a chance to meet the enemy. Rumors began circulating in June 1918 that pilots would be needed for an American-run bombing group with land-based aircraft to bomb the submarine pens located along the Belgian coast. There was a push to attach themselves to this new unit. MacLeish had been one of them.

Additional naval aviators served with distinction while attached to Allied air services and were awarded the Navy Cross.

Walter L. Seiler, Quartermaster First Class, US Navy, served with a French aviation unit and was awarded the Navy Cross. His citation reads: "The Navy Cross is awarded to Quartermaster First Class Walter L. Seiler, US Navy, for extraordinary heroism and devotion to duty while serving in the French Unit of the US Naval Aviation Service. Quartermaster Seiler engaged with an enemy submarine on 13 August 1918, off Dunkirk, and displayed courage and daring in answering enemy shell fire with a machine gun." (Courtesy of the US Naval History and Heritage Command, NH 118845)

Right: Ensign Clyde Palmer, USNRF, Naval Aviator No. 396. A 1918 portrait photograph taken before his death at Saint-Inglevert, France, on September 14, 1918. He was awarded the Navy Cross for service with Allied forces. (Courtesy of the US Naval History and Heritage Command, NH 47588)

Above left: Ensign Mosely Taylor, USNRF, Naval Aviator No. 118. He was awarded the Navy Cross while serving with 214 Squadron RAF. (Courtesy of the US Naval History and Heritage Command, NH 43963)

Above right: Ensign George Moseley, USNRF, Naval Aviator No. 566. He received his French brevet on October 17, 1917, and was assigned to French Squadron 150 before receiving a commission as an ensign with the NRFC. He earned his naval certification on February 4, 1918, and was assigned to 218 Squadron RAF in July 1918. He was then transferred to the French Escadrille de Saint-Pol in September. Moseley was awarded the Navy Cross for service while serving with the French between September and November 1918. (Courtesy of the Naval History and Heritage Command, NH 47625)

Chapter 12

Naval Air Operations in Italy

Italy declared war on Austria-Hungary on May 23, 1915, on the Allies' side (Britain, France, and Russia). However, it had held membership in the Triple Alliance with Germany and Austria-Hungary since 1882. The possibility of its soldiers participating in trench meat grinders was unpalatable. Nevertheless, the Italians were more than willing to take the carrots dangling from the stick of the Treaty of London in April 1915. The Allies promised Italy control over a large border region stretching from South Tyrol to Trieste, parts of Dalmatia along Austria-Hungary's coast, and unknown territory from the Ottoman Empire, once the latter was defeated. Unfortunately, sound reasoning behind the threat evaporated not long after Italy declared war on May 23 against Austria-Hungary by opening a 600km front, most of which lay in steep mountainous terrain along the northern border between the warring nations. The landscape offered commanding defensive opportunities but was ill suited to conducting offensive operations, and a three-year stalemate ensued. This front became a meat grinder of its own; for over three years, the Austrians and Italians fought 11 significant battles along the Isonzo River, with barely a meter taken by either side at the cost of thousands of dead, missing, or captured. American pilots, primarily naval, were needed to supplement Italian air units for reconnaissance and bombing missions, especially against the Austrian naval stronghold of Pola, located at the very tip of the Austrian-Hungarian border at the northern Adriatic Sea.

The decision to deploy American aviation personnel was agreed in November 1917, with the Italians offering to train 50 aviators at the Regia

American and Italian dignitaries at the US NAS Porto Corsini, Italy, on April 29, 1918, watching Italian and American flown aircraft apparently in a dogfight with enemy planes. (Courtesy of the US Naval History and Heritage Command, NH 2804)

Marina Scuola di Aviazione on Lake Bolsena. The original Italian request for aid from Washington resulted in an agreement drawn up in Rome by Lieutenant John L. "Lanny" Callan, USNRF, Naval Aviator No. 1442. Callan, with members of the Italian Navy, quickly began work.[1]

On December 17, 1917, detached from Rome, Callan, together with members of the Ispettorato d'Aviazione della Regia Marina (aviation inspector of naval aviation) and Tenete di Vascelle Mario Calderara (who was a pioneer of Italian aviation and the commander of Bolsena) began preparations. American use of the base at Porto Corsini and Pescara was authorized. Callan and Ludovico De Filippi, the commander of Italian naval aviation, agreed the United States would take control of the Italian naval air stations at Bolsena, Porto Corsini, and Pescara. Bolsena was a training station situated on a lake, about 60 miles northeast of Rome. The first group of 32 student aviators arrived at Bolsena on February 19, 1918,

Inspection of NAS Lake Bolsena, Italy, in World War One, 1917. Front row (left to right): Captain Charles Russell Train, USN; Lieutenant William B. Atwater, USNRF (Naval Aviator); Admiral Henry Thomas Mayo, USN; Capitano Di Corvette Mario Calderara, RIN; Senior Italian at Naval Training Base, Bolsena, Lieutenant Commander John L. Callan, USNR; Capitano De Conchita L. Di Villa-Rosa. Second row (left to right): Captain Ernest King, USN; Captain O. P. Jackson, USN; Lieutenant Mark Walton (Naval Aviator); Commander A. B. Cook, USN; and an unknown Italian officer. (Courtesy of the US Naval History and Heritage Command, NH 120095)

A seaplane landing at Bolsena, Italy, located northeast of Rome. The site was for training US naval aviators and observers in 1918. Those trained here went on to Porto Corsini for combat operations. (Courtesy of the US Naval History and Heritage Command, NH 113868)

followed by 18 more on March 25. Lieutenant Calderara of the Italian Navy transferred the command to Ensign William "Bull" Atwater, USNRF, Naval Aviator No. 112. After 12 hours of training, American naval aviators flew their first solo. The best students were assigned to fly the Macchi M-5 seaplane fighter.

The first American naval pilot to fly was Quartermaster E. M. Smith, who flew with Italian instructor 2° Capo Vakdimiro on March 7, 1917. The first US naval aviator to solo was possibly John B. Stanley, Naval Aviator No. 1495. The first fatality among the naval aviators occurred on March 20, 1918, when Machinist Mate First Class Clarence A. Nelson took off on his first solo in FBA No. 7637. He and his plane disappeared in a cloud, flying vertically into the water a few moments later. Local townspeople and authorities from the base found neither wreckage from the plane nor Nelson's body. In his memory, the town of Bolsena named the road leading from the village to the hangars Via Nelson. The total number of officers and men who underwent instruction at the Bolsena training station was

An unknown American aviator stands by an Italian Nieuport-Macchi M.5 flying boat fighter. US naval personnel flew Italian aircraft as American planes were unavailable. (Courtesy of the National Archives via the Alan C. Carey Collection)

134. After completing advanced schooling, pilots and observers were sent to air stations in France or Italy. By mid-July, 11 naval pilots had qualified out of the 49 taking instruction. Another 26 arrived on August 24, but they did not have the time to be eligible before the Armistice. At that time, the NAS Bolsena had 79 flying boats on hand.

The Porto Corsini station was located on the Adriatic Sea, about seven-and-a-half miles from the town of Ravenna, while the Pescara station was located near the village of Pescara. These two stations aimed to bomb the Austro-Hungarian naval base at Pola on the Istria Peninsula, only 55 miles south of Trieste, Italy. The headquarters of the Austrian Navy at Pola commanded the northern Adriatic, causing considerable worry among the Italians.

Regia Marina's 263° Squadriglia already occupied the base, operating FBA-type seaplanes and M.5 seaplane fighters. Within weeks, the Porto Corsini station became known as Goat Island City. In response, the nose art of a winged goat adorned American-operated planes. The American naval

During operations from the Italian base of Porto Corsini from July 1918 until the Armistice, the US Navy operated at least eight single-seat Italian Macchi M.5 fighter flying boats. Here is a side view of the aircraft. One such plane was sent to the US for evaluation in 1917. (Courtesy of Rex Beisel's Collection via Jim Sullivan and Thomas Doll)

Frontal three-quarter view of a Macchi M.5 at Porto Corsini, Italy, in November 1918. (Courtesy of Rex Beisel's Collection via Jim Sullivan via Thomas Doll)

personnel, as with the FNAF in Britain and France, lacked experience, and the Italians found themselves training many of the Americans from scratch.

The war with Austria became a backwater conflict with very little coverage in the United States. France and the Western Front garnered the attention of newspaper readers. American and British soldiers were not engaged in it, and few Americans, if any, possibly cared since their sons and fathers were fighting and dying along the French and Belgian fronts. Bylines within periodicals briefly discussed the Italian–Austrian front in southern Europe, but it might as well have been in another world. Like France, the two warring nations were caught at a standstill but did not get coverage. The arrival of American naval personnel in Italy increased the number of brief news articles. However, an aerial battle between Austrians and a combined force of Italian and American seaplanes caught the attention of the average American reader. Afterward, they knew American naval aviators served with distinction while patrolling the Adriatic and Mediterranean Seas.

An Italian seaplane with Italian markings on Lake Bolsena, Italy. This was one of the types operated by American naval aviators for training. Lake Bolsena, located north of Rome, was the primary training base for the Americans. (Courtesy of the Naval History and Heritage Command, NH 121959)

Those naval aviators stationed in Italy, just like their counterparts in Britain and France, initially relied on the host country to provide flight instructors until American pilots were assigned to become instructors themselves after proficiently handling Italian planes. In the beginning, FBA flying boats were used exclusively for instruction purposes, but later, some Macchi L-3 and M-5 flying boats arrived.

On July 23, 1918, the first American aviation personnel arrived at Porto Corsini, consisting of a detachment of 377 officers and men from Pauillac, France, under Lieutenant Haviland, USNF, Naval Aviator No. 577. The following day Haviland took over the Porto Corsini station from the Italians and placed it in commission as a United States naval air station. A native of Minnesota, he was born on March 10, 1890. His history includes attending Iowa State College for two years. He left his studies at some point before joining the military; maybe it was due to economic reasons or boredom.

Hence, his interesting military career began with serving in the Navy from 1907 to 1911 as an enlisted rate. He then served in the Illinois National Guard from 1912 to 1917. Afterward, he enlisted in the French Flying Corps, serving as a pilot. His experience with the French served him well as he enrolled in the NRFC as a lieutenant in Paris. His duties before arriving in Italy consisted of assignments at Moutchic and Dunkerque (Dunkirk). He found himself commanding the American Porto Corsini Naval Air Station at 28 years old.

Naval aviators assigned to Italy flew routine patrols above the northern Adriatic Sea. They carried out propaganda flights by dropping leaflets onto the Austrians stating their cause was lost, flew reconnaissance flights, and combined with the Americans in bombing operations against the Austrian naval base at Pola. The Americans flew operations under the direction of the Italian naval aviation district's commander in Venice. The first air raid

A second image of officers at Porto Corsini, taken on August 1, 1918. Back row (left to right): R. H. Clark, E. L. Smith, C. W. Gates, W. White, A. P. Taliaferro, K. Stewart. Front row (left to right): L. W. Knowles, E. I. Tinkham, C. H. Hammann, J. A. Goggins, J. Stanley. (Courtesy of the US Naval History and Heritage Command, NH 113899)

upon Pola on August 21 consisted of one M-8 and four M-5s whose mission was to drop propaganda matter. Besides antiaircraft fire, the Austrians sent up five pursuit planes at Pola, and the Americans immediately attacked them. Ensign Ludlow shot one enemy plane down, and the others returned to their base. No American pilot suffered any injuries as a result of the engagement. Telegrams were sent from the Italian district commander and United States aviation forces commander in Italy, commending the pilots for their brilliant work. On the following night, the enemy carried out an air raid in reprisal. On August 21, 24, and 29, naval air forces carried out return air raids upon Pola, dropping bombs on the arsenal.[2]

During one propaganda flight in the late morning of August 21, 1918, five M.5 fighter seaplanes were escorted by two Macchi M.8 bombers (Italian reconnaissance/bomber flying boats). The planes swept over Pola at 12,000ft, and the flight came under sporadic, ineffective antiaircraft fire. While the last propaganda leaflets left the group, Ensign George H. Ludlow,

A seaplane trainer on Lake Bolsena, Italy. (Courtesy of the US Naval History and Heritage Command, NH 121960)

The ex-Austro-Hungarian naval base, Pola, on August 11, 1920. The island seaplane base was often the target of bombing and propaganda flights. (Commander H. L. Pence, USN; courtesy of the US Naval History and Heritage Command, NH 121368)

the lead pilot, saw five Austro-Hungarian Albatroses in pursuit and two seaplanes below the aircraft. He gave the signal to attack; Ludlow dove toward the Austrians, followed by Ensigns Austin Parker and Charles H. Hammann. The aerial fight began at 7,500ft while still under intense antiaircraft fire. Ludlow singled out the center Austrian pursuit plane, giving it bursts from machine guns while handling his controls with his knees. He swung to the right to engage a second enemy plane, enabling Parker to attack the first. Hammann, in the meantime, engaged two other Austrian aircraft.

The Austrians were tenacious in their fighting ability to protect their base. Parker's guns jammed at this juncture, forcing him out of the fight. Ludlow brought down his target, sending it into the harbor in flames. However, his plane was badly shot up. The right magneto was shot away, the propeller shattered, and the engine crankcase punctured, spewing out oil that quickly burst into flames. Ludlow immediately slipped into a tailspin, and the rush of air extinguished the fire. One Austrian aircraft followed Ludlow to 1,500ft above the fire and fired a burst, which wrecked his engine; two bullets passed through his helmet, one grazing his scalp.

Ensign Charles Hazeltine Hammann, Naval Aviator No. 1494, USNRF. He was awarded the Medal of Honor for heroism in rescuing Ensign George M. Ludlow during aerial operations off Pola, in the Adriatic Sea, on August 21, 1918. (Courtesy of the US Naval History and Heritage Command, NH 79440)

Ludlow sent his plane into another spin before leveling out, conducting a smooth water landing three miles from Pola.

Hammann drove off the remaining Austrian aircraft through his expert flying ability, firing first on their tails, then on their flanks, and, finally, with head-on attacks that forced the remaining enemy planes to abandon the attack. Those attacks enabled pilots Parker and Voorhees to escape and return to Porto Casini. During a lull in the battle, Hammann landed his seaplane beside Ludlow's crippled plane, which was still buoyant. The pilots saw Austrian destroyers heading toward them while another flight of enemy aircraft took off. Ludlow opened the photographic port, enabling the plane to flood, and then kicked holes in the wings before slipping overboard to swim toward Hammann's aircraft, climbing up on the fuselage of the single-seat seaplane, sitting under the motor, and hanging on to the struts. The extra load forced the hull into the choppy sea, where the bow, already damaged by gunfire, was broken in, and one of the wing pontoons was smashed.

The damaged plane finally managed to rise from the water and into the air. Before heading home, Hammann fired a burst of machine-gun fire into

Ludlow's plane, finally sinking it as an Austrian destroyer and seaplanes headed toward them. Hammann flew the 60-mile trip back to Porto Casini without mishap until the plane landed on the water when the smashed-in bow took in enough water to nose the plane over and caught a wing tip in the heavy swell; the aircraft turned over on its back. Both pilots extricated themselves from the wreckage, and a motorboat from the air station rescued them. Both men sustained injuries, with Ludlow having a nasty gash on his forehead and a scalp wound received from enemy fire, while Hammann suffered significant bruising.

The Italian government awarded the Silver Medal of Valor to Ensign Hammann and a similar bronze medal to Ensign Ludlow. Ludlow also received the Navy Cross. In addition, the President of the United States presented Hammann with the Medal of Honor, the first awarded to a US naval aviator. The US Navy cited him for heroism in landing on the water alongside Ludlow's disabled airplane. It is one of life's bitter ironies that less than a year later, on June 24, 1919, Ensign Hammann met his death in a Macchi plane of the same type he had used in the aerial battle over Pola.[3]

Ensign Hammann's air rescue of downed aviator Ensign George H. Ludlow. On August 21, 1918. (Artwork by H. Townsend; courtesy of the US Naval History and Heritage Command, 9538-B)

A halftone reproduction showing two images of Hammann sitting in a Macchi M.5 flying boat. He was killed in a flying boat crash at Langley Field, Virginia, on June 14, 1919. (Courtesy of the US Naval History and Heritage Command, NH 49249)

The following report by the chief-of-staff of the Italian Navy on August 25, 1918, wrote about the contribution of American naval personnel:

American aviation recently began its support for our operations in the Adriatic. An American squadron energetically attacked and forced to return to Pola, Austrian airplanes near the Istrian coast. During the pursuit one American machine was obliged to land but a very intrepid aviator took the pilot on board and destroyed the machine. Military works at Pola and especially aviation installation and submersible bases were bombarded by day on the 21st, during the night of the 22nd, and at dawn on the 23rd, by several Italian machines and some Americans. Four tons of explosives were dropped and numerous explosion and fires were seen.[4]

Similar attacks against Pola were conducted by the following:

Macchi-8: Lieutenant (jg) Russell "Bart" Read (pilot), Lieutenant W. B. Haviland (observer)
Macchi-8: Ensign Walter White (pilot), Machinist Mate First Class (MM1c), A. L. Pierce (observer)
Macchi-8: Ensign Albert P. Taliaferro (pilot), Machinist Mate First Class (MM1c), H. H. Pierce (observer)
Franco British (FBA): Ensign Edward Tinkham (pilot) and Machinist Mate Second Class (MM2c), J. H. Charroin (observer)
Franco British (FBA): Chief Quartermaster E. W. Smith (pilot) and Ensign H. Gartner (observer).
Macchi-5: Ensign E. L. Johansen
Macchi-5: Ensign James M. Grier
Macchi-5: Charles H. Hammann
Macchi-5 Ensign George H. Ludlow
Macchi-5: Ensign Wayne Duffett
Macchi-5: Ensign Austin Parker
Macchi-5: Lieutenant Derisses (Italian Naval Aviation Forces)
Macchi-5: Sergeant Guarneiri (Italian Naval Aviation Forces)[5]

Reconnaissance missions over Pola continued through October 1918. On October 7, six Macchi M.5s were subjected to antiaircraft fire and attacks from enemy planes, but the patrol returned safely to Porto Corsini. American and Italian planes conducted a bombing mission over Pola comprising eight M.5s, three Macchi M.8s, and two FBAs, along with an Italian squadron from Venice. The flight met minimal antiaircraft fire while dropping 14 bombs along Austrian airdromes. On October 22, three M.8s, two FBAs, and eight M.5s left in the afternoon for a bombing offensive against Pola in conjunction with the Italian Venice squadron. It is noteworthy that 13 out of the 43 planes taking part in this operation were from Porto Corsini, although there were only 16 planes at the Porto Corsini station at the time. The barrage put up by the Austrians was very poor, causing little inconvenience, and 14 bombs were dropped by American and Italian planes.

On November 4, 1918, Austria-Hungary and Italy signed the Armistice of Villa Giusti, ending the war between the two warring powers. The insufficient number of pilots, the small number of planes compared to what the Italians had promised, and a lack of spare parts hindered operations. The Italians had promised sufficient aircraft by December 1918, but the Armistice negated that promise. However small in number, the Americans and their Italian compatriots flew 745 operational flights. Besides Nelson, American casualties of those stationed in Italy numbered four killed in non-combat accidents: James L. Goggins, Quartermaster, killed on August 11, 1918 when he fell out of an M-5; Ensign Louis J. Bergen, Naval Aviator No. 351 and Thomas L. Murphy, both killed on September 15 when they fell from an M-8; and George B. Killeen who died from burns on September 18.[6]

In addition to missions flown against the Austrian naval base, American naval personnel ferried Italian Caproni bombers from Italy to France to participate in night-bombing missions against German submarine bases located along the Belgian coast. This operation did not go as well, and blame was placed on the bombers' inability to function well and the lack of sufficient numbers to conduct strategic bombing operations. Edward "Eddie" McDonnell inspected the aircraft, and American army and naval personnel ferried the planes back to France. He made the best out of a difficult situation. Initially, he observed the Caproni as a quality aircraft having a maximum range of approximately

Above left: Ensign Edward I. Tinkham, Naval Aviator No. 1498, USNRF, at Porto Corsini in September 1918. He received the Navy Cross posthumously. He died of pneumonia on March 30, 1919, in Ravenna, Italy. (Courtesy of the US Naval History and Heritage Command, NH 43704)

Above right: Ensign Walter White, USNRF, Naval Aviator No. 1496, was awarded the Navy Cross and Italian War Cross for distinguished service in World War One as a seaplane pilot. (Courtesy of the US Naval History and Heritage Command, NH 119463)

10,000ft, maneuverable, and able to carry 1,000lb of bombs. According to McDonnell: "I had a number of interviews with Signor Caproni and made several flights in Caproni planes. During one of these flights with an Italian officer we looped the loop in a three-motor Caproni which seemed to me quite a demonstration for a larger plane of this type."[7] McDonnell interviewed Italian officers who participated in bombing missions along the Austro-Italian front and found no issues with the aircraft. He evaluated the 450 (Ca-3) and discussed with Signor Caproni the latest bomber – the 600-series with 600hp engines (the 600-type/Ca-5) – which could carry 1,800–2,000lb of bombs, and he was impressed. McDonnell returned to France and was assigned to RNAS No. 7 Handley Page Squadron to inspect the aircraft's characteristics, flying a few combat missions aboard the bombers. He believed the Caproni had several advantages over the British-built aircraft: "Greater ceiling with full load, about 15,000 as compared with 10,000. Greater speed, about 100 to 105 miles-per-hour compared with 75 or 80. Greater safety factor in case of motor failure, the Caproni with a light load being able to fly with two motors of the three whereas the Handley-Page could not maintain altitude with single motor when one motor failed."[8]

However, compared to the Caproni, McDonnell found the Handley Page was more ruggedly built and had better defensive gun positions. He returned his observations to the Navy Department and Admiral Sims to procure materiel and personnel for the NBG. The group needed heavy bombers, and Handley Pages were unavailable; thus, it fell to obtaining Italian Capronis. McDonnell and those who operated them found an aircraft known for having a weak frame and malfunctioning Fiat engines: "Subsequent experience proved the Fiat Capronis were a failure due to the entirely poor design and workmanship of the Fiat motors…Crank-shafts were not properly machined, gaskets were left out of the crank-shaft

American naval aviators and personnel ferried Italian Caproni bombers from Italy. This image shows one such aircraft departing from Milan. (Courtesy of the US Naval History and Heritage Command, NH 112974)

housing. A very poor carburetor…was adopted and this was largely responsible for the great fire risk in these planes."[9]

He and others respectfully found the Italians (Gianni Caproni, and Italian officers) had stretched the truth about the quality of the aircraft. Caproni admitted it. Admiral Sims, understanding the inferiority of the plane, still ordered them anyway, since the NBG needed bombers for night missions. Army pilots flew the first five orders back to Saint-Inglevert, France.

Bob Lovett, a strong supporter of the project, did not want it to "fizzle" and needed the support of the naval brass and those within the NBG, or his reputation would be tarnished. But, according to McDonnell, "They refrained from cabling complaints to Washington which might have injured the prestige of Lieutenant Lovett, Chief Politician…"[10]

Naval officials quickly hid information on the aircraft's faults, despite rumors the Caproni had significant issues. However, increasing production of the Handley Page still could not meet American demand, as the British needed a higher number of them and their requirement took precedence over that of the US. Gianni Caproni and the Italian government claimed they could meet the need for the -450 and -600 models. The Caproni, with its shortcomings, was the heavy bomber that could enable the NBG to engage in the strategic bombing of German submarines located along the Belgian coast against supply dumps and marshaling yards. Lieutenant Commander John Callan supported the purchasing of Caproni bombers in a memorandum sent to Captain Hutchinson Cone, dated August 19, 1918:

> […] arrangements have been made with the Italian Government for the purchase of 600-H. P. Caproni bombing planes. Fifteen Naval Aviators were sent to the Italian School at Malpensa, and obtained their brevets on Capronis. Of these pilots, seven were lent to the Italian Navy to ferry their machines from Milan to Gioja del Colle, near Brindisi, but they are now all being used to ferry the American Navy Capronis from Milan to Paris.[11]

McDonnell stated, "Of the seventeen planes, eight were delivered safely, and five pilots were killed in this enterprise." In one plane flown by him and Harry Davison, they had to change an engine, a radiator, one carburetor, and eight magnetos and had four engine failures in the air.[12] The Italians fared worse than the Americans, according to Lieutenant (jg) Sam Walker, a former member of the Second Yale Unit, who went to Italy for instruction on the Caproni. He conveyed serious problems while training with the Italians: "…we couldn't agree with the Italians as to their methods of instruction and their lack of eagerness they showed for flying. Perhaps this was because so many of them were killed in practice. In thirty days, they mad a record of wiping out forty men!"[13]

Five members of the USNRF and the NBG were killed while attempting to ferry the bombers from Italy to France, mainly due to engine failures. Ensign Sam S. Walker, Naval Aviator No. 86 and a former member of the Second Yale Unit, was killed early in August 1918 when his bomber crashed in the Italian Alps. On August 17, Ensign Alan La Motte Nichols, Naval Aviator No. 268, and an individual named Turner, possibly a mechanic, were killed on take-off; their plane smashed to bits upon hitting the ground. Ensigns Clyde N. Palmer, Naval Aviator No. 395, and Philp B. Frothingham, Naval Aviator No. 250, were killed upon landing at Saint-Inglevert, France, on September 15, 1918.

Lieutenant Reginald Coombe, an eyewitness, recalled watching Palmer and Frothingham's aircraft taxiing in at St. Inglevert when the wheels hit a soft piece of ground and got stuck. The pilots attempted to free the plane, but it would not budge; the tail came up, and the nose dropped to the ground, causing the fuselage to break just forward of the pilot's seat. The dashboard came down, pinning the pilots. Both propellers, hitting the ground, broke off, and a motor started racing. The mechanic seated in the rear machine-gun cage was thrown clear and attempted to cut the engines but succeeded in stopping only one. In a few seconds, the whole machine was a mass of flames: "It was impossible to get anywhere near the two men, Frothingham and Palmer, and fire extinguishers were of no use whatever. It was an awful sight to be there and see these two men burn up, but there was absolutely nothing that could be done."[14]

Chapter 13

The First Marine Aviation Force

The war forced the United States military to enter a period of accelerated growth in personnel and arms. Marine Aviation developed its units and bases while the Navy Department adopted anti-submarine warfare as naval aviation's principal mission. Marine Corps personnel strength at the time of the declaration of war was 419 regular officers, 49 warrant officers, and 13,725 enlisted personnel. Of those numbers, the aviation branch consisted of around 4 commissioned officers and 30 enlisted. Commandant of the Marine Corps, Major General Commandant George Barnett's primary goal was to send a brigade to France to fight alongside the Army Expeditionary Force (AEF) as quickly as possible. As a result, the Marines under his leadership would see accelerated growth in personnel to 2,400 officers and 70,000 men and the creation of an independent air arm, consisting of 250 commissioned officers and 2,180 enlisted. Alfred Cunningham planned to support those Marine ground forces: "From this time, we began to work energetically for expansion. Our ambition was to organize a first-class aviation force to operate with the Marine forces we hoped would be sent to the front."[1]

The Marine Corps aviation section comprised five officers and 30 enlisted men based at Pensacola. The plan called for organizing an entire squadron of land planes, with intensive training, and for Marine Corps ground forces to be ready for France. Yet, Cunningham found no support from the War Department, the Army, or the Navy. He lamented:

> This officer made every possible effort, both with the War Department in Washington and the American Expeditionary Forces authorities in France,

to secure authority for our Marine aviation squadron to serve with the Marine Brigade in France. No success whatever attended these events. Army aviation authorities stated candidly that if the squadron ever got to France, it would be used to furnish personnel to run one of their training fields, but that this was as near the front as it would ever get.[2]

Cunningham was frustrated but relentless, even though it appeared discouraging. Confronted with this depressing outlook, the squadron commander set out to find another way to get his squadron into the fight. He had to, or Marine Aviation would have no role in Europe.[3]

Cunningham began an aggressive effort for his fledgling organization to participate in combat operations. In January 1918, he appeared before the General Board of the Navy and requested that Marine aircraft conduct special missions in Europe. The only naval air operations at the time were anti-submarine operations performed by flying boats and seaplanes.

Major Alfred Cunningham led the Day Wing of the NBG in France in 1918. (Courtesy of the Alfred A. Cunningham Collection [COLL/3034] at the Archives Branch, Marine Corps History Division)

In that, he saw an opportunity for Marine Aviation to participate in such air operations. According to Cunningham:

> Submarines were causing enormous shipping losses: The main operating bases and repair shops were at Ostend, Zeebrugge, and Bruges (along the southern Belgian Coast), all within easy reach by planes from Dunkirk. If these waters could be patrolled continuously during daylight with planes carrying heavy bombs, submarines attempting to enter these bases could be destroyed. Destroyers were prevented from patrolling…efficiently in daylight by the heavy shore batteries.[4]

Those waters were also protected by mines, preventing destroyers from patrolling the areas. The Germans were aware of British seaplanes conducting anti-submarine operations and sent out land-based fighters to shoot down the Allied seaplanes. Cunningham asked why the British did not patrol this area with bombing planes protected by fighting land planes; the British responded that they were hard-pressed on the front in Flanders and northern France, and could not spare the aircraft for the work.[5]

Cunningham presented the idea to the Marine Commandant and the General Board of the Navy. As a result, they supported the proposal and cut orders to organize four Marine landplane squadrons as quickly as possible and to secure suitable planes from the Army. His resolve kept Marine Corps aviation in existence.

Cunningham realized a significant part of Marine Aviation would require flying land planes. At the same time, the Navy emphasized establishing seaplane units for anti-submarine operations in the western hemisphere and European waters. Cunningham's persistence resulted in the establishment of the First Marine Aviation Force. As the senior at Miami, Geiger commanded Squadron A and was acting CO of the force. The other squadron commands went to Captain McIlvain (B Squadron), Captain Douglas Roben (C Squadron), and First Lieutenant Russell A. Presley (D Squadron).[6]

The force was four squadrons on paper, yet there were not enough aviators to outfit them. So, Cunningham and Geiger turned to the Navy to fully equip the organization with pilots. In the summer of 1918, the Marines began drawing their flying students from the school the Navy had set up in April at MIT. Promising volunteers were sent there and given the rank of chief petty officer or gunnery sergeant during their preliminary training; Cunningham feared they would not be prepared for combat. Those naval pilots selected for the fledgling Marine Aviation Force were not pleased to join the unit, according to Freddy Beach. Another echoed aviator Freddy Beach's comments: "Unfortunately for the Navy fliers… Washington had assigned the day bombing role in the Northern Bombing Group to the Marine Corps, leaving… newly qualified aviators without hope of promotion to flight or squadron leader—and even without a mission."[7]

At this time, the Marines operated mainly with Curtiss Jenny training planes. That changed in May 1918 when the first British-designed, American-manufactured de Havilland DH-4s arrived. That type

Captain Roy S. Geiger served as CO of the First Marine Aviation Force during training at Miami, and briefly served as the Marine Day Group commander of the NBG. (Official USMC Photograph)

would become the standard Marine combat plane used in the war and throughout the mid-1920s. The Philadelphia Navy Yard initially served as a combination land-and-water air station for the Marine Aviation section. The section was officially designated as the Marine Aeronautic Company in late April 1917. The following month saw it divided into two units: the First Marine Aeronautic Company – Advanced Base Force and the First Aviation Squadron, commanded by Captain Francis T. "Cocky" Evans. The detachment consisted of ten officers, only two qualified pilots, and 93 enlisted men. The company was then divided on October 12 into the 1st Aeronautic Company (seaplane) and transferred to Cape May, New Jersey. The 1st Aviation Squadron, comprising 24 officers and 237 men, commanded by Captain McIlvain, was transferred to Hazlehurst Field, Mineola, Long Island, on October 17.

Before the reorganization, on February 26, 1917, Cunningham received orders to form the Marines' first tactical aviation unit at the Marine Flying Field, Philadelphia Navy Yard, by transferring a Marine section of naval aviation based at Pensacola. On April 27, 1917, the Corps authorized the Marine Aeronautics Company of the Advance Base Force organization at the Marine Barracks, Philadelphia Navy Yard.

Personnel and equipment from the Marine Aviation section formed the nucleus of the Marine Aeronautic Company in the rapid expansion of Marine Aviation following the declaration of war against Germany. Cunningham scored a significant victory when Major General George Barnett secured Navy Department approval in the summer of 1917 for the First Aviation Squadron to provide reconnaissance and artillery spotting for the Marine brigade sent to France. Captain Cunningham went to the recently established officer training course at Quantico in August to select potential aviators and, according to Lieutenant General Karl S. Day, a second lieutenant at the time recalled, "We were looking for adventure. At the time, I was barely 21; I was one of the youngest; I don't think there was anybody there over 24 or 25. He told us that we were going to have an aviation section, that we would go to France, and that he was down there to talk to anybody who was interested in becoming a pilot."[8]

According to Second Lieutenant Day, 18 men were selected from the training battalion; six were detached to the Azores to fly seaplanes under Francis Evans. The other 12, including Second Lieutenant Day, were sent to Hazlehurst Field for flight training under civilian instructors. "We had three civilian instructors, some of whom weren't very good, and some were very good."[9]

At Mineloa in Hazlehurst Field, the squadron flew JN-4B Jenny trainers with civilian instructors, and the unit's main body lived in tents. Marine Corps aviation had no formal training school at the time and relied on civilians to teach fledgling aviators how to fly. One morning, after one hour and 53 minutes of dual instruction, one of the instructors – a Lafayette Escadrille veteran – staggered out drunk. "'All right,' he said. 'You son-of-a-bitch, go out and kill yourself.' That was my first solo."[10]

Marine Aviation in 1917 consisted of only seven qualified pilots, with six selected to command units not yet formed, and thus required civilian instructors. Training progressed reasonably well, but temperatures dropped rapidly by December, and something had to be done to remedy the situation. Several cold weeks at the field were the worst on record, with -17°F on the night of December 27. Without any other orders, Captain McIlvain packed his troops, equipment, and aircraft on a train he had requisitioned. He headed south on January 1, 1918, for the Army's Gerstner Field at Lake Charles, Louisiana.

Meanwhile, Captain Geiger was forming another Marine unit at NAS Coconut Grove, Florida, to train for seaplane duty. This force was augmented in February and March by the arrival of six newly commissioned second lieutenants and a dozen more reserve second lieutenants. These student officers were trained and designated as naval aviators for seaplane duty. Geiger took several of the first qualified flyers to the Curtiss Flying School for training in land planes, primarily with the OX-5 Jenny. Captain Cunningham heard about a shortage of suitable planes for his men training in Florida and acquired 20 Curtiss Jennies with Hispano-Suiza engines. On April 1, 1918, McIlvain arrived in Miami with his aeronautic company at Curtiss Field, renamed the Marine Corps Flying Field – the first Marine Corps Air Station (MCAS).

An oblique photograph shows the Marine Corps air station outside Miami, circa 1918. In the rear center are probably Curtiss JN-4 training planes before the arrival of the first de Havilland DH-4. (Courtesy of the National Archives via the Alan C. Carey Collection)

Tents were used as hangars for aircraft based at the Marine Flying Field near Miami. The planes are JN-4Ts. In the center-right is a Curtiss JN-6HG-1. (Courtesy of the Goodyear W. Kirkman Collection [COLL/3336] at the Archives Branch, Marine Corps History Division)

De Havilland DH-4, bureau number A-3273, at the United States Marine Corps Flying Field, Miami, circa 1918. This plane has been obtained from the Army and still carries its Army serial number. (Courtesy of the US Naval History and Heritage Command, NH 43438)

One might imagine the Marines stationed in Miami enjoyed its luxurious hotels, restaurants, and beaches. Yet, the field was in the outer rural fringes of Dade County, where they lived in tents, planes were housed in canvas hangars, and the landing field was made of soft sand where grass refused to grow. The area was characterized as land almost entirely wild and uncultivated. The company was split into a headquarters detachment and four land plane squadrons – A, B, C, and D. In February 1918, the Marine Aviation section of eight officers and 40 enlisted men was organized and stationed at Miami's naval air station. The number of personnel in this section was later increased and served at that station throughout the war, taking over its deep-sea scouting role. Captain Thomas R. Shearer was in command during the entire time. By March, a British officer declared the force fit for combat, but one Marine flyer, First Lieutenant Ford Rogers, disagreed: "We had flown nothing but Jennies [Curtiss JNs]. We got one DH-4, and all of us got one flight…"[11]

After their morning flight, student pilots lined up their training planes on June 17, 1918. By July, such men were heading overseas for duty in France as part of the NBG. (Courtesy of the National Archives, 165-WW-516F-010)

Student pilots at Marine Flying Field on June 17, 1918. Behind them are Thomas-Morse Scouts and Curtiss "Jennies." Those stationed at the base more than likely became part of the Marine element of the NBG. (Courtesy of the National Archives 165-WW-516F)

Contact!: Early US Naval and Marine Corps Aviation, 1911–18

Curtiss JN "Jennies" training planes stage a flyover at the Marine Flying Field, circa 1917–18. Below them is the main road of the airfield. The Marine Corps operated the field from 1918 to 1919. (Courtesy of the National Archives via the Alan C. Carey Collection)

US naval base, Ponta Delgada Harbor, Azores. At the bottom center is the First Marine Aeronautical Company, 1918. (Courtesy of the US Naval History and Heritage Command, NH 122243)

In mid-October 1917, the First Marine Aeronautical Company of ten officers and 93 men, initially equipped with two R-type Curtiss seaplanes, received orders from Captain Noble E. Irvin, Officer in Charge of Naval Aviation, to report for sea patrol duty at the Navy Coastal Air Station at Cape May, New Jersey. Upon arrival, Captain Irvin directed: "The Aeronautical Company will immediately take up patrol duty along the coast within the vicinity of Cape May, doing daily reconnaissance, covering as much territory, and extending seaward as far as will be considered advisable within the judgment of the commanding officer of this unit."[12]

Major Evans, CO of the aeronautic squadron at Cape May, found very little to do defending the eastern seaboard from German submarines. His superiors agreed that such a unit would benefit more if transferred overseas. Any thoughts of duty in the United Kingdom or France near the action were dashed on December 7, 1917, when Major Evans, 12 officers,

Personnel of the First Marine Aeronautical Company, at the US naval base in the Azores, pose for an official photograph. (Courtesy of the US Naval History and Heritage Command NH 122248)

Major Francis T. Evans, US Marine Corps CO of the First Marine Aeronautical Company in the Azores. (Courtesy of the US Naval History and Heritage Command, NH 49658)

and 133 enlisted men were ordered to embark upon the transport ship USS *Hancock* for Naval Base 13 on the island of Ponta Delgada, Azores.[13]

One of the Marine pilots was 27-year-old Lieutenant Walter Smith Poague, who served with the company, and his musings on the war and life are contained in his diary and letters he sent to family members. He was stationed at Aviator Ponta Delgada, Azores Islands, as a First Marine Aeronautic Company member. A Chicago native, he enlisted in the Marine Corps in June 1917, trained at Quantico, Virginia, and was appointed a second lieutenant. He transferred to Aviation Department Flying Field, Cape May, New Jersey, in October 1917 and sent the *Hancock* with First Contingent Marine Corps flyers abroad. The old military saying, "Hurry up and wait," defined the week he stayed aboard the ship in port for seven days before setting sail on the eighth. But, like most military members, Poague found time to write and think about life. On January 13, he wrote about the uselessness of war:

Sunday, 13 January,

I'm tired and blue, for the whole war is such a useless thing. I don't want to waste my time as I am doing—my years are too few, war is too long, and this is all so useless and idle. The prospect of death tends to enter one's specialty for those heading into harm's way.

He wrote on Thursday, January 17, that he was not afraid, "at least not yet." He saw death as a splendid gamble, but he loved life and was not frightened about his prospects:

Was it Seeger who said: "I find no fear in death, No horror to abhor; I never thought it aught But just to cease to dwell spectator And resolve most naturally once more Into the dearly loved eternal spectacle." I can't say I have achieved that sublime attitude, but I am tranquil. More, I am curious.[14]

On Wednesday, January 23, the *Hancock* arrived at Ponta Delgada on the island of São Miguel, and it took over a month to unload the ship and set up camp. By February 15, two aircraft were ready for operations. This organization operated an anti-submarine patrol station with ten R-6

A Curtiss R-type floatplane of the First Marine Aeronautical Company over the harbor at Ponta Delgada, Azores, March 1918. (Courtesy of the US Naval History and Heritage Command, NH 122255)

seaplanes, two N-9 seaplanes, and six HS-2L flying boats from its base. In addition, it flew regular patrols to deny enemy submarines ready access to the Azores convoy routes. It was not the stuff of great heroes, but the First Aeronautic Company was the first American aviation unit to deploy with a specific mission. His life along with the company's was dull. So dull that one pilot dared write Major General Commandant Barnett, complaining of the "most unpleasant continued inactivity" and requesting to be sent to France. General Barnett wrote back that a Marine officer's paramount duty was to carry out his assignment, no matter how unpleasant. Furthermore, while orders relieving the bored young aviator were sent, the General revoked them.

The squadron carried out patrols around the waters surrounding the islands from dawn to dusk, and the only sighting they had of the enemy was on September 11, 1918. A Curtiss R-6 was on patrol with pilot Lieutenant Poague and his crew member, Gunnery Sergeant Zeigler, when they saw a German U-boat on the surface. They circled, then came in to attack and drop their only bomb. Unfortunately, not only did the bomb miss, but it also failed to explode, and the two flyers could only watch as the submarine's crew leisurely battened down the hatches and then submerged out of sight.

Marines working on a Lowe-Willard-Fowler HS-1L, bureau number A1107, Azores, 1918. (Courtesy of the US Naval History and Heritage Command)

Lieutenant Poague's first patrol took place on February 19, and he wrote of his experiences in a series of letters and diary entries:

> Today I had my first flight in the Azores, 19 February, an hour hop. The most distinct reaction is the surprise at finding how instinctive flying has become. It is now two and a half months since I have flown, and yet the former control came to me as easily as ever. Flying is like swimming, I am sure, or skating, or riding a bicycle, in that once it is learned and the muscles become adapted, it is never forgotten. From the air this rolling, fertile country looks even better than from the sea. We had expected bad air currents, due to the mountains, but to date haven't found.

His preoccupation with life and death is displayed throughout his writing about the beauty and splendor of the Azores.

> I want to get on and on to big things which will build me. I want to get into this scrap all the way up to my eyes and to live life madly. And then I want

An HS-L1 is being towed with the pilot in front and a mechanic in the rear. (From the Hugh Squares Collection [COLL/3015] at the Archives Branch, Marine Corps History Division)

to write life. I want life and I want to live. I do not want to die, but I think I'd rather die in the big fight than live and never enter the fighting. Patience is necessary—and hard, I have eaten life too ravenously to nibble at the crumbs of this thing. I hope I'll always be a glutton when life is served, hot, savory and entrancing.

I've been watching life go by for a year and I've speculated a good deal upon it. We're just ugly, squawking little animals squeezed out of an oblivion and dropped here to run a certain course and mature, breed and, fading away, drop back into those same vast silences. I've wondered why of it all. And I've rebelled.

His last letter to his family, dated October 18, discusses his hatred for the "Hun" (Germans), the talk of an armistice, and his plans after the war. He also lamented about the hell hole that was his temporary home: "The prospect of months more in this hole leaves me flattened out like a steam roller had gone over me, for I never expect to be so weary, so utterly tired of a town again as I am of this nameless place to which your letters come. It's a dead, monotonous existence and no joy in it anywhere."

Marine mechanics working on a seaplane, possibly an HS-1L, Azores, 1918. The company operated H-1s, H-2s, N-, and R-type planes between 1917 and 1918. (From the Hugh Squares Collection [COLL/3015] at the Archives Branch, Marine Corps History Division)

Poague's death occurred on November 5, 1917, and his observer, Sergeant Ziegler, riding in the plane's back seat, wrote a letter to the family explaining the circumstances of Poague's death. He found it hard to explain how Walter perished that day and tried to discuss the events in a letter thoroughly, explaining that he would meet the family upon returning to the US if they still had questions. He wrote:

> On 5 November we started from the beach at 6:00 A.M. on what we called the sunrise scout patrol. The motor and plane seemed and tested all O. K. But the wind was against us, as there is only one way to take off in that harbor. We had what we call a downwind of about twenty-five miles per hour and the sea just outside the harbor was very rough. To get off in a downwind you must have flying speed of the machine plus the speed of the wind. Walter was Officer of the Day and that night had received several submarine warnings and some of them were within our range, so that made the sunrise patrol all the more important. When we left the beach, we both expected to take off before we passed the sea buoy which is at the mouth of the harbor, but when we passed the buoy, we were still planning.
>
> Mr. Poague was in the rear seat and had the controls and I in the front seat with the wireless. After leaving the buoy I expected to feel it take off any moment, but the pontoons just seemed to be touching the top of the waves. We traveled for quite a distance when the plane rose several feet and then settled, and the pontoons struck the top of a wave and gave way. I saw one come through the right lower wing, and I loosened my belt to jump, but we bounded and turned over too fast to jump. We turned over twice and stopped with us hanging head down underwater. I fought my way out between the tangled wires and wreckage and was about exhausted when I reached the surface, but was not hurt badly, teeth knocked loose and stiff neck. I called for Mr. Poague, but received no answer, so I climbed around the wreckage and found him still hanging in his seat with the top engine panel—that is the top wing—just over the front seat against his chest and blocking all of the rear cockpit except that occupied by Mr. Poague's body.

I took his arm and tried to pull him out, but his safety belt was still fastened and the panel was tight against him. He appeared to be dead then, for he did not move all the while I worked to get him out. I loosened his belt by kicking in the bottom of the fuselage, but I still could not pull him out, so I kicked every section of the panel that was floating it against the fuselage so I could push it away from the cock-pit. I did succeed in moving it some, but he wore a life preserver over a large leather coat which was caught inside the fuselage, and in going under the water so often to get it loose. I became too exhausted to lift him on the wreckage after I did get him loose, so I hung to the wreckage with him until we were picked up by a native fishing boat, which was about one-half hour after the accident occurred, and about ten minutes later the Admiral's boat with the doctor reached us. They did everything they could to bring him back, and after working three hours without getting any signs of life, the doctors pronounced him dead. I myself think Mr. Poague was killed without knowing what happened.[15]

Walter Smith Poague made the ultimate sacrifice during a typical aerial patrol. He may have drowned or may have suffered internal injuries that killed him. Nevertheless, the result was the same. He was the only member of the company to lose his life while stationed in the Azores. Throughout 1918 the Aeronautical Company maintained a full schedule covering convoy lanes around the Azores, flying 70 miles out with only two hours' gasoline capacity, finding nothing of the enemy. Finally, on July 24, 1918, half the company was pulled out of the Azores and sent back to the US to train new pilots for duty in Europe. The remainder of the company was pulled out on January 24, 1919, arriving at the Marine Flying Field, in Miami, Florida, on March 15. The First Marine Aviation Detachment was the first Marine force to operate overseas, and it did fulfill its goal of patrolling the waters around the Azores, searching in vain for German U-boats. "Khaki" Evans received the Distinguished Flying Cross for an aerial flight on February 13, 1917, conducting the first successful loop of a seaplane. He remained the detachment's CO until its disestablishment in 1919. He remained in the Marines before retiring on December 1, 1944, after serving 35 years.

Right: Lieutenant Walter Poague, shown here, wrote detailed letters and diary entries about his duty with the First Marine Aeronautical Company. (From *Diary and Letters of Marine Aviator by Lieutenant Walter S. Poague*)

Below: A damaged seaplane, possibly the one in which Lieutenant Poague was killed. (From the Hugh Squares Collection [COLL/3015] at the Archives Branch, Marine Corps History Division)

Chapter 14

The Northern Bombing Group: Marine Corps Operations

Lieutenant Kenneth Whiting recommended that American naval aviation (primarily seaplanes and flying boats) be employed from Dunkerque in bombing the German submarine pens at Zeebrugge, Ostend, and Bruges, located along the North Sea coastline of Belgium. However, such aircraft on hand did not have sufficient range from their base at Killingholme, nor could such planes carry an adequate bomb load to inflict significant damage on the submarine-pens. Moreover, those American, British, and French seaplane units attached to patrolling would not undertake such missions. Instead, their operations consisted of convoy coverage and anti-submarine duty. Nevertheless, seaplanes escorted more than 6,000 ships from this station along the important traffic lane bordering the east coast of England. Not one troop transport ship became a victim of an enemy submarine.[1]

Lieutenant Robert "Bob" Lovett, a former member of the First Yale Unit, studied the feasibility of establishing a bombing group with the primary duty of operations against enemy submarine bases, and became a staunch advocate of doing so. His meticulous research covered the theory and practical application of aircraft used in war, which aided in the creation of the NBG. It became the Marine Corps' task to raid the submarine bases. Yet, that mission would change during the months to come.

On January 28, 1918, Lovett submitted a memorandum, and this document exerted a significant influence on the creation of the NBG. His reports may also have influenced Major Cunningham to push for such a force. Lovett believed the British Handley Page and the Italian Caproni bombers would be the most effective at conducting such missions at night. He further elaborated, "It is my conviction that the US Naval Air Service can take part in the warfare ahead of anything at present contemplated, by specializing upon large bombing planes…"[2]

Lovett may have been behind the idea of sending some to train and operate with British squadrons. Regarding the concept, he said: "For the start, we should send the best pilots and observers we have right out to

Lieutenant (jg) Robert "Bob" Lovett, Naval Aviator No. 66, is shown here in 1917 at US NAS Moutchic, France. He graduated from the First Yale Unit and was instrumental in establishing the NBG. (From the scrapbook of John Lansing Callan; courtesy of the US Naval History and Heritage Command, NHF-039-RR. 10.05)

the front with Handley-Pages and Capronis and work them in with the British squadrons. The British can easily accommodate enough pilots and observers to give us a start, and we would not have to wait for our school in the States, which will probably take some time to get going."[3]

An argument then ensued between the Army and Navy about which branch could conduct such strike missions. The Navy won the debate when General Pershing intervened; the Navy would bomb the submarine pens, and the Army would provide pursuit fighters as escorts. The Navy requested 75 bombers and 40 single-seat fighters, but the Army denied the request, leaving the Navy stuck with its seaplanes and whatever aircraft foreign allies could supply. Thus, lacking adequate aircraft and personnel, the Navy began to form the group. The project initially included 12 squadrons of bombing and fighters (pursuit) planes to be based at various points near Calais and Dunkerque. The yet unnamed group would explicitly bomb the German submarine bases along the coast of Flanders, Belgium. Captain Cone then set the requirements for what turned out to be an enormous project in a cablegram to Admiral Sims: "First, establish six squadrons [of] night bombers of ten planes each, either Handley-Page or Caproni type. Personnel requires 180 officers and 1764 men, including 72 pilots, 72 observers, and 144 gunners. Second, establish six squadrons [of] day bombers of 18 planes each, either DH or Bristol Types. Personnel required 282 officers, 1,266 men, 120 pilots, and 120 observers."[4]

However, naval authorities scaled back the number of squadrons to eight; acquiring a sufficient number of aircraft remained an issue well into early October 1918. The lack of planes forced the group to attach pilots and observers with British and French units before and after the group was organized.[5]

The Navy group officially organized the unit as the NBG between mid-June and August 1918 under Captain David C. Hanrahan, USN, with the wing headquarters at Autingues, France. Hanrahan was a non-aviator and did not fully understand the intricacies of commanding an aviation unit. Some liked him, but others did not. Placing non-aviators in command of aviation units had become standard practice

The Northern Bombing Group: Marine Corps Operations

NBG Commanding Officer Captain David C. Hanrahan (center) with other staff members at either Oyé or La Fresne, France. (Courtesy of the US Naval History and Heritage Command, NH 52890)

since Commander Mustin, who briefly commanded the seaplane tender *North Carolina*, was relieved of duty by a non-aviator in 1915.

It appeared the Marines would not play an active role in the group. However, Major Cunningham insisted the corps had a prior claim on the strategic bombing of German submarine bases and was outraged that the Navy planned to cut Marine participation in the bombing program. His viewpoint resulted in the plan's adjustment to include the Marines in daily operations. Accordingly, the four squadrons of Cunningham's First Marine Aviation Force, including the headquarters section, were organized to operate under Navy command. They would serve as the Day Wing of the NBG in northern France, which worked in the Dunkerque area against German submarines and their bases at Ostend, Zeebrugge, and Bruges.

Setting the operational goal of equipping the NBG with aircraft became a logistical nightmare. Other air units targeted railway junctions, railway yards, canals, canal docks, ammunition dumps, supply dumps, and aerodromes. These targets were located at or near the southern Belgian towns of Turnhout, Tielt, Steenbrugge, Eecloo, Ghent, Deinze, and Lokeren in connection with the Belgian offensives during the fall of 1918. Such raids hindered the enemy's retreat as much as possible. However, during this period, enemy aircraft were incredibly active on the front lines, and planes were generally attacked while on the raids.[6]

By August 10, two Handley Page bombers with naval personnel operated in night-bombing raids in conjunction with the British as part of the newly established NBG, beginning in mid-August. Acquiring Capronis proved difficult as the aircraft needed to be ferried over the Italian Alps to France and Britain. American and Italian authorities agreed to deliver 30 Caproni bombers in June and July 1918, and 80 in August. However, the actual number supplied was nine during July, and another nine in August.

On August 11, 1918, the group received its first Caproni bomber equipped with three Fiat engines. It was flown by Ensign Leslie R. Taber, with Ensign Charles Fahy as co-pilot and D. C. Hale as the gunner, from the acceptance field at Furino, Italy, to the aerodrome at Saint-Inglevert. On August 15, 1918, this plane made a successful night raid on the submarine shelters at Ostend, Belgium, four days later. After August 15, Caproni bombers conducted no combat flights as they needed constant maintenance work to render them fit for service. It was quickly proven that the Fiat engines were defective, showing poor quality and construction, which required nearly all of them to be taken apart and rebuilt.

The troubles experienced by the Fiat engines resulted in inquiries on obtaining a substitute, as naval officials claimed the better Italian Isotta-Fraschini motor was available in small numbers. Testing proved them considerably superior to the Fiat; the Americans arranged the delivery of the preferred engines with the Italian government to equip future deliveries of Capronis with motors and transport the planes by rail. However, the first Caproni fitted with Isotta-Fraschini engines did not arrive until November 8, three days before the Armistice with Austria-Hungary.

The Marine aspect of the group also proved troublesome in becoming operational. On approval for a land-based Marine air group, Cunningham campaigned to bring his squadrons to full strength in men and aircraft.

He made repeated recruiting visits to the officers' school at Quantico, Virginia, and collected other volunteers elsewhere. As long as they seemed willing, able, and possessed valid credentials as potential pilots or mechanics, they received orders for Miami. However, even with this influx of strength, the two detachments could not furnish enough pilots for the planned four squadrons of the First Aviation Force. So, Cunningham toured the Navy air installations and recruited naval aviators, mostly young reservists who wanted to go to France. Those five officers (already qualified Navy seaplane pilots) transferred from the Navy to the Marine Corps and reported to the Marine field at Miami for landplane training. Of 135 pilots who eventually flew in France with the First Aviation Force, 78 were transferred naval officers who obtained Marine Corps commissions.

Major Cunningham commanded the Day Wing from its organization until December 7, 1918, except for the period from August 1 to 7, 1918, during which Major Roy D. Geiger assumed temporary command of the group. Geiger absorbed the entire school at Miami into an MCAS, arranging to commission the instructors in the reserves and requisition the school's Jennies.

Major John W. Cunningham, USMC (center), no relation of Major Alfred Cunningham, and staff of the First Marine Corps Aviation Force in Paris, France, 1918. (Courtesy of the US Naval History and Heritage Command, NH 61292)

By June 16, 1918, Cunningham and Geiger had organized the force into a headquarters and four complete combat squadrons designated as A, B, C, and D. In France, the alpha designation would change to the numerical 7th, 8th, 9th, and 10th squadrons. The four squadrons and the headquarters company organized and trained at the Marine Flying Field in Miami, and secured Curtiss JN Jenny planes and equipment from the Army. However, before the First Marine Aviation Force went aboard, a cablegram was received from United States naval aviation headquarters in France recommending the number of squadrons for this project should double, and that these additional squadrons be composed of Navy personnel. Upon approval of this recommendation, the revised project was named the "Northern Bombing Group."

By June 1, 1918, the First Marine Aviation Force reported having 124 "satisfactory" pilots on hand: 64 regular Marines, 23 reserve second lieutenants, 17 second lieutenants (ex-Navy), and 20 ensigns awaiting enrollment in the Corps. In addition, it had ten Navy cadets pending enrollment and 47 enlisted Marine pilots. On July 13, 1918, the First Marine Aviation Force, consisting of squadrons A, B, C, and headquarters company, left Miami and then embarked on USS *Dekalb* at New York City for France on July 18, 1918. This organization consisted of 107 officers and 654 enlisted men. The Day Wing disembarked at Brest on July 30, 1918, and found an entire bag of administrative and supply problems, including that there were no aircraft and equipment waiting for them.[7]

Acquiring additional personnel and training Squadron D became a priority, along with providing air patrols off the Florida coast. Finally, in September 1918, Squadron D, comprising 41 officers and 189 enlisted men, arrived in France, completing the four squadrons of the Day Wing.

Once in France, Cunningham and his men moved the 400 miles to their base locations near Calais. In addition, authorities at Brest had no quarters for or orders covering the disposition of the Marine Aviation Force, so personnel spent the day of July 31 aboard the ship until the French made arrangements for them ashore. The force disembarked again a day later and moved into pup tents at Camp Pontanezen while awaiting further orders.

On August 3, Cunningham procured a French-manned freight train, loaded the personnel of the three squadrons, plus some rations, into the boxcars, and headed north toward Flanders. After a slow railroad journey of 400 miles, the force detrained at Calais on August 5 and marched to the British rest camp. Afterward, they proceeded to airfields located between Calais and Dunkerque. Squadrons A and B camped near Oyé, a town between Calais and Dunkerque. La Fresne became the base for Squadron C, a small village about 10 miles northeast of Calais. Unfortunately, no airfields existed at Oyé, and Marine personnel from La Fresne constructed the base.

The First Marine Aviation Force wing of the NBG would be composed of four squadrons with 18 DH-4s, each with six planes. In comparison, six Navy squadrons would receive six Italian Caproni bombers for operations. The Marine squadrons became organized as the 7th, 8th, 9th, and 10th squadrons under the command of Cunningham, and the Navy's Night Wing consisted of squadrons 1, 2, 3, and 4, commanded by Lieutenant Robert Lovett, USN. The bombing group established four operating bases behind French and Belgian lines in the Calais–Dunkerque region. Navy Squadrons 1 and 2 operated from Saint-Inglevert, while Champagne became the base

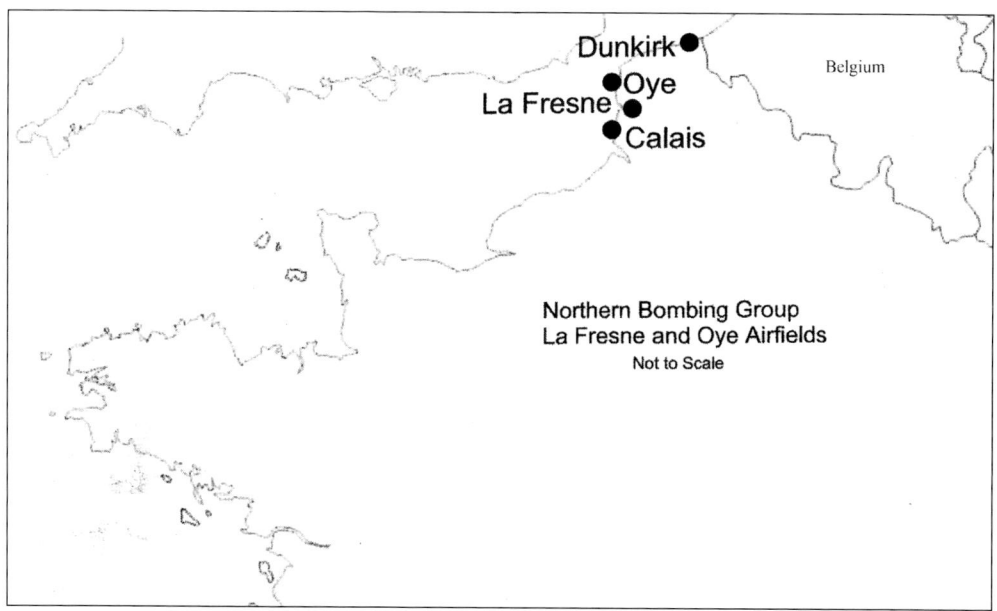

Northern Bombing Group
La Fresne and Oye Airfields
Not to Scale

for Squadrons 3 and 4. Oyé housed Marine Squadrons 7 (A) and 8 (B), while La Fresne became the base for Squadrons 9 (C) and 10 (D).[8]

Additionally, naval personnel supplemented the Day Group. Five naval aviators and the same number of enlisted observers are known to have been utilized by the day group to complement Marine personnel; they were:

Pilots
Lieutenant (jg) Albert R. Johnson
Lieutenant (jg) Delzie R. Lee
Ensign Charles W. Greenough
Ensign Charles E. Hodges, Jr.
Ensign Elmer B. Taylor

Observers/Gunners
Jay R. Jones, MM1c
George E. Sprague
Horton E. Tatmen, CCM
Alva M. Turnball, MM2c
Anthony J. White, MM2c

Cunningham found his group without planes, equipment, and materiel. When it became clear delays were in the offing, Cunningham received the Navy's approval to make a deal with the British to send marine personnel to RAF units. Although there is no corroborating evidence, Cunningham brokered the negotiations since three Marine pilots were serving with RAF units before the First Marine Aviation Force arrived in France. Those men were William M. McIlvain, Roy S. Geiger, and Edmund Gillette Chamberlain.[9]

Until the delivery of aircraft to the First Marine Aviation Force, Cunningham had no desire to leave his pilots and observers idle, and, without the means to train for combat duty, he took the initiative to have some personnel assigned to RAF squadrons 213, 217, and 218 until the end of the Armistice. As a result, approximately 63 Marine flying personnel served with British squadrons. Of those, 50 were pilots/observers, 11 were enlisted observers, and two enlisted were gunners.[10]

When the Meuse–Argonne began on September 26, 1918, Marine Squadron "C" had one American-built DH-4 powered by a Liberty engine; Major Cunningham placed the plane with its pilot, Captain Lytle, and observer, Sergeant Amil Wiman, at the disposal of No. 218 Squadron, RAF. This crew and aircraft began combat operations on October 1, dropping bombs on the railway yards at Lichtervelde. On October 3, 1918, Captain Lytle and Sergeant Wiman participated in a raid against Westende, Nieuwpoort, and Ostend railway yards, as well as Lichtervelde.

The German evacuation of their submarine bases at Ostend, Zeebrugge, and Bruges in late October, which had been the particular objectives of the NBG, left no assigned mission for the Marine Day Wing. After that, with approval from the US Navy, the RAF placed the Marine bomber squadrons under the operational control of the No. 5 Group, RAF. The Marine's primary operational mission was supporting the first Allied advance in Flanders, beginning on September 28, 1918. Equipped with DH-9s borrowed from the British, Cunningham sent pilots and observers to 217 and 218 Squadrons.

Jesse Floyd Dunlap, Naval Aviator No. 593, was a member of the NBG and became the first member to deliver a DH-4 to the Day Wing stationed in France. (Courtesy of the Alfred A. Cunningham Collection at the Archives Branch, Marine Corps History Division)

Those serving with 218 Squadron carried out the following raids on the dates indicated: Oye on October 5, Westende on October 7, and Ardoye on October 8. On returning from the raid on October 8, nine German fighters attacked a Marine DH-4, quickly cutting it off from the British bombers. In the fight that followed, they brought down one enemy plane. On October 11, Cunningham sent two pilots and observers from Marine Squadron "A" to 217 Squadron equipped with DH-4s, to fly with the British.

Marines operating with the RAF participated in bombing missions flying the DH-9. In contrast, others served in pursuit squadrons equipped with the Sopwith Camel. Captain Lytle participated in 11 bombing missions while Second Lieutenant Donald Whiting participated in eight bombing raids against German-held Ostend, Zeebrugge, Bruges, and Westende, Belgium – a 15–45-minute flight from RAF bases. Captain Karl S. Day participated in five raids, dropping 1,000lb of bombs on the enemy at Bruges and Ghent. First Lieutenants Herman Peterson and Arthur

Wright and Second Lieutenants William McSorley and Charles Needham participated in four raids on Ostend and Bruges. Marines operating with the RAF participated in bombing missions using the de Havilland DH-9, with Captain Day participating in five attacks, dropping 1,000lb of bombs on the enemy at Bruges.

The First Marine Aviation Force suffered its first combat casualties while operating with the RAF. Flying through heavy antiaircraft fire and evading enemy planes, First Lieutenant Everett Brewer and his observer, Sergeant Harry Wershiner, were wounded over Corteinarcke, Belgium, on September 28.

Second Lieutenant Everett R. Brewer (pilot), Naval Aviator No. 585. He is credited with destroying two enemy planes, although he and his observer were wounded. (Courtesy of the Alfred A. Cunningham Collection at the Archives Branch, Marine Corps History Division)

On September 29, Second Lieutenant Chapin C. Barr became the first Marine aviator to lose his life due to enemy air action, dying of a leg wound that severed an artery. Others killed in action while flying with the RAF were Second Lieutenants Harvey C. Norman and Caleb W Taylor, killed on October 25. First Lieutenant Mulcahy and his observer, Corporal McCullough, became the first Marines to shoot down an enemy plane. While flying with No. 218 Squadron (equipped with the DH-9) on September 29, they shot down a Fokker D. VII over Coremarch, Belgium.

Chapin C. Barr, Naval Aviator No. 823, was mortally wounded in aerial combat on September 28, 1918. He was awarded the Navy Cross for extraordinary heroism. (Courtesy of the Alfred A. Cunningham Collection Archives Branch, Marine Corps History Division)

Second Lieutenant Harvey C. Norman (pilot), Naval Aviator No. 783, was killed in action on October 22, 1918, and was awarded the Navy Cross posthumously. (Courtesy of the Alfred A. Cunningham Collection at the Archives Branch, Marine Corps History Division)

Second Lieutenant Caleb W. Taylor (pilot), Naval Aviator No. 840, was killed in action on October 25, 1918, and was awarded the Navy Cross posthumously. (Courtesy of the Alfred A. Cunningham Collection at the Archives Branch, Marine Corps History Division)

The following extracts from the report of Major Bert S. Wemp, Officer Commanding 218 Squadron RAF, to Major Cunningham, dated October 6, 1918, on the services of the Marine pilots and observers during that period:

> Herewith attached Squadron Record Books and narratives of Combats in the Air, in which American pilots shot down enemy aircraft. Official credit is given to Lieut. E. R. Brewer, USMC, and Sgt. Werner, USMC, for bringing down one E A [enemy aircraft], and he may have brought down another, but we are unable to get particulars owing to his precarious state,
>
> On the 29th, Lieut. F. P. Mulcahy, USMC, and Corp. McCullough, USMC, shot down an E. A. [enemy aircraft], which was witnessed and confirmed by two of our officers.
>
> Lieutenants Mulcahy, Brewer, Lytle, Talbot and Nelms, and the late Lieut. Barr, with their N. C. O. observers, have done wonderful work in this push during the past week, and when the time comes for those nowhere to leave the squadron, I can assure you I will hate to part with their services.[11]

Some Marine pilots and observers remained with the RAF, such as First Lieutenant "Tex" Rogers and his observer, Corporal Ross W. Winkler, who were among those serving with 218 Squadron flying DH-9s on bombing missions. By October 12, the Marines had received enough DH-4s and 9As to begin flying missions independently of the British. With the aid of the British, the Day Wing of the NBG became a viable fighting force. Absorbing men into RAF units to gain combat experienced enabled Cunningham to possess trained personnel when the time came to field an independent fighting force. Yet, precious time was wasted between August and September 1918 when there were no planes or equipment to form such a force.

While Marine pilots and observers were serving with the RAF, Cunningham continued dealing with a two-month delay (August–September 1918) in receiving American-built DH-4s that seriously

First Lieutenant Karl "Wild" Day, Naval Aviator No. 601, served as executive officer for C/3rd Squadron and also served with 218 Squadron, RAF from August to November 1918 (Alfred A. Cunningham Collection [COLL/3034] Archives Branch, Marine Corps History Division)

impeded operational readiness. When the planes arrived, they were assembled and ferried directly to the two Marine bases in the Calais–Dunkerque area. The first American-built DH-4 arrived at La Fresne aerodrome from Pauillac on September 7, 1918, piloted by First Lieutenant Jesse F. Dunlap with Gunnery Sergeant Floyd B. Smith as his aerial gunner.[12]

The Marines would have to wait for their full complement of DH-4s. However, negotiations in obtaining aircraft for the NBG appear to have been brokered by Admiral Sims, which involved trading American-produced

Unknown members of the First Marine Aviation Force, Day Wing, standing in front of a DH-4 either at La Fresne or Oyé between October and November 1918. (Courtesy of the National Archives, 127-G-35KK-518981)

Left is Major Douglas B. Roben, Naval Aviator No. 535 and USMC Aviator No. 774, with Major Cunningham in France. Roben died from complications due to the Spanish flu epidemic. (Courtesy of the Alfred A. Cunningham Collection [COLL/3034] at the Archives Branch, Marine Corps History Division)

Liberty engines for DH-9 planes. The Americans made arrangements to swap three Liberty engines, and, in return, the British would return one Liberty-powered DH-9. The First Marine Aviation Force would conceivably operate 20 DH-9s and between 16 and 70 DH-4s. The following order came from Vice Admiral Sims to solve the supply issue:

> Vice Admiral William S. Sims, Commander, United States Naval Forces Based In Europe, To Office Of The Chief Of Naval Operations, First Cable Of The Day
> Sub-Area: <Serial IV-E>
> Subject: Exchange of Liberty Engines for British Planes.
> Source: Adm. Sims.
> Date 1 September 1918.
> Cablegram, 25 September 1918
> From: Sims
> To: Opnav.

He agreed with the US Army Air Service and RAF to exchange Liberty engines for British planes. The United States Army Air Service agreed to deliver 120 Liberty engines by September 1, 1918. After that, 90 more would be delivered in 30 days, another 60 in the following 30 days, and 15 per month for the following three months. He then pushed for the NBG to receive six FE2B2 planes. Sims then pressed the British to maintain a maximum of:

> Eighteen machines per month and ten engines per month in addition to full spares for planes and engines, the whole to cover a total period of six months, unserviceable engines to be returned to the Royal Air Force, also 54 DH-9A3 machines complete without engines as soon as possible, delivery to be complete in 3 months from date. Also, 20 Handley-Page machines complete without engines as soon as possible, delivery to be complete within 2 months from the date, the DH9A machines and the Handley-Page machines to be delivered with initial airplane spares. Of the planes to be received the Navy

is to get the ten Handley-Page. To carry out this agreement, arrangements have already been made by the Navy to turn over 60 liberty engines to the British now and 90 additional by January 15. Certain modifications are embodied in agreement as to receiving ten Handley-Page with eagle eight engines.

Thereafter, the number of DH-4s and DH-9s arriving at the NBG increased. On October 18, the group received 15 train cars of DH-4 materiel from Glasgow, Scotland. By October 23, 17 planes were flown from Eastleigh to the NBG fields in France.[13]

The First Marine Strategic Bombing Force took form as the group received an adequate supply of DH-4 and DH-9 aircraft, enabling it to become an independent fighting force. The first all-Marine bombing force undertook its first combat mission on October 14, 1918, by Squadron 9 [ex-"C" Squadron] from La Fresne aerodrome. They targeted a German-held railway junction and yards at Thielt, Belgium, with the squadron aircraft dropping 2,128lb of bombs without damaging the attacking aircraft. However, some dozen Fokker D. VIFs and Pfalz IIIs intercepted the group on the return trip back to home base. The Germans approached the bombing force head-on, splitting into two groups: one of four, and one of eight aircraft.

The Germans succeeded in separating one aircraft from the rest of the formation. Then, they concentrated their attack on Second Lieutenant Ralph Talbot, one of the Naval Reserve officers who had transferred to Marine Aviation. Talbot's gunner, Corporal Robert G. Robinson, quickly shot down one attacker. Still, two others closed in from below, spraying the DH with fire and wounding Robinson in the left elbow, rendering his arm useless. Despite his wounds, Robinson cleared the jam in his gun and continued to fire until he was hit twice – once in the stomach and once in the thigh.

Meanwhile, Talbot took frantic evasive action. With Robinson unconscious in the rear seat, Talbot brought down a second German with his fixed guns

Ralph "Dick" Talbot, Naval Aviator No. 456, was posthumously awarded the Medal of Honor for his exceptionally meritorious service and extraordinary heroism during air raids over France and Pittham, Belgium, in October 1918. (Alfred A. Cunningham Collection [COLL/3034] Archives Branch, Marine Corps History Division.)

and put the plane into a steep dive to escape the remaining German fighters. Crossing the German lines at an altitude of 50ft, he landed safely at a Belgian airfield where Robinson was hospitalized.[14]

It was a savage head-on encounter. The action was so fast and deadly that it was difficult to comprehend. Robinson recovered from his wounds, but Talbot was later killed in a test flight. Both men were awarded the

Congressional Medal of Honor for this fight and an accumulation of other daring deeds during that period. Talbot's citation reads:

> For exceptionally meritorious service and extraordinary heroism while attached to Squadron C, 1st Marine Aviation Force, in France. Second Lieutenant Talbot participated in numerous air raids into enemy territory. On 8 October 1918, while on such a raid, he was attacked by nine enemy scouts, and in the fight that followed shot down an enemy plane. Also, on 14 October 1918, while on a raid over Pittham, Belgium, 2d Lt. Talbot and another plane became detached from the formation on account of motor trouble and were attacked by 12 enemy scouts. During the severe fight that followed, his plane shot down 1 of the enemy scouts. His observer was shot through the elbow while his gun jammed. 2d Lt. Talbot maneuvered to gain time for his observer to clear the jam with one hand, and then returned to the fight. The observer fought until shot twice, once in the stomach and once in the hip and then collapsed, Lt. Talbot attacked the nearest enemy scout with his front guns and shot him down. With his observer unconscious and his motor failing, he dived to escape the balance of the enemy and crossed the German trenches at an altitude of 50 feet, landing at the nearest hospital to leave his observer and then returning to his aerodrome.

Robert G. Robinson was awarded the Medal of Honor for his extraordinary heroism during air raids with Ralph Talbot in which he was wounded over Pittham, Belgium, in October 1918. (Courtesy of the US Naval History and Heritage Command).

The Northern Bombing Group: Marine Corps Operations

A burned wing section and engine of Ralph Talbot's plane in which he was killed in October 1918. (Courtesy of the Alfred A. Cunningham Collection [COLL/3034] at the Archives Branch, Marine Corps History)

Morning line of the First Marine Aviation Unit, France, 1918. The planes are DH-4s. (Courtesy of the US Naval History and Heritage Command, 61294)

Mechanics turning the prop to start a DH-4 for a bombing mission against German targets in Flanders, Belgium, by the Day Wing of the NBG. (Courtesy of the National Archives via the Alan C. Carey Collection.)

A DH4, bureau number A3280, in squadron number D-5, was operated by both B and C squadrons. Note the Marine Corps logo and roundel on the fuselage. (Courtesy of the Alfred A. Cunningham Collection Archives Branch, Marine Corps History Division)

The Northern Bombing Group: Marine Corps Operations

The roundel for the Marine Day Wing of the NBG. The colors are gold eagle and anchor with the roundel colors of blue, red, and white. This emblem was kept on Marine Corps planes into the 1920s. (Courtesy of the Alfred A. Cunningham Collection Archives Branch, Marine Corps History Division)

Day and night raids against German forces at Steenbrugge, Eceloo, Ghent, Deynze, and Lokeren continued throughout October, weather permitting, against German-held railways, canals, supply dumps, and airfields. On October 22, another raid was made on Melle in East Flanders, under the direction of Captain Day. Nine aircraft took off, but due to the dense fog and the necessity of flying 65 miles by compass, only four planes could reach the objective. Second Lieutenant Charles B. Todd, Jr., the pilot of one of the four striking aircraft, described the mission:

> We received our orders to proceed to Melle, a railroad center near Ghent, and to bomb the place [sic]. We left the aerodrome, nine planes in all, at 8:40 AM and started toward the lines gaining altitude as we flew. When we crossed the lines at an altitude of about 11,000 feet, we ran into a thick fog bank and were forced to descend to about 7,000 feet. The five ships in the

rear of our formation left us and turned back, thus leaving but four of us to proceed on our mis s ion. We flew in a diamond formation with Captain Day leading, Captain Presley was on the right, I was on the left and Lieutenant H. C. Norman was in the rear corner of the diamond.

The fog was very dense and we had much difficulty in seeing the earth a great part of the time and we used our compass for direction. Near Ghent we ran into a heavy Archie barrage [antiaircraft fire] which first burst above us, then below us and soon when the correct range was obtained the shooting was very accurate and the bursting shells came so close that they fairly seemed to bounce off our wings, engine and tail. They burst so close to my tail that my machine was thrown about as if I were flying in a heavy wind storm.

It was very difficult to stick to the formation, and we dared not separate because we would be lost to one another in the fog and thus be an easy mark for the Huns who fly in droves and not singly. Indeed, I feared that I would run my Leader down and still I stuck to the formation as did we all.

Suddenly three Huns [Germans] darted out of the haze in the rear and firing at Norman, came right on after me. Two were below and one behind. I banked my machine to give my observer a chance at them and then closed in behind my own leader. The Huns did not remain long, however, because of the dense fog and the fire from their Archie. We dropped our bombs on the railroad, and then the formation became scattered. An official Belgian report states was attacked by 7 Hun planes and brought down. His aircraft crashed near the Bruges-Ghent canal on the allied side of the lines, and both Lieutenants Norman and Taylor were killed.[15]

The retreating Germans caused the aerodrome at Oyé and La Fresne to be so far behind the lines that it was necessary to establish an advanced aerodrome. Cunningham chose an abandoned German air base at Knesselare, Belgium, in East Flanders on October 26, with Major McIlvain taking command of Squadron 8 (ex-"B" Squadron). This change in the front lines interrupted some flights for several days while Squadron 8 moved to the forward field. Squadron 8 did manage to conduct missions,

DH-3, bureau number A3269, was operated by squadrons A, B, and C. It had a forced landing at Bervyse, Belgium, on October 14, 1918. (Courtesy of the National Archives, 35kk 529570)

Marine Corps Day Group DH4s and DH9s prepare for another bombing sortie against German targets in southern Flanders in late October 1918. (Courtesy of the Alfred A. Cunningham Collection (COLL/3034) at the Archives Branch, Marine Corps History)

A scene at La Fresne aerodrome. The DH4 (right) of the C Squadron and DH9 (left) of the A Squadron have completed a day bombing mission in support of the British Army in Flanders. Ground crews (left) are reading the E8504, E-12, of the C Squadron for the next mission. (Courtesy of the Alfred A. Cunningham Collection (COLL/3034) Archives Branch, Marine Corps History Division)

A line-up of Marine Corps DH-4s and DH-9s during the fall or winter of 1918 when the Marine Day Wing conducted independent operations. (Courtesy of the National Archives 127-G-35KK-529554)

Above: Pilots and gunners of Marine Squadron C at La Fresne, France, in November 1918. Standing in the back row, in the center of the photo, and wearing a Sam Browne belt, is Captain Robert S. Lytle, Naval Aviator No. 605, CO. The gunners are holding their single, twin Lewis machine guns of .30 caliber. (Courtesy of the National Archives, 35KK-529922)

Right: Second Lieutenant John F. Gibbs, 2nd Squadron, Naval Aviator No. 830. He was forced down by engine failure in Holland on October 27, 1918, and he and Frank Nelms were interned. (Courtesy of the Alfred A. Cunningham Collection [COLL/3034] at the Archives Branch, Marine Corps History)

beginning on October 27, by sending a six-plane raid against a railway junction and yards at Lokeren, Belgium, in East Flanders. During this mission, the aircraft flown by Second Lieutenants Frank Nelms and John F. Gibbs was hit by antiaircraft fire, causing a forced landing in neutral Holland, where the two men were interned until the Armistice.[16]

Inclement weather, a shortage of planes, and the arrival of Spanish influenza during the end of October and into November curtailed air operations. Cunningham lamented on October 31 in official correspondence, "… today I tried… to form a raid and found that I could only muster ten well pilots out of all four squadrons… I have practically had to abandon operations."[17]

Second Lieutenant Frank Nelms, Jr., 2nd Squadron, Naval Aviator No. 871. He was forced down in Holland with Gibbs. (Courtesy of the Alfred A. Cunningham Collection [COLL/3034] at the Archives Branch, Marine Corps History)

The first aerial resupply mission in Marine Aviation history occurred on October 23, 1918, when Marine Captain Robert S. Lytle (right) and Gunnery Sergeant Amil Wiman helped to resupply a beleaguered French battalion. (Courtesy of the Alfred A. Cunningham Collection Archives Branch, Marine Corps History Division)

Second Lieutenant Charles B. Todd, USMCR, reported the following:

> The Spanish Influenza epidemic broke out in the camp on 25 October 1918, and 30 took ill. Influenza spread the following day with 102 cases. The base changed from combat operations into a hospital: Several officers and men, including the former Major Douglas B. Roben, Captain Arthur H. Wright, and Ensign Elmer B. Taylor, were sent to the British General Hospital owing to the gravity of the illness; three of those died, as did five enlisted men. Four officers and approximately 17 enlisted men of the Marine day wing died from exposure to the complications of the Spanish Influenza epidemic.[18]

On November 11, the group consisted of 130 officers in the group headquarters in the Night Wing and 164 officers in the Day Wing, including 88 and 80 pilots in the respective air wings. Enlisted men totaled 1,336 in the Night Wing and 818 in the Day Wing. Aircraft on hand on the same date would have been troublesome if the war had continued as the number

Arthur H. Wright (pilot), Naval Aviator No. 148/803, Marine Corps Aviator No. 883. He died from complications due to Spanish influenza. (Courtesy of the Alfred A. Cunningham Collection at the Archives Branch, Marine Corps History Division)

of operational aircraft diminished. The entire Day and Night Wings comprised six Caproni bombers (two in commission), 12 DH-4s (eight in commission), and 17 DH-9s (seven in commission). Operations would have been considerably better if the planned 40 Caproni bombers and 72 DH-4s had arrived. Such a plan would have increased the effectiveness of the group. Still, the NBG, both night and day sections, dropped 155,998lb of bombs on targets in Belgium between October and November 1918.

After the Armistice, the squadrons were all moved back to their original airfields before sending them back to the United States. The complete demobilization of the group was finished on February 10, 1919. The force in the field on the Armistice date was about 250 officers and 2,400 enlisted men; at the group assembly and repair base at Eastleigh, there were about 220 officers and 2,200 enlisted men, totaling around 470 officers and 4,600 enlisted men for the entire group.

William McIlvain, commander of B Squadron, on the right, holding the pole, is with other unknown officers displaying the flag of the First Marine Aviation Force after the Armistice during its demobilization in late November 1918. (Courtesy of the Alfred A. Cunningham Collection Archives Branch, Marine Corps History Division)

Chapter 15

Lighter-Than-Air Operations

The success of the early naval air operations during World War One overshadowed the creation of lighter-than-air (LTA) operations. Not a glamorous occupation for those wishing to fly a flying boat, seaplane, pursuit aircraft, or bomber, but pilots were needed to operate such craft according to naval doctrine. The primary purpose of balloons was to observe enemy movements, spot artillery, and conduct anti-submarine spotting. The Navy's LTA activities began in September 1915 with the construction of the unsuccessful non-rigid airship DN-1. The contract for the construction of the DN-1 between Goodyear and the Navy included a provision to train two naval officers. Lieutenant Commander Frank R. McCrary and Lieutenant Louis H. Maxfield were the two selected for training and ordered to Akron, Ohio, in August 1915; both would become prominent figures in LTA operations.[1]

Training of student pilots began at Pensacola under McCrary and Maxfield following a syllabus proposed by Captain Bristol in January 1916. On May 16, McCrary sent a revised syllabus to Commander Mustin, commander of the Pensacola NAS, who approved it and sent it up through the chain of command. Captain Bristol supported the idea and was included in a second revision of the training syllabus signed by Secretary of the Navy Daniels on June 3, 1916. The Bureau of Navigation issued the training syllabus for LTA operations, including meteorology, handling free balloons, solving problems relating to piloting, navigation, and theoretical instruction in weather forecasting and studying weather maps.[2] Specifically:

Commander Frank R. McCrary photographed circa 1918, likely taken at NAS Queenstown, Ireland, where he was assigned as CO in October of 1917. (Courtesy of the US Naval History and Heritage Command, NH 47976)

Student pilots were required to complete flights covering instruction in ascension, control of ballast under varying air conditions, methods of sounding air currents and checking descent, reading of instruments, keeping the log, navigation, valving, use of appendix and drag rope, making a landing and ripping the bag. In addition, one of the flights required an intermediate landing wherein the instructor was dropped off, and the student continued a solo flight for not less than one hour.[3]

The need for naval LTA aviators became crucial with the declaration of war. Yet, the only qualified airship pilots at that time were McCrary and Maxfield. Therefore, on May 29, 1917, Goodyear was given a contract to train Navy personnel in free ballooning, kite balloons, and airships. By June, the first LTA class began training. Prospective pilots trained primarily at

Akron, Pensacola, and Rockaway, New York. Operations were conducted exclusively in the North Atlantic, the Gulf of Mexico, and the Caribbean Sea while operating the B- and C-class dirigibles.

Specifications for the B-class were requested by the Chief of Naval Operations in October and modified on December 13, 1916. The requirements for the B-1 consisted of the following: a top speed of 45mph, an in-flight endurance of 12 hours, a crew of three, a radio range of 150 miles, and the capability of landing at sea and being towed. Plans for the B series were approved by the General Board and by Secretary of the Navy Daniels on January 27, 1917, with an order for 16 dirigibles with construction between six companies: Goodyear, Goodrich, the Connecticut Aircraft Company, Curtiss Aeroplane, the Motor Corporation, and the US Rubber Company. All the airships operated for coastal patrol during World War One at the following naval air stations: Chatham, Montauk, Rockaway, Cape May, and Key West. In addition, NAS Hampton Roads had B-class airships assigned, but used them primarily for experimentation. Those used for coastal patrol flew over 13,600 hours and roughly covered an astonishing 400,000 miles. One of the primary functions of the B-class was

This was the first series of airships operational in the United States Navy. There were 20 airships in the series. They were designed from the meager, non-classified data obtained from wartime Great Britain. They used a two-seat airplane fuselage as the control car. (Courtesy of the US Naval History and Heritage Command, NH 72906)

as a trainer. Many of the pilots trained on the B-class went on to duty at American naval air stations in Europe, flying European-built airships. The Navy ordered a contract for 16 B-class airships on March 19, 1917, which was fulfilled with the delivery of the last B-1 airship in June 1918.

Improvements made to the B-class resulted in the construction of the C-class. Modifications to the series provided increased endurance for longer on-station time for convoy and patrol duties, more power for additional speed to handle headwinds, and more power reliability with the addition of twin engines. It also had a much larger lift capacity, which enabled a more significant load of depth charges carried in its anti-submarine warfare role. The Navy contracted Goodyear and Goodrich to build 30 of the C-class. However, only a few of the C-class were completed before the Armistice. The first C-class made its maiden flight on September 30, 1918, and was delivered to the Navy on October 22 after flying nonstop from Akron to Anacostia, DC; it refueled, and then continued to NAS Rockaway, New York.

US Navy Aeronautic Station, Pensacola, Florida. Inflation of a free balloon, circa 1916. Kite and dirigibles operated along the eastern seaboard. (Courtesy of Mr. D. M. McPherson, Corte Madera, California, 1972; US Naval History and Heritage Command, NH 76001)

Britain and France led LTA in connecting bodies of water, such as the English Channel and the Bay of Biscay. Those operations meant there were two theaters of operations: primarily the eastern seaboard of the United States and European waters. Convoy duty was the connecting link between the two and was largely covered by LTAs. On the eastern seaboard of the Americas, LTA was operational at naval air stations: Chatham (non-rigid airship and kite balloon), Key West (non-rigid airship and kite balloon), Cape May (non-rigid airship), Montauk (non-rigid airship and kite balloon), Coco Solo (kite balloon), Pensacola (non-rigid airship and kite balloon), Hampton Roads (non-rigid airship and kite balloon), Rockaway (non-rigid airship and kite balloon), and Halifax (kite balloon). Meanwhile, the air station at Akron was devoted exclusively to training, and NAS Pensacola was primarily used for training, with a brief period during the war when its secondary mission involved some operational patrolling. NAS Hampton Roads served as a training and experimental station during the early part of the war, later becoming a vital patrol station for seaplanes and LTA.[4]

Approximately 170 individuals were trained as pilots of the B-1 airship. The total number of regular naval students trained for dirigibles and as free balloon pilots was 57 and 12, respectively. In addition, civilian and naval instructors trained pilots to operate 205 dirigibles, 222 kites, and free balloons at Akron or Pensacola during the war.

In Britain, most American LTA operations involved personnel assigned to British units operating kite balloons, primarily to protect merchant shipping. In July 1918, most of the US LTA personnel and kite balloon equipment was transferred to NAS Brest, France, as more enemy submarines were operating in the Bay of Biscay. The first contingent of dirigible pilots arrived in Europe in November 1917, beginning LTA operations there. The French bases at Brest, Paimboeuf, Guipavas, Gujan, La Pallice, and La Trinite became US naval air stations for LTA activities. Several additional air stations were planned, but they never materialized. NAS Paimboeuf was the most significant station for dirigibles. There, Lieutenant Frederic P. Culbert, Naval Aviator No. 95, and three other personnel received flying instruction in French dirigibles. On January 4, 1918, Maxfield arrived to take command of the American detachment. The French Astra Torres sent an airship (AT-1) on January 30 from Rochefort, with Americans comprising part of the crew. That was followed on February 3 by the French Zodiac Vedette dirigible (VZ-3). American naval personnel began patrolling on February 24, 1918, while the airships and air stations were still under French control. Paimboeuf was established as an American naval air station on March 1, 1918. Lieutenant Commander Maxfield was designated CO; Lieutenant Culbert was the executive officer, and six members of the first LTA class from Akron were assigned as pilots there.

The AT-1, under American control, made its first flight on March 3, 1918. On March 20, the French transferred the VZ-3 to American control. NAS Paimboeuf engaged in a variety of operations with its assigned dirigibles. Besides patrol duties and training, the air station performed experimental

Lieutenant Commander Zachary Lansdowne, photographed on July 7, 1919, following his arrival at Mineola, New York, on board the British airship R-34, which had flown to the United States from the United Kingdom. (Courtesy of the US Naval History and Heritage Command, 48388)

The first lot of pilots, instructors, and mechanics at Cranwell, England, during World War One. (Part of the US Naval Aviation French Unit Collection; US Naval History and Heritage Command, UA 80.02.04)

work. On June 9, the AT-1 tested a submarine listening device. The Assistant Secretary of the Navy, F. D. Roosevelt, visited the station on August 17, 1918 and made a flight on the AT-1. On October 1, 1918, another of the airships under American control, the AT-13, encountered a German submarine during patrol operations. The airship had escorted a southbound convoy from Brest and then returned to its patrol area. En route, the AT-13 conducted practice shots with its 47mm gun. The firing spring broke on firing a second round, and the gun was out of commission. However, the airship continued to its patrol station. The AT-13 picked up a northbound convoy and began providing escort coverage. The airship left the convoy for a short time to avoid an approaching storm, and it was during this time its crew sighted a U-boat. The submarine immediately fired on the airship. There was no damage, and unable to return fire because of its inoperable gun, it rejoined the convoy to warn them of the submarine's presence and reassumed its escort duties. The airships out of Paimboeuf continued their patrols during the remainder of the war, but

Naval personnel at Guipavas, France, waiting to tie down an airship. (Courtesy of the Naval History and Heritage Command, NRL16177)

Astra-Torres airship, AT-13, preparing for flight at NAS Paimboeuf with Assistant Secretary of the Navy Franklin D. Roosevelt. (Part of the US Naval Aviation French Unit Collection; courtesy of the US Naval History and Heritage Command, UA 80.02.50)

Hangar and a kite balloon at the La Trinite air station. (Courtesy of the US Naval History and Heritage Command, UA 80.02.41)

no other submarines were sighted. The effectiveness, or ineffectiveness, of LTAs in European waters is open to debate as the appearance of LTAs covering merchant shipping in the North Atlantic waters connecting to it may have kept U-boats from striking but were ineffective in identifying enemy submarines and conducting successful attacks.

Chapter 16

Impact and Legacy of Early Naval Aviation

Although the first use of the airplane in combat was during the Balkan War (1911–12), World War One entrenched an aerial arm into the militaries of every industrialized nation. Beginning barely a decade after Orville and Wilbur Wright launched the first heavier-than-air flying machine, World War One saw dramatic leaps in the development of aircraft technology: the first aircraft carrier was put to sea, a plane launched the first aerial torpedo, and aircraft assisted with convoy escorts for the first time. In the aftermath of the war, while it was clear to American naval leaders that aviation would play a significant role in the future, there was no shortage of debate over the exact nature and extent of that role. As a result, naval air operations during World War One seem insignificant in terms of the overall operations conducted during the conflict. Still, they paved the way for establishing permanence within the Navy and Marine Corps.

Admiral Fiske foresaw the future of naval aviation as a significant component of the United States Navy, especially during World War Two. The admiral envisioned and campaigned for developing a large aviation force, including arming large airplanes with torpedoes and bombs. He invented such a concept and a new type of warfare. Such a program may have succeeded if given a chance, beginning in 1914 when Europe went to war, but it is doubtful that such a plan would have proceeded. Moreover, it would have taken millions of dollars to train and equip the massive force Admiral Fiske desired – allocations that Congress would never have appropriated. Nevertheless, Fiske's concepts would be realized by the 1920s, as naval aviation began mounting torpedoes onto planes. Likewise, other nations adopted the idea, which would be used extensively by such military powers as Britain, Japan, and the United States.

Upon the United States' entry into World War One, the US Navy had one air station at Pensacola. Available for service were 48 aviators and students, along with 54 aircraft. Before World War One, the only war experience naval aviation had was with photoreconnaissance at Veracruz, Mexico, in 1914. At the date of the Armistice, naval aviation forces in Europe comprised 1,100 officers, 18,000 enlisted men, 400 planes, 50 kite balloons, and three dirigibles. It constructed 27 operating bases, some of which were enormous, distributed to cover most of the coastline of Ireland, England, France, and eastern Italy. Contemporaneous with this building of bases and expansion of personnel and equipment, the naval aviation forces in Europe made 22,000 flights, nearly 6,000 of which were combat missions. They covered almost one million miles of flying, almost wholly over the area of submarine operations.

In 1918, United States Navy seaplanes flew 40,883 hours off the continental United States on patrol duty. Patrols during the last three months of the war covered 1,305,000 nautical miles. Lighter-than-air patrols in home waters flew a total of 5,145 hours. Officially, the US Naval Air Force foreign service executed 39 attacks against enemy submarines, of which, at that time, ten were considered at least partially successful. Despite the unpreparedness in aviation, the first American force to land in Europe was the First Aeronautical Detachment, consisting of six officers and 63 enlisted men. This detachment reached France on June 5, 1917, and immediately went into training for active service. From this modest beginning, the naval air force grew steadily until, at the date of the Armistice on November 11, 1918, it included in its organization 1,147 officers and 18,308 enlisted personnel operating more than 400 aircraft, 50 kite balloons, and three dirigibles. It had to its credit a total of 22,000 flights and had patrolled over 800,000 nautical miles, with only 19 casualties.[1]

Marine Corps aviation had few aviators and planes at the beginning of its entry into World War One. As a result, Navy brass saw very little usefulness of Marine Aviation except for supplementing the Navy's seaplane program. Without Alfred Cunningham's tenacity, no First Marine Aviation Force would have existed. Moreover, the initial lack of trained aviation personnel and aircraft probably delayed the fielding of an adequate force in France for months, causing the loss of some combat effectiveness. The same can be said of the NBG, since both had to rely on British and French aircraft, and absorbed American pilots and observers to train and provide combat experience.

The Navy's demobilization process after the Armistice significantly impacted naval aviation, such as liquidating its overseas air stations in France, Britain, and Italy. However, those air stations within the continental

Post-Navy flying boat. World War One saw the first transatlantic crossing by a US NC-4 in May 1919. Albert C. Read commanded the flying boat. (Courtesy of the Naval Heritage and History Command, NH 112451)

United States remained for the most part, and by the 1920s, the rise of aircraft carriers began. Men under instruction were allowed to complete their coursework, but the assignment of new students stopped. Miami, Key West, and San Diego continued training until those on board qualified, and then reverted to the patrol mission. The LTA school at Akron and ground schools at MIT (Boston), Washington State, and Dunwoody (Minneapolis) began closing. Postwar plans were approved, calling for the return of all flight training to Pensacola, and the concentration of technical training at Great Lakes. Officers and men of the Reserve Flying Corps were released to inactive duty as rapidly as possible.

The Navy saw an overall decrease in personnel from 530,338 in 1918 to approximately 94,000 by 1923. When Captain Thomas T. Craven became Director of Naval Aviation in May 1919, only 669 officers and 7,100 enlisted men remained in naval aviation. Some naval flight personnel chose to stay

Aerial torpedo testing became an essential aspect of the postwar US Navy. A Curtiss F-5L torpedo test drops a 1,000lb dummy torpedo in tests conducted by the Naval Aircraft Factory, Philadelphia, November 28, 1918. The facility in the background appears to be the Hog Island Shipyard. (Courtesy of the US Naval History and Heritage Command, NH 44237)

In the aftermath of World War One, the collier *Jupiter* was converted into the US Navy's first aircraft carrier, and *Langley* (CV-1) was recommissioned on March 20, 1922. (Courtesy of the US Naval History and Heritage Command, NH 63546)

in the service, later transferring to the USN, as provided by law. Many of those who went home became active in the Naval Reserve when it began reorganizing in the 1920s. Many, whether in the reserve or not, returned to active duty to serve with distinction during World War Two.

The military demobilization after World War One nearly eliminated Marine Corps aviation with a reduction of more than half its size, going from a personnel strength of 2,462 to 1,020. However, permanent air stations were established at Quantico, Parris Island, and San Diego. Remarkably, the brief experience of Marine Aviation in World War One marked a starting point for its increased involvement in supporting ground operations. Major Cunningham as CO of the NBG's Day Wing, and Colonel John A. Lejeune as CO of the 4th Marine Brigade and the Army's 2nd Infantry Division during the war, envisioned the integration of Marine Aviation with ground forces. The lessons learned in World War One provided the initial framework from which the Marine Corps planned to support its ground forces, and the development of the amphibious doctrine in World War Two.

Naval and Marine Corps planes in Nicaragua, circa 1928. They supported Marine ground forces during the Nicaraguan civil war. Note the DH-4HT has the Army serial number 38332. (From the Alfred A. Cunningham Collection [COLL/3034] at the Archives Branch, Marine Corps History Division)

Counterinsurgency operations conducted by US armed forces during the "Banana Wars" in Cuba, Haiti, Honduras, Nicaragua, and the Dominican Republic were instrumental in establishing the permanence of the Marine Corps aviation section. Although those interventions were in the future, men such as Alfred Cunningham would lead the fight to develop, maintain, and expand Marine Aviation during the postwar years. It was the incursions in those countries where the concept of close air support came to fruition, with Major Cunningham initially conceiving the idea. That concept became a valuable tactic of Marine Aviation during amphibious landings in World War Two. The golden age of naval and Marine Corps aviation would follow during the 1920s and '30s. Still, by 1941, as in World War One, the United States military would initially be unprepared for another worldwide conflict.

One final note: those who served in aviation units during World War One had sons who fought in the air in during World War Two; only one generation separated the two.

Appendix A

Course of Instruction for Naval Aviators, Dated May 1, 1917

1. In accordance with the department's order of 10 April, 1913, the following instructions for the training of officers and enlisted men for the Air Service are issued:

    (a) Classes of officers and men to be trained for the Air Service will be detailed every three months beginning 1 January, 1916.
    (b) The course of instruction will not exceed 2 years for officers and 18 months for enlisted men.
    (c) Only officers and men who hold certificates of qualification as herein prescribed or have heretofore qualified will be eligible to detail for duty in aircraft in actual service. -
    (d) The classes of officers will be composed of eight-line officers. The officers must have served at least two years in seagoing ships.
    (e) An officer desiring instruction in aeronautics must make official application and pass the physical examination prescribed by the Bureau of Medicine and Surgery. The senior officer present will at once have applicants examined physically.
    (f) The classes of enlisted men will be composed of:
       Eight chief petty officers, seaman branch.

      Two chief petty officers, preferably machinist's mates.
      Two petty officers, first class, preferably carpenter's mates.
      Two petty officers second class, preferably electrician's or gunner's mates.
      Two seamen

(g) Enlisted men, to be eligible for this duty, must have had at least two years' service in a seagoing ship, must be under forty years of age.

(h) The eight chief petty officers of the seaman branch will be trained to steer aircraft and will be required to pass the same physical examination required of officers detailed to aeronautic duty. The remainder of each class will be trained in handling aircraft machinery.

(i) The commander in chief, Atlantic Fleet, will select these classes of enlisted men, and all requests for upon requests for instruction in aeronautics if away from an Atlantic home port and facilities exist for carrying on the instructions under his command.

(j) Officers detailed for aeronautic duty will be classed as, viz.
    Student naval aviators
    Naval aviators.
    Navy air pilot aeroplane.
    Navy air pilots, dirigible.
    Military aviator.

(k) Enlisted men detailed for aeronautic duty will be classed as, viz:
    Student airmen.
    Airmen.
    Quartermasters, aeroplane.
    Quartermasters, dirigible.
    Machinists, aeronautics.

Appendix B
Major Naval Aircraft Production Models (1916–18)

Model	Number Built
Aeromarine 39A/B	50
Aeromarine 40F	50
Boeing C-1	51
Curtiss F5	144
Curtiss F5-L	198
Curtiss F-5MF	102
Curtiss N-9/H9	560
Curtiss R-6	76
Curtiss HS-1L/Curtiss HS-2L	1,092
Curtiss H-12 or Model 6A	104
Curtiss H-16 or Model 6C	334

Appendix C

US Naval Air and Marine Corps Stations

World War One Naval Air Stations

Akron, Ohio: Lighter-than-air training

Anacostia, DC: Experimental station

Bay Shore, Long Island: Elementary flying school, and emergency patrol station

Brunswick, Georgia: Patrol station

Cape May, New Jersey: Patrol station

Chatham, Massachusetts: Patrol station

Dunwoody Institute: Ground school

Great Lakes, Illinois: Mechanics school

Hampton Roads, Virginia: Experimental and patrol station

Key West, Florida: Elementary flying school

Marginal Parkway, New York: Supply station

Massachusetts Institute of Technology: Ground school

Miami (Dinner Key), Florida: Elementary flight station and patrol station

Miami (Curtiss Field), Florida: Marine Corps landplane training station

Montauk, Long Island: Patrol station

Morehead City, North Carolina: Patrol station

North Sydney, Nova Scotia: Patrol station

Pensacola, Florida: Advanced ground and flight school

Philadelphia, Pennsylvania: Naval aircraft factory manufacturing plant

Rockaway, Long Island, New York: Patrol station
San Diego, California: Elementary flying station
The University of Washington: Ground school

World War One Marine Corps Air Stations

Marine Flying Field, Miami, Florida
Balloon Company, Marine Barracks, Quantico, Virginia
Naval Base No. 13, Azores
Marine Flying Field, Philadelphia, Pennsylvania
Naval Air Station, Cape May, New Jersey
Naval Air Station, Pensacola, Florida
Hazelhurst Field Mineola, Long Island
Gerstner Field, Lake Charles, Louisiana
Army Balloon Schools at St. Louis, Missouri, and Omaha, Nebraska

Appendix D

Overseas Naval Air Stations

Commissioned stations include training, patrol, assembly, and repair, and where American naval personnel were assigned.

Arcachon, France
Brest, France
Calais, France
Champagne, France
Bolsena, Italy
Cazaux, France
Coco Solo, Canal Zone patrol station, Panama
Camp Borden, Canada
Castletownbere, Ireland
Dunkerque, France
Eastleigh, England
Felixstowe, England
Fromentine, France
Great Yarmouth, England
Guînes, France
Hourtin, France
Île-Tudy, France
Killingholme, England
L'Aber Vrach, France
Le Croisic, France
Lough Foyle, Ireland

Moutchic, France
North Sydney, Nova Scotia, Canada
Oyé, France
Paimboeuf, France
Pauillac, France
Portland, England
Porto Corsini, Italy
Queenstown, Ireland
Saint-Inglevert, France
Saint-Raphaël, France
Saint-Trojan-les-Bains, France
Stonehenge, England
Tours, France
Tréguier, France
University of Toronto, Canada
Wexford, Ireland
Whiddy Island, Ireland

Selected Bibliography

Government Publications

Center of Military History, *Order of Battle of the United States Land Forces in the World War: American Expeditionary Forces: Divisions*, vol. 2, Center of Military History: Washington, DC (1988)

Gorrell, Edgar S., *Gorrell's History of the American Expeditionary Forces Air Service, 1917-1919*, US Army Air Service Information Section: Washington, DC (1921)

Headquarters, Northern Bombing Group, US Naval Aviation Forces, Autingues, France, "The Facts Concerning Any Flights or Combats Participated in by Captain Edmund G. Chamberlain, US Marine Corps, on July 27 and 29, 1918." Record of Proceedings of a Court of Inquiry (November 25, 1918)

Johnson, Edward C., *Marine Aviation: The Early Years 1912-1940*, History and Museums Division, Headquarters Marine Corps: Washington, DC (1977)

Marine Corps History Division, Marine Corps University, "Muster Rolls of 1st Squadron, B Squadron, and C Squadron, August-November 1918." (microfilm)

Marine Corps History Division, Marine Corps University, "Muster Rolls of 1st Air Squadron, 1919-1923." (microfilm)

Marine Corps History Division, Marine Corps University, "Muster Rolls of Aircraft Squadrons, Second Brigade 1927-1928." (microfilm)

McClellan, Edwin N., *The United States Marine Corps in the World War*, Washington Government Printing Office: Washington, DC (1920)

Mersky, Peter, *US Naval Air Reserve. Deputy Chief of Naval Operations (Air Warfare) and the Commander*, Naval Air Systems Command: Washington, DC (1987)

Navy Department Office of Naval Intelligence, Historical Section, *Publication Number 7: The American Naval Planning Section London*, Published under the direction of The Hon. Edwin Denby, Secretary of the Navy, Washington Government Printing Office: Washington, DC (1923)

Navy Department Office of Naval Records and Library, Historical Section, *Publication Number 1: German Submarine Activities on the Atlantic Coast of the United States and Canada*, Published under the direction of The Hon. Josephus Daniels Secretary of the Navy, Washington Government Printing Office: Washington, DC (1920)

Sitz, W. H., *A History of US Naval Aviation (Bureau of Aeronautics Technical Note No. 18, Series of 1930*, United States Government Printing Office: Washington, DC (1930)

The American Naval Planning Section in London, *Memorandum No. 12: Further Development of United States Naval Air Effort in European Waters* (February 15, 1918)

Published Diaries, Letters, Memoirs

Cunningham, Alfred A., *Marine Flyer in France*, "The Diary of Captain Alfred A. Cunningham. November 1917–January 1918." Graham Cosmos, ed., History and Museums Division, Headquarters Marine Corps: Washington, DC (1974)

Day, Karl S., "Oral History Program," (January 1, 1973)

Ingalls, David S., "Hero of the Angry Sky: The World War I Diary and Letters of David S. Ingalls, America's First Naval Ace," Geoffrey L. Rossano, ed., Ohio University Press: Athens (2013)

Rossano, Geoffrey L., ed., "The Price of Honor: The World War One Letters of Naval Aviator Kenneth MacLeish," Naval Institute Press: Annapolis (1991)

Published Aviation History

Arthur, Reginald Wright, *Contact! Careers of US Naval Aviators Assigned Numbers 1 to 2000* (Vol. I), Naval Aviator Register: Washington, DC (1967)

De Chant, John A., *Devilbirds: The Story of United States Marine Corps Aviation in World War II*, Harper & Brothers Publishers: New York and London (1947)

Coletta, Paolo E., *Patrick N. L. Bellinger and Naval Aviation*, University Press of America: Lanham, New York, London (1987)

Hudson, James J., *In Clouds of Glory: American Airmen Who Flew with the British During the Great War*, The University of Arkansas Press: Fayetteville (1990)

Layman, R. D., *Naval Aviation in the First World War: Its Impact and Influence*, US Naval Institute Press: Annapolis (1996)

Morton, John Fass., *Mustin: A Naval Family of the 20th Century*, Naval Institute Press: Annapolis (2003)

Naval Aviation War Book Committee, *Flying Officers of the USN*, Washington DC (1919)

Paine, Ralph D., *The First Yale Unit: A Story of Aviation 1916-1919* (Vol. I), Riverside Press: Cambridge (1925)

Paine, Ralph D., *The First Yale Unit: A Story of Aviation 1916-1919* (Vol. II), Riverside Press: Cambridge (1925)

Reynolds, Clark G., *Admiral John H. Towers: The Struggle for Naval Air Supremacy*, Naval Institute Press: Annapolis (1991)

Rossano, Geoffrey L., *Stalking the U-Boat: US Naval Aviation in Europe During World War I*, University Press of Florida: Gainesville (2010)

Treadwell, Terry C., *America's First Air War: The US Army, Naval and Marine Air Services in the First World War*, Airlife: Shrewsbury (2000)

Turnbull, Archibald, and Clifford Lord, *History of United States Naval Aviation*, Yale University Press: New Haven (1949)

Van Deurs, George, Admiral (Ret.), *Anchors in the Sky: Spuds Ellyson the First Naval Aviator*, Presidio Press: San Rafael, California (1978)

Van Deurs, George, Admiral (Ret.), *Wings for the Fleet*, United States Naval Institute: Annapolis (1966)

Van Dyke, Adrian O., and the editors of *Naval Aviation News*. *Naval Aviation in World War I*, Chief of Naval Operations: Washington, DC (1969)

Woodhouse, Henry, *Text Book of Naval Aeronautics*, The Century Company: New York (1917)

Wortman, Marc, *The Millionaires' Unit: The Aristocratic Flyboys Who Fought the Great War and Invented American Airpower*, Public Affairs: New York (2006)

Yockelson, Mitchell A., *Borrowed Soldiers. Americans Under British Command, 1918*, University of Oklahoma Press: Norman (2008)

Journal and Periodical Articles

Anonymous, "Marine Downs Five Planes in One Day," *The Recruiters' Bulletin*, p. 10 (September 1918)

Anonymous, "Not a Princeton Man," *Princeton Alumni Weekly*, vol. 21, no. 6, p. 138 (November 10, 1920)

Anonymous, "Marine Aviation, a Record of Achievement," *Marine Corps Gazette*, vol. 15, no. 3, pp. 33–39 (November 1930)

Boggs, Jr., Charles W., "Marine Corps Aviation: Origin and Growth," *Marine Corps Gazette*, vol. 34, no. 11, pp. 68–75 (November 1950)

Burke II, Laurence Mitchell, "Water Wings: The Early Years of Navy and Marine Corps Aviation," New Interpretations in Naval History: Selected Papers from the Symposium Held at the United States Naval Academy, pp. 23–37 (September 10–11, 2009)

Cunningham, Alfred A., "Aviation in the Navy," *Marine Corps Gazette*, vol. 1, no. 4, pp. 333–42 (December 1916)

Cunningham, Alfred A., "Value of Aviation to the Marine Corps," *Marine Corps Gazette*, vol. 5, no. 3, pp. 221–33 (September 1920)

Camp, Dick, "Rugged Roy Geiger and the Northern Bombing Group," *Leatherneck*, vol. 89, no. 5, pp. 34–38 (May 2006)

De Chant, John A., "Marine Aviation Observers in Africa and Europe," *Marine Corps Gazette*, vol. 30, no. 7 (July 1946)

Edwards, W. Atlee, "The US Naval Air Force in Action 1917-18," *Proceedings*, pp. 1,863–882, United States Naval Institute (November 1922)

Emmons, Roger M., "The First Marine Aviation Force," *Cross and Cockade Journal*, pp. 173–86 (summer 1965)

Emmons, Roger M., "The First Marine Aviation Force," *Cross and Cockade Journal*, pp. 272–92 (fall 1965)

Emmons, Roger M., "Marine Combat Squadrons in WWI," *Marine Corps Gazette*, vol. 60, no. 2, pp. 79–80 (November 1978)

Ford Walter G., "The US Marines in World War I: The US Marine Corps," *Marine Corps History*, pp. 17–30 (summer 1916)

Halstead, J. Sterling., "Trained by the Royal Flying Corps," *Proceedings*, pp. 26–29, US Naval Institute (February 1965)

McClellan, Edwin N., "The Birth and Infancy of Marine Aviation," *Marine Corps Gazette*, vol. 15, no. 5, pp. 11–13 and 43–44 (May 1931)

McClellan, Edwin N., "Marine Corps Aviation," *Marine Corps Gazette*, vol. 16, no. 2, pp. 56–59 (August 1931)

McClellan, Edwin N., "Marine Corps Aviation," *Marine Corps Gazette*, vol. 16, no. 4, pp. 45–49 (February 1932)

Morris, Michael J., "Combat Effectiveness: United States Marine Corps Aviation in the First World War," *Over the Front*, vol. 12, no. 3, pp. 232–38 (fall 1997)

Robb, Izetta Winter, "Navy's First Ace," *Naval Aviation News*, pp. 82–83 (1969)

Websites and Digital Articles

Marine Corps History Division. "End Strengths." Marine Corps University, https://www.usmcu.edu/Research/Marine-Corps-History-Division/Research-Tools-Facts-and-Figures/End-Strengths/ (accessed December 18, 2022)

Naval History and Heritage Command. https://www.history.navy.mil (accessed June 12, 2020)

Selected Bibliography

Simmons, Brigadier General Edwin H. (Ret.), "Marines Over the Western Front." *Naval History Magazine*, vol. 20, no. 3 (June 2006) https://www.usni.org/magazines/naval-history-magazine/2006/june/marines-over-western-front (accessed on July 16, 2022)

Evans, Mark L., "Performed All Their Duties Well," Naval History Magazine, vol. 23, no. 5 (October 2009) https://www.usni.org/magazines/naval-history-magazine/2009/october/performed-all-their-duties-well (accessed December 15, 2021)

Cavagnaro, Major Dennis A. (Ret.), "Devil Dog of the Air," *Leatherneck* (October 1991) https://www.worldwar1centennial.org/index.php/usmc-in-ww1/851-devil-dog-of-the-air-sam-richards.html (accessed January 2022)

World War I Diary of Charles Fahy, The Historical Society of the District of Columbia, https://dcchs.org/sb_pdf/fahy-wwi-diaries-final/ (accessed June 21, 2022)

Poague, Walter S., *Diaries and Letters of a Marine Aviator*, https://archive.org/details/diarylettersofma00poag/page/n15/mode/2up (accessed June 8, 2022)

A Few Pioneers: 1896–1916, https://www.history.navy.mil/content/dam/nhhc/research/publications/1910/1%20Chapter1.pdf (accessed March 17, 2020)

Lindley, John M., "A History of Sea-Air Aviation," *Naval Aviation News*, https://www.history.navy.mil/research/histories/naval-aviation-history/a-history-of-sea-air-aviation-wings-over-the-ocean.html.

Ray, Thomas, "Naval Aviation: The Beginning." *Proceedings*, vol 97, no.1, https://www.usni.org/magazines/proceedings/1971/january/naval-aviation-beginning

"The History of Naval Aviator and Naval Aviation Pilot Designations and Numbers, The Training of Naval Aviators and the Number Trained (Designated)," *United States Naval Aviation 1910–1995*, https://www.history.navy.mil/content/dam/nhhc/research/histories/naval-aviation/Aviation%20Appendices/APP01.PDF (accessed July 15, 2021)

"The American Naval Planning Section in London," Publication No. 7 (1923) https://www.history.navy.mil/research/library/online-reading-room/title-list-alphabetically/a/american-naval-planning-section-london.html (accessed February 2022)

Unpublished Theses and Dissertations

Amerman, Annette Dee, "Integration of US Marine Corps Aviation with the Royal Air Force in First World War: Legacy and Impact," Master's thesis, University of Birmingham (2018)

Ritchie, Matthew T., "The Influence of Marine Aviation on the Development of the Tentative Landing Operations Manual," Master's thesis, Elon University (2001)

Notes

Chapter 1

1. Laurence Mitchell Burke II, BS, MA Dissertation. "What to do with the Airplane? Determining the Role of the Airplane in the US Army, Navy, and Marine Corps, 1908-1925".
2. See, A Few Pioneers, 1896-1916, p. 2. See https://www.history.navy.mil/content/dam/nhhc/research/publications/1910/1%20Chapter1.pdf
3. Cowle's request originated from a report by Sweet, which outlined the specifications for aircraft. See Dissertation of Lance Mitchell Brooke II.
4. By this time, Metcalf had resigned and was replaced by Truman Newberry. Source: Dissertation of Lance Mitchell Brooke II.
5. John M. Lindley, "A History of Sea-Air Aviation: Wings Over the Ocean," *Naval Aviation News*. See https://www.history.navy.mil/research/histories/naval-aviation-history/a-history-of-sea-air-aviation-wings-over-the-ocean.html.
6. Ibid.
7. Burke II, "What to do with the airplane? Determining the role of the airplane in the US Army, Navy and Marine Corps, 1908-1925," p. 237.
8. George van Deurs, *Wings for the Fleet*. Annapolis, Maryland, p. 14 (1966).
9. Admiral Dewey became an ardent supporter of naval aviation until his death in 1917.
10. Irving Chambers, "Aviation and Aeroplanes," *Proceedings*, p. 180, United States Naval Institute (March 1911).
11. Ibid.
12. John Alexander Douglas McCurdy, with the support of Curtiss, attempted to take off from the ocean liner *Kaiserin Auguste Victoria*

on November 9, 1910, but was unsuccessful. See *Hero of the Air*, *The World War I Diary and Letters of David S. Ingalls, America's First Naval Ace*, Ohio University Press, pp. 99–100.
13. Ibid., pp. 98–99.
14. Van Deurs. *Wings for the Fleet*, p. 15.

Chapter 2

1. Admiral George van Deurs, *Wings for the Fleet*, Naval Institute Press: Annapolis, Maryland, p. 17 (1966). Curtiss told both men that it was too dangerous.
2. Ibid., p. 18.
3. Ibid., p. 19.
4. Thomas Ray, "Naval Aviation: The Beginning," *Proceedings*, vol 97, no.1 (1971). See https://www.usni.org/magazines/proceedings/1971/january/naval-aviation-beginning.
5. The primary source for the Navy's disinterest can be found in "A History of Sea-Air Aviation" by John M. Lindley in *Naval Aviation News*.
6. Ibid.
7. Ray, "Naval Aviation: The Beginning."
8. Van Duers, *Wings for the Fleet*, pp. 28–29.
9. Ray, "Naval Aviation: The Beginning."
10. Laurence Mitchell Burke II, BS, MA, "What to do with the Airplane? Determining the Role of the Airplane in the US Army, Navy, and Marine Corps, 1908-1925." See, A Few Pioneers, 1896-1916.
11. Ray, "Naval Aviation: The Beginning."
12. Ibid.
13. Ibid.
14. Burke II, "What to do with the Airplane? Determining the Role of the Airplane in the US Army, Navy, and Marine Corps, 1908-1925." See, A Few Pioneers, 1896-1916. p. 246.
15. William W. Trimble. *Hero of the Air: Glenn Curtiss and the Birth of Naval Aviation*. Naval Institute Press: Annapolis, p. 103 (2012)

Chapter 3

1. Admiral George van Deurs, *Anchors in the Sky: Spuds Ellyson the First Naval Aviator,* Presidio Press: San Rafael, pp. 54-55 (1978)
2. Ibid., pp. 54–55.
3. Ibid., p. 102.
4. Irving Chambers, "Aviation and Aeroplanes." *Proceedings* (March 1911).
5. Chambers, "Aviation and Aeroplanes."
6. Van Deurs, *Anchors in the Sky*, p. 83.
7. Ibid.
8. Thomas Ray, "Naval Aviation: The Beginning," *Proceedings*, vol. 97, no.1 (1971).
9. Ibid.
10. Chambers, "Aviation and Aeroplanes."
11. Ibid.
12. William B. Trimble, *Hero of the Air: Glenn Curtiss and the Birth of Naval Aviation,* Naval Institute Press: Annapolis, p. 112 (2010)
13. Ibid., p. 113. Ellyson suggested to Chambers that North Island be purchased for naval aviation, p. 115.
14. Amphibian aircraft remained in the Navy and Coast Guard inventory until the late 1950s and '60s, operating such aircraft as the HU-16 Albatross.
15. The A-2 was converted to a landplane; afterward, it had floats and landing gear attached and became known as the OWL (over water and land).
16. Early aviators were initially issued ACA certificates and given naval aviator numbers retroactively based on their reporting date to the aviation school.
17. Trimble. *Hero of the Air*, p. 131.
18. Paolo E. Coletta, *Patrick N. L. Bellinger and Naval Aviation*, University Press of America: Lanham, New York, London, p. 52 (1987).
19. Ellyson and Towers soon taught Richardson, who was given ACA certificate number 174 on October 15, 1912.
20. Van Deurs, *Anchors in the Sky*, pp. 117–19.

21. See '"What to do with the Airplane?': Determining the role of the airplane in the US Army, Navy and Marine Corps, 1908-1925" for a more concise history of Chambers versus pilots, pp. 255–6.
22. Ibid., p. 140.
23. Another contemptuous event occurred between Chambers, Ellyson, Lawrence Sperry, and the latter's father. Lawrence, a 17-year-old mechanical genius, invented an airplane gyro stabilizer – a form of automatic pilot. Ellyson supported the invention, but Captain Chambers did not. Indeed, according to Spuds, the captain was "most insulting to both Sperrys." Spuds sent Lawrence to work with Curtiss in San Diego.

Chapter 4

1. Colonel Joseph A. Alexander, "Close Air Support: The Pioneering Years," November 19, 2012, https://news.usni.org/2012/11/19/close-air-support-pioneering-years.
2. There have been several calls to disband the Marine Corps over the years.
3. Laurence Mitchell Burke II, BS, MA Dissertation, "What to do with the Airplane? Determining the Role of the Airplane in the US Army, Navy, and Marine Corps, 1908-1925." See, A Few Pioneers, 1896-1916. p. 60.
4. Burke II, "What to do with the airplane?" pp. 261–62.
5. Ibid., p. 262.
6. Two of the three men assigned to aviation training in 1912 were Marines – Cunningham and Bernard Smith – the other being Vic Herbster of the Navy. Cunningham soloed on August 20, 1912, operating the Wright B-1, nicknamed the "Bat Boat."
7. Annette Dee Amerman, "Integration of US Marine Corps Aviation with the Royal Air Force in First World War: Legacy and Impact," Master's thesis, University of Birmingham, p. 62 (2018).
8. Cunningham had to give up flying in August 1913 at the request of his fiancée.
9. Smith would remain on active duty until January 1920, when he took a position with Pan American Airways. He returned to the Marines as

Notes

a reservist in 1931, staying in that capacity until 1946. He was killed in an automobile crash in 1947.

10. Smith was to take over the A-1 but Ellyson demolished it and it was scrapped.
11. Clark G. Reynolds, *Admiral John H. Towers: The Struggle for Naval Air Supremacy*, Naval Institute Press: Annapolis, p. 59 (1991).
12. He continued to be assigned to shipboard duty, serving through the World War One. He returned to naval duty aboard the seaplane tender Wright (AV-1) and then as the executive officer aboard the Lexington (CV-2). He was killed in an airplane crash on February 27, 1928, on his 43rd birthday.

Chapter 5

1. Reynolds, *Admiral John H. Towers: The Struggle for Naval Air Supremacy*, Naval Institute Press, p. 46 (1991).
2. Ibid., p. 48.
3. There were differences between Chambers other aviators as well. See *Anchors in the Sky*, those included that Chambers was a non-flyer, Ellyson was grounded and was attached to Chambers as his aide, and there were differences in policy, to name a few, pp. 148–51.
4. Ibid., p. 151.
5. See *Patrick N. L. Bellinger and US Naval Aviation* by Paolo Colleta for a detailed look at his life as an aviator. He was known to be a troublemaker during his early years as an aviator. In one instance at Guantanamo, he became drunk and jumped into the water from a warship in an effort to reach the aviation camp, pp. 56–57.
6. Reynolds, *Admiral John H. Towers*, p. 54. On February 7, 1913, Bellinger broke several altitude records with the A-3.
7. Reginald Wright Arthur, *Contact! Careers of US Naval Aviators Assigned Numbers 1 to 2000* (Vol. 1), Naval Aviator Register: Washington, DC, pp. 520–21 (1967). Lieutenant (jg) James M. Murray, Naval Aviator No. 10, was killed on February 16, 1914, flying the D-1 when the plane crashed into Pensacola Bay.

8. Reynolds, *Admiral John H. Towers* Towers, pp. 66–67.
9. The term "bumpy air" was used to describe updraft, downdraft, and turbulence during the early years of aviation.
10. Robert Sherrod, "Marine Corps Aviation: The Early Years," *Marine Corps Gazette*, vol. 16, no. 4, p. 55 (May 1953)
11. Mustin would face allegations as commanding officer of NAS Pensacola for over $1m in damages to the station on October 18, 1916. Officials additionally accused him of inappropriate flying instructions, which were deemed a contributing factor to the death of Lieutenant (jg) Richard Saufley. His naval aviator designation was revoked on January 30, 1917. He would become the the first assistant chief of BuAer in September 1921. He died at the Naval Hospital, Newport, Rhode Island, on August 23, 1923.
12. Annette Dee Amerman, "Integration of US Marine Corps Aviation with the Royal Air Force in First World War: Legacy and Impact." Master's thesis, University of Birmingham, p.69 (2018).
13. Richardson graduated from the Naval Academy in 1901.
14. Mark L. Evans, "Performed All Their Duties Well." *Naval History Magazine* (October 2009)
15. Ibid.
16. Ibid.
17. Paolo E. Coletta, *Patrick N. L. Bellinger and Naval Aviation*. University Press of America: Lanham, New York, London, pp. 72–73 (1987).
18. John A. De Chant, *Devilbirds: The Story of United States Marine Corps Aviation in World War II*, Harper & Brothers Publishers: New York and London, p. 3 (1947).

Chapter 6

1. Alexander Graham Bell, "Preparedness for Aerial Defense," and address delivered before the Eleventh Annual Convention of the Navy League of the United States, Washington, DC, April 10–13, 1916.
2. Ibid.

Notes

3. W. Atlee Edwards, Lieutenant Commander USN, "The US Naval Air Force in Action 1917-18," US Naval Institute: Annapolis, pp. 1,865–866 (1922).
4. Ibid., p. 1,866.
5. Source: Captain Mark L. Bristol, Director of Naval Aeronautics to Rear Admiral Victor Blue, Chief of Bureau of Navigation.
6. Anonymous, "Marine Corps Aviation, a Record of Achievement," *Marine Corps Gazette*, vol. 15, no. 3, p. 37 (November 1930).
7. When war broke out in 1917, he returned to the US for duty on naval operations; he then established the Navy's school for aerial gunnery and bomb dropping at Miami before leaving again for Paris. In 1919 he helped build the NCs, which flew the Atlantic, but the Navy kept him from making the flight. He resigned from the Marine Corps in 1920 but returned to service as a lieutenant commander in the Naval Reserve in 1931 (at which time the Marine Corps was accepting no reserve officers). In 1937, B. L. Smith returned to the Marine Corps. In World War Two, as a lieutenant colonel, he set up the Marine Corps barrage balloon program and later served as naval attaché in Central America. He was killed in an automobile accident at Coral Gables, Florida, on December 2, 1946; Robert Sherrod, "Marine Corps Aviation: The Early Years," *Marine Corps Gazette*, vol. 16, no. 4, p. 54 (May 1953).
8. In January 1915, McIlvain was the only Marine left at the Navy flying school. It was at this time the Marine Section, Navy Flying School was officially formed. See Adrian O. Van Wyen's *Naval Aviation in WWI*, Chief of Naval Operations: Washington, DC, p. 6 (1969)
9. Annette Dee Amerman, "Integration of US Marine Corps Aviation with the Royal Air Force in First World War: Legacy and Impact," Master's thesis, University of Birmingham, pp. 71–72 (2018)
10. Ibid.; Edwin N. McClellan, "Marine Corps Aviation," *Marine Corps Gazette*, vol. 16, no. 4, p. 45 (February 1932)
11. Edwards, "US Naval Air Force in Action," p. 1,867.

12. Ralph D. Paine, *The First Yale Unit: A Story of Naval Aviation*, Riverside Press: Cambridge, pp. 35–36 (1925).
13. Marven Matthews Smith, Lieutenant Commander, US Naval Reserve. "An Analysis of the Development and the Future of the Naval Selected Air Reserve." Submitted in partial fulfillment of the requirements for the degree of Master of Science in management, United States Naval Postgraduate School, Monterey, California, (1965).
14. Ibid.
15. Allan Ames, Naval Aviator No. 67; Henry P. Davison, Jr., Naval Aviator No. 72; John D. Farwell III, Naval Aviator No. 76; Artemus L. Gates, Naval Aviator No. 65; Erl Gould, Naval Aviator No. 68; Robert A. Lovett, Naval Aviator No. 66; Albert Sturtevant, '16; John Vorys, '18; and Yale graduate C. D. Wiman, '15. In addition, two non-Yale men, Wellesley Laud-Brown and Albert Ditman, rounded out the first dozen of the Yale First Unit.
16. The First and Second Yale Units' contribution to naval aviation in World War One has been told through an extensive series of books and articles since their formation in 1916 with Ralph D. Paine's two-volume series, *The First Yale Unit: A Story of Naval Aviation*, written in 1925, being the most extensive.
17. Ralph Paine, *The First Yale Unit: A Story of Naval Aviation 1916-1919*, Riverside Press: Cambridge (1925).
18. Marc Wortman, *The Millionaires' Unit: The Aristocratic Flyboys Who Fought the Great War and Invented American Airpower*, Public Affairs: New York, p. 80 (2006).
19. Paine, *The First Yale Unit*, p. 29.
20. Charles Beach, '18; Graham Brush, '17; Reginald Coombe, '18; David Ingalls, '20; Robert Ireland, '18; Francis Lynch, 18; Kenneth MacLeish, '19; Archibald McIlwaine, '18; Curtis Read, '18; Russell Read, '20; William A. Rockefeller, '18; Kenneth Smith, '18; W. P. Thompson, '18; C. M. Stewart, '17.
21. Paine, *The First Yale Unit*, p. 157.

Chapter 7

1. Ralph D. Paine, *The First Yale Unit: A Story of Naval Aviation 1916-1919*, Riverside Press, p. 34 (1925).
2. Rear Admiral George van Deurs, *Wings of the Fleet*, Naval Institute Press, p. 85 (1966).
3. "They left behind a trail of bitterness." See Paolo E. Coletta, *Patrick N. L. Bellinger and US Naval Aviation* (1987).
4. Ibid., p. 148.
5. There is reference that Stoltz was killed while flying an AH-8 and Stoltz was killed in AH-9 while flying at Pensacola. See "US Navy and Marine Corps Serial and Bureau Numbers 1911–present." http://www.joebaugher.com/navy_serials/navyserials.html.
6. Ibid.
7. Van Deurs, *Wings for the Fleet*, p. 150.
8. Other sources state Saufley flew an AH-8 and Stolz flew an AH-9. See US Navy and US Marine Corps Military Aircraft Serial Numbers and Bureau Numbers 1911–present, http://www.joebaugher.com/navy_serials/secondalphaseries.html.
9. Reginald Wright Arthur, *Contact! Careers of US Naval Aviators Assigned Numbers 1 to 2000* (Vol. 1), Naval Aviator Register, p. 524 (1967); Van Deurs, *Wings for the Fleet*, p. 151.
10. Clarence Bronson was killed in a premature bomb explosion in flight.
11. Van Deurs, *Wings for the Fleet*, pp. 151–4. However, the book did not fully explain the causes of accidents.
12. John Fass Morton, *Mustin: A Naval Family of the 20th Century*, Naval Institute Press, p. 108 (2003).
13. Ibid.
14. Ibid., pp. 87–9.
15. Bellinger returned to Pensacola as a test pilot setting new records. In April 1915, he set a new American altitude record for a seaplane reaching 10,000ft in one hour and 19 minutes piloting a Burgess-Dunne AH-10. In 1916, he returned to the *North Carolina* for experimental aviation

duty while Chevalier was reassigned as an inspector of seaplanes at the Burgess plant at Marblehead, Massachusetts, in 1915.
16. Captain Mark L. Bristol, Director of Aeronautics to Lieutenant Commander Henry E. Yarnell, Secretary of the Naval War College.
17. See Captain Mark L. Bristol, Director of Naval Aeronautics, to Lieutenant Commander Henry E. Yarnell, Secretary of the Naval War College, dated October 21, 1916; Also see, Clark G. Reynolds, *Admiral John H. Towers: The Struggle for Naval Air Supremacy*, Naval Institute Press, p. 95 (1991).

Chapter 8

1. Lieutenant Edward O. McDonnell may have been alluding to the period between 1914 and 1915.
2. Unknown author, "The History of Naval Aviator and Naval Aviation Pilot Designations and Numbers, The Training of Naval Aviators and the Number Trained (Designated)." See https://www.history.navy.mil/content/dam/nhhc/research/histories/naval-aviation/Aviation%20Appendices/APP01.PDF.
3. Adrian O. Van Wyen, "Naval Training at MIT," *Naval Aviation News*, p. 16 (July 1967).
4. Sterling J. Halstead, "Trained by the Royal Flying Corps," *Proceedings*, US Naval Institute, pp. 26–29 (1965); "Naval Aviation in World War I," *Naval Aviation News*, pp. 26–29 (1969).
5. Ibid.
6. "History of the Naval Aviator and Designations and Numbers," p. 199.
7. Unknown author, *Enlisted Naval Aviation Pilots*, Turner Publishing [Compiler] (1995).

Chapter 9

1. "A Few Pioneers: 1896–1916," p. 24. https://www.history.navy.mil/content/dam/nhhc/research/histories/naval-aviation/pdf/part01.pdf.
2. W. H. Sitz, Captain (USMC), *A History of US Naval Aviation*, Bureau of Aeronautics Technical Note No. 18, Series of 1930, US Government

Notes

Printing Office. The Aircraft Procurement section was extracted from the United States Navy Department Bureau of Aeronautics.

3. Ibid.

Chapter 10

1. Memorandum No. 12: "Further Development of United States Naval Air Effort in European Waters."
2. The *Deutschland* had previously arrived in the United States in June 1916 for commercial purposes and was not seen as a combative vessel. The submarine conducted a second visit to the US in November 1916.
3. Navy Department Office of Naval Records and Library, Historical Section, *Publication Number 1: German Submarine Activities on the Atlantic Coast of the United States and Canada*, pp. 8–9 (1920).
4. Jake Klim, "How a Tiny Cape Cod Town Survived World War I's Only Attack on American Soil." https://www.smithsonianmag.com/history/how-tiny-cape-cod-town-survived-world-war-is-only-attack-american-soil-180969691/.
5. The Felixstowe–Dunkerque region comprised areas between Felixstowe, England, and Dunkerque, France, as part of the Spider Web patrol sectors.
6. The American Naval Planning Section in London, Publication No. 12, p. 99 (1923). https://www.history.navy.mil/research/library/online-reading-room/title-list-alphabetically/a/american-naval-planning-section-london.html.
7. Ibid.
8. Josephus Daniels, *Our Navy at War*, Pictorial Bureau: Washington, DC, pp. 220–40 (1922).
9. Geoffrey L. Rossano (ed.), *Hero of the Angry Sky: The World War I Diary and Letters of David S. Ingalls, America's First Naval Ace*. Ohio University Press: Athens, p. 44 (2006).
10. Ibid.
11. US Naval History and Heritage Command, "US Navy Aeronautic Detachment No. 1: The First American Unit Overseas in World War I."

https://www.history.navy.mil/content/history/nhhc/browse-by-topic/wars-conflicts-and-operations/world-war-i/ships-aircraft/usn-aero-det-no-1.html.

12. W. Atlee Edwards, Lieutenant Commander USN, "The US Naval Air Force in Action 1917-18." US Naval Institute (1922).
13. Ibid., p. 1,875.
14. Miscellaneous Records of the Navy Department. Record Group 45, Roll 411, p. 10,064.
15. John B. Kneip is listed as Naval Aviator No. 2888.
16. See https://www.history.navy.mil/content/history/nhhc/research/publications/documentary-histories/wwi/february-1918/lieutenant-john-l-ca.html.
17. Miscellaneous Records of the Navy Department. Capt. Hutchinson I. Cone, a cablegram to the Office of the Chief of Naval Operations dated July 29, 1918. Source Note: Cy, DNA, RG 45, Entry 517B. In a cablegram to the Office of the Chief of Naval Operations dated July 29, 1918.
18. Ibid. Capt. Hutchinson I. Cone, a cablegram to the Office of the Chief of Naval Operations dated July 29, 1918.
19. Source Note: Cy, DNA, RG 45, Entry 517B. In a cablegram to the Office of the Chief of Naval Operations dated July 29, 1918, Capt. Hutchinson I. Cone, commander of the United Stations Naval Aviation Forces, Foreign Service, expressed similar concerns about the state of American airplanes; he raises many of the same concerns Roosevelt expresses.
20. The number of aircraft allocated can be found in *Cross and Cockade*, vol. 4, no. 1, pp. 59–60 (spring 1963).

Chapter 11

1. W. Atlee Edwards, Lieutenant Commander USN, "The US Naval Air Force in Action 1917-18," US Naval Institute (1922).
2. Naval aviator numbers if not shown in the text are unknown. Ensigns Leslie Taylor, James Nisbet (Naval Aviator No. 318), Jesse Easterwood,

Phillip Frothingham, William Gaston (Naval Aviator No. 294), and Alexander McCormick (Naval Aviator No. 123). McCormick was killed when he walked into a moving propeller. Ensign Thomas Mickinnon, Sidney Clark (Naval Aviator No. 442/800), John McMurran (Naval Aviator No. 508/791), Peter Lawson (Naval Aviator No. 875), Marcus Whitehead, Yeoman Marolon O'Gorman, and Archibald McIlwaine (Naval Aviator No. 82), with observers Randall Brown, Irving Shelly, and Sidney Huey, served with 217 Squadron. Lieutenant Charles Freddie Beach and Ensigns Joe Mosley, Charles "Chet" Bassett (Naval Aviator No. 1316), and "Babe" Johnson.

3. Ibid., p. 254. Names complied from Ralph D. Paine's *The First Yale Unit 1916-1919*, Vol. II.
4. The SPAD was a French fighter plane developed and manufactured by Société Pour L'Aviation et ses Dérivés (SPAD).
5. Ralph D. Paine, *The First Yale Unit*, pp. 89–90 (1925).
6. Charles Sheehan, "World War I Diary of Charles Fahy," The Historical Society of the District of Columbia, p. 15.
7. Ibid., pp. 19, 21.
8. Ibid., p. 23.
9. Ibid., pp. 19–26.
10. Varsenare is located in the Belgian province of West Flanders, Belgium.
11. Source: *Naval Aviation in World War I* by Adrian O. Van Wyen, historian, Deputy of Naval Operations (Air). Published by the Chief of Naval Operations: Washington, DC (1969).
12. Ibid.
13. The Rumpler C.IV was a German single-engine, two-seat reconnaissance biplane.
14. Van Wyen, "Navy's First Ace."
15. Ibid.
16. Geoffrey L. Rossano, "The Price of Honor: The World War One Letters of Naval Aviator Kenneth MacLeish," Naval Institute Press, pp. 134–35 (1991).

Chapter 12

1. Luigino Caliaro, "Waging War Goat Island City," Key Aero. https://www.key.aero/article/waging-war-goat-island-city.
2. Adrian O. Van Wyen, *Naval Aviation in World War I*, Chief of Naval Operations: Washington, DC (1969).
3. Ibid.
4. Ibid., p. 52.
5. Russell "Bart" Read, former member of the Second Yale Unit, Naval Aviator No. 78; Lieutenant Willis B. Haviland, Naval Aviator No. 577; Ensign Walter White, Naval Aviator No. 1496, awarded War Cross by Italy; Ensign Albert P. Taliaferro (pilot), Naval Aviator No. 1497; H. H. Pierce (observer); Franco British (FBA): Ensign Edward Tinkham, Naval Aviator No. 1498, awarded War Cross by Italy; Ensign Elmer "Joe" L. Johansen, Naval Aviator No. 325, awarded Navy Cross, Letter of Commendation, and Silver Life Saving Medal; Ensign James M. Grier, Naval Aviator No. 1006; Ensign George H. Ludlow, Naval Aviator No. 342. Awarded Navy Cross; Ensign Wayne "Piccoloissmo" Duffett, Naval Aviator No. 327; Ensign Austin Parker. Awarded Navy Cross.
6. Approximately 60 US naval aviators, commissioned and enlisted, died overseas due to operational mishaps, combat, and illness.
7. Ralph Paine, *The First Yale Unit: 1916-1919*, Riverside Press: Cambridge, Massachusetts, pp. 213–15 (1925).
8. Ibid.
9. Ibid., p. 217.
10. Ibid., p. 218.
11. Lieutenant Commander John L. Callan USN.R.F., commander, United States naval air forces in Italy, to Captain Hutchinson I. Cone, commander, United States naval aviation forces, foreign service US naval forces operating in European waters, US naval aviation forces, foreign service in Italy. https://www.history.navy.mil/content/history/nhhc/research/publications/documentary-histories/wwi/august-1918/lieutenant-commander.html.
12. Ralph D. Paine, *The First Yale Unit: 1916-1919*, Vol 2, p. 217.

Notes

13. Ibid., p. 221.
14. Ibid., pp. 238–9.

Chapter 13

1. Alfred Cunningham, "Value of Aviation to the Marine Corps," *Marine Corps Gazette*, vol. 5, no. 3, pp. 221–33 (1920).
2. Annette Dee Amerman, "Integration of US Marine Corps Aviation with the Royal Air Force in First World War: Legacy and Impact," Master's thesis, University of Birmingham, p. 76 (2018).
3. Alfred Cunningham, *Marine Corps Gazette*, vol 5., no. 20 (1920).
4. Ibid.
5. Ibid.
6. Major Douglas B. Roben brought combat experience to the First Marine Aviation Force, having been cited for his initiative in combat against bandits in Haiti prior to transferring to aviation. He passed away from the Spanish flu in October 1918. His citation reads, "The President of the United States of America takes pleasure in presenting the Navy Cross to Major Douglas B. Roben (MCSN: 0-3220), United States Marine Corps, for distinguished service in the line of his profession as airplane Pilot and Squadron Commander of Airplane Squadron No. 3, 1st Marine Aviation Force, attached to the Northern Bomb Group (USN), in which capacity he led the Squadron on many active bombing raids against the enemy during World War I."
7. David S. Ingalls, *Hero of the Angry Sky: The World War I Diary and Letters of David S. Ingalls, America's First Naval Ace*, Geoffrey L. Rossano, ed., Ohio University Press: Athens, p. 185 (2013). Beach was also a graduate of the First Yale Unit.
8. Interview with General Karl S. Day (1968).
9. Ibid.
10. Ibid.
11. Simmons, Edwin H., "Marines Over the Western Front," *Naval History Magazine*, vol. 20, no. 3 (June 2006).
12. Interview with General Day

13. Capt Francis T. Evans, the fourth Marine flyer (and 26th naval aviator). At Pensacola on February 13, 1917, defying the experts who believed it was probably impossible to loop a seaplane, Evans looped an N-9 (floatplane Jenny) from 3,000ft, not once but twice. Then, he forced it into a spin and pulled it out safely – the experts also had serious doubts that a seaplane could be brought out of a spin. For this contribution to the science of aviation and the security of flight, Evans was finally awarded the Distinguished Flying Cross on June 10, 1936 (nine years after the decoration was created).
14. Poague, Walter S., *Diaries and Letters of a Marine Aviator*. Alan Seeger was an American war poet who fought and died in World War One during the Battle of the Somme, as a member of the French Foreign Legion.
15. All the quotes are from the diary that I believe is important in understanding the life of a young man whose life was cut short by a tragic accident.

Chapter 14

1. Josephus Daniels, *Our Navy at War*, Pictorial Bureau: Washington, DC, pp. 220–40 (1922).
2. Ralph D. Paine, *The First Yale Unit: A Story of Naval Aviation*, Vol. 2, Riverside Press: Cambridge, p. 169 (1925).
3. Ibid., pp. 184–85.
4. Ibid., pp. 185–86.
5. An unknown number of naval pilots and observers served with French flying units.
6. Adrian O. Van Wyen, *Naval Aviation in WWI*, Chief of Naval Operations: Washington, DC (1969).
7. Edwin H. Simmons, "Marines Over the Western Front," *Naval History Magazine*, vol. 20, no. 3 (June 2006).
8. Roger Emmons, "The First Marine Aviation Force." *Cross and Cockade*, p. 272–92 (fall 1965).
9. Annette Dee Amerman, "Integration of US Marine Corps Aviation with the Royal Air Force in First World War: Legacy and Impact,"

Master's thesis, University of Birmingham, p. 100 (2018). Chamberlain was an interesting character as he was court-martialed after the war for falsifying combat reports and information regarding his service with the RAF.
10. Roger M. Emmons, Master Sergeant (ret.), "Marine Combat Squadrons in World War I," *Marine Corps Gazette*, p. 80 (November 1978).
11. Ibid.
12. Roger M. Emmons, "The First Marine Aviation Force Part I," *Cross and Cockade*, vol. 6, no. 2, p. 273 (summer 1965).
13. Miscellaneous Records of the Navy Department, Record Group 45, Roll 0412, p. 1,053.
14. John P. Condon, Major General USMC (ret.), *Marine Corps Aviation*, John M. Elliott, ed., Washington DC, p. 6 (1987).
15. *Roger M*. Emmons, "The First Marine Aviation Force: Part II," *Cross and Cockade*, vol. 6, no. 3, pp. 278–79 (fall 1965).
16. Ibid.
17. Geoffrey L. Rossano and Thomas Wildenberg, *Striking the Hornet's Nest*: *Naval Aviation and the Origins of Strategic Bombing*, Naval Institute Press, p.191 (2015).
18. *Cross and Cockade*, p. 186 (summer 1965).

Chapter 15

1. Maxfield was lost on August 24, 1921, when the British-built R-38 crashed near Hull, England.
2. McCrary, as pilot of the DN-1, which he flew in April 1917, is credited as being the first LTA pilot in the Navy.
3. The primary source for LTA operations comes from the *History of Naval Aviation*, Chapter XII.
4. Ibid.

Chapter 16

1. The US Navy lost over 200 aviation personnel in combat and accidents during the war, both overseas and domestically.

Index

Note: page numbers in bold refer to photographs and captions. Designations for aircraft and squadrons in brackets refer to former appellations.

ACA (Aero Club of America), the 54–55, 57, 61, 62, 64, 82, 98, **101,** 121, 140, 170
Aerial Coast Patrol, the 128, 134, 136–137, **137,** 146
Air-Ground Task Force, the 107
aircraft:
    Burgess D-1 107, 150, **151, 184,** 198
    Burgess D-2 90; C-4 98, 337
    Caproni 229, 255, 278, **280,** 303, 304, 306, 332
    Caproni 400 281;
    Caproni 600 279–281, 282
    Curtiss A-1 (Triad) (E-1) **52, 56,** 57, **57,** 59, 60, 62, 63, **64, 65, 68,** 69, **71,** 74, **75, 77,** 82, 95, **97, 99,** 106
    AH-1 **72, 110, 114, 116**
    AH-2 **100,** 111
    AH-3 **65, 67,** 74, **97, 100,** 102, 112–113
    AH-8 155
    AH-9 155
    AH-14 **77,** 155
    Curtiss A-2 (E-1) **57,** 60, 63, **63, 65,** 69, 74, **76, 77,** 82, 83, 85, 86, **93, 94,** 95

Curtiss E-1 (OWL) 59, **65,** 74, 85, **89,** 106
Curtiss F-5 **108, 114,** 214, 216
Curtiss F-5L **206,** 214, **217, 220, 346**
Curtiss H-12 **187,** 197, 203, 206, 210–212, **215,** 220, 251, 252
Curtiss H-16 (F-3) 186, **187,** 203, 210, **212,** 212–214, 220, **225, 230,** 231, **232, 238, 239, 244,** 245, 249
Curtiss HS-1 186, 210, **211,** 220, **220,** 234, 236, **237, 242, 248, 257**
Curtiss HS-1L **192, 207, 216,** 220, **232, 241, 244,** 245, **296, 297, 298**
Curtiss HS-2L **192, 215, 244,** 296
Curtiss Jenny JN-4 201, **289,** 290, **292**
Curtiss JN-4B 288
Curtiss N-9 158, 168, **169, 174, 184, 191, 193,** 197–198, 199–201, **200,** 203, 220, **220,** 296
Curtiss R-3 197, 206, **209**
Curtiss R-6 158, 197, 203, **205, 209,** 295–296

380

Index

de Havilland (AirCo) DH-4 8, 201, **202,** 229, 304, 311, **311,** 316, 317, **318,** 319, 320, **323, 324, 327, 328,** 332, **348**
de Havilland DH-9 8, 259, 313, 314, 316, 319, 320, **327, 328,** 332
Handley Page **141,** 254, 255, **257,** 280, 281, 303, 304, 306, 319–320
June Bug 32, **34**
Wright B-1 **57,** 59, 60, **60,** 63, 64, **64,** 82, 83, **83, 84,** 85, **88, 99,** 336–337
Wright B-2 85, **96,** 99, **99,** 102–104, **103, 104,** 150
Aircraft Production Board, the 166, 201, 203, 204, 206, 238

Barrett, Thomas W. 246
Bellinger, Lt Patrick N.L. 63, **76, 77, 89, 97,** 98, **99,** 102, **102,** 112–113, **113, 115, 116, 117,** 129, 151, 155, **155,** 156–157, 160, **160,** 161, 170, **172, 175**
Biddle, Gen William 79–80, 82
Billingsley, Ensign William **96,** 98, **99, 102,** 102–104, **103,** 150, 156, **175**
Bristol, Rear Adm Mark L. 107, 119, 121, 126–128, 150, 151, 153, **153,** 154, **154,** 156, 158, **159,** 159–160, 161–164, 182, 334

Callan, Lt Cmdr John L. "Lanny" **239,** 240–241, 265, **266,** 281
Chambers, Capt Washington Irving 23, 24–25, **26,** 27, 28–31, **30,** 33–35, 38–39, 44, 45–49, 51, 52–53, 57–59, 60–61, **63, 64,** 67, 72–73, 74, 80, **81,** 82, 84, 89–90, 95, 96–97, 107, 119, 150, 151, 179
Chapman, Thomas H. 186
Chevalier, Lt Godfrey de **74,** 90, 98, **99, 102,** 112, **155,** 170, **175, 177**
Cowles, Rear Adm William 22–23
Cunningham, Maj Alfred A. 7, 8, 79, **80,** 80–85, **81, 83,** 88–90, **91,** 92, **99, 101,** 105, 132, **172, 174,** 176–177, 189, 201, 283–285, **284,** 286, 287, 288, 303, 305, 306–309, 310, 311, 312, 316, **318,** 326, 330, 345, 347, 348
Curtiss, Glenn 13–14, **21,** 30, 31–35, **33, 34,** 40–41, 44, 46, 48, 51–52, **53,** 53–54, **54,** 55, 60, 61, 62, 67, 72, 74, **75,** 82, 96, 198, 204

Davison, F. Trubee **135, 136,** 137, **137, 138,** 139–141, **141,** 142, 146
Day, Lt Gen Karl S. 287–288, 312, 313, **317,** 326
Dewey, Adm George 26, 27, **27,** 31, 45

Edwards, Lt Cmdr W. Atlee 123, 125, **177**
Ellyson, Lt Theodore "Spuds" 7, 49–57, **50, 52, 56,** 60, 61, 62, 63, **63, 64, 65, 67,** 67–72, **68, 70, 71, 72,** 73, 74, **75,** 78, 81, 82, 86, 89, 90, 95, 96, 97–99, **101,** 170, 174, **174**
Ely, Eugene 31, 34, 35, **35, 36,** 36–44, **37, 38, 40, 43, 44, 45,** 46, **46,** 47–48, **48,** 53, 57, 73
Evans, Maj Francis T. "Khaki" **87,** 87–88, **172, 175,** 189, 287, 293, **294,** 300

Fahy, Ensign Charles 254–256, 306
FAI (Fédération Aéronautique Internationale), the 17, 54
First Aeronautical Company, the 8, 88, 227, 228, **292**, 293, **293**, 296, 300, **301**
First Marine Aeronautic Company, the 287, 294
First Marine Aviation Force **286**, 288, 307, **307**, 308–310, 313, 318, 319, **323**, 332–333, **333**, 345
  Squadron 7 (A) 285, 290, 308, 309, 312, **328**
  Squadron 8 (B) 285, 290, 308, 309, 326–330, **333**
  Squadron 9 (C) 285, 290, 308, 309, 311, 320, **328, 329**
  Squadron 10 (D) 285, 290, 308
First Naval Aeronautical Detachment **222**, 226–227, 246–248, **251**, 344
First Yale Unit, the 122, 135, **135, 140, 144, 145,** 226, 250, **252,** 254, 256, 261, 302, **303**
Fiske, Adm Bradley A. 26–27, **27**, 31, 107, 134–135, 144, 148–149, 161, 170, 343–344
Fletcher, Rear Adm Frank F. 25, 35, 111
FNAF (First Naval Aviation Force), the 8, 223–226, 249, 250, 269

Geiger, Maj Roy Stanley 7, 88, **90**, 92, **173**, 190, 285, 286, **286**, 288, 307–308, 310
General Order No. 153 121, 124
General Order No. 375 129
Gibbs, Second Lt John F. **329**, 330, **330**
Guantanamo Bay 78, 79, 85, 86, 90, 95, 98, **99**, 100, **101, 102**

Hammann, Ensign Charles H. 273, **274**, 274–275, **275, 276,** 277
Hammondsport, New York 32, 33, **34, 56,** 61–62, **63, 64, 65, 68, 71, 75, 76, 77, 83, 89,** 90, **94,** 99
Hanrahan, Capt David C. 304, **305**
Haviland, Lt Willis B. **265,** 270–271, 277
Herbster, Lt Victor D. "Vic" 64, **66,** 85, 96, **96,** 99–100, **99,** 102, **102,** 104, **155,** 160, 170, **174**

Ingalls, Lt David S. 142, 226, 249, 256–261, **258**

Joint Army and Navy Airship Board, the 201
Joint Technical Board, the 201, **202,** 203, 210

Langley, Prof Samuel Pierpont 14, **15,** 16
Liberty engines 201, 203, 206, 210, 212, 216, 243, 311, 319
Lovett, Ensign Robert A. **136,** 140, **141, 143, 145,** 226, 233, 281, 302–304, **303,** 309
LTA (lighter-than-air) operations 334–342, **336, 337, 341, 342,** 346

MacLeish, Lt Kenneth 249, **261,** 261–262
Marine Barracks, Philadelphia Navy Yard 287
McCrary, Lt Cmdr Frank R. 334, 335, **335**
McDonnell, Lt Edward O. 179, **179,** 249, 254, **255,** 278–279, 280, 281–282
McIlvain, Lt William M. "Mac" **86,** 87, **88,** 92, **93,** 106, 107, 132,

155, 170, **175, 177,** 189, 285, 287, 288, 310, 326, **333**
McIntee, William 22, **25,** 28, 36
Meyer, George von L. 24, **25,** 28, 35, 36, 39, 45, 46, 48, 51, 52, 57, 58–59, 73
Mitscher, Lt Marc A. "Pete" 7, **173, 175, 179**
Murray, Lt James M. 107, 150, **151,** 152, 156, 157, **175**
Mustin, Lt Cmdr Henry "Rum" 106–107, **115,** 129, **131, 149,** 150–151, **152,** 153, **154, 155,** 156–157, 158–159, 160, 161, 164–166, **165, 166,** 170, **172, 175,** 305, 334

NAS Hampton Roads, Virginia 36, **38, 39,** 63, 178, 186, 209, **336,** 338
NAS Killingholme, England 212, **225,** 229, **230,** 302
NAS Pensacola **133,** 149, **149, 152,** 155–156, **156,** 160, **162, 163, 166, 167, 168, 169, 171, 173,** 178, **178, 179,** 181, 184, 185, **185,** 187, **187,** 191, **191, 200, 207, 214,** 246, 254, 283, 334, **337,** 338, 344
naval militia, the 121, 124, **127,** 135, 136
NBG (Northern Bombing Group), the 8, 229, 238, 255, 256, 280, 281, 282, **284,** 286, **286, 291,** 302–303, **303,** 304–306, 309, 311, **311, 312,** 316, 317, 319, 320, **325,** 332, 345, 347
NRFC (Naval Reserve Flying Corps), the 126–128, 134, 135–136, 137–139, 141, 184

Office of Naval Aeronautics, the 29, 30, 49, 107, 119

Peary, Rear Adm Robert E. 126, **126,** 136, 140, 142, 144
Poague, Lt Walter Smith 294–295, 296–300, **301**
Pond, Cmdr Charles "Frog" **40,** 41, 42, 43–44, **48**

RAF, the 310, 313, 316, 319
  7 Squadron 249, 254
  213 Squadron 249, 256–260, 262, 310
  214 Squadron 249, 254–255
  217 Squadron 249, 310, 312, 316
  218 Squadron 249, **263,** 310, 311, 312, 314, 316, **317,** 320
RFC (Royal Flying Corps), the 182, **186,** 198
Richardson, Lt Holden "Dick" 67, 73, 74, **77, 89,** 90, **94,** 105, 107, 151–152, 170, **175**
RNAS (Royal Navy Air Service), the 164, 228, 229, 231, 249, 250, 279
Robinson, Cpl Robert G. 320, 321–322, **322**
Rockwell, Lt James V. 153–154, 156, 157, 158
Rodgers, Lt John "Jang" **60,** 61, 69, 72, 73, 81, 82, 95, 96, 99, **174**
Roosevelt, Franklin D. 104, 243, 340
Roosevelt, Theodore 14, 16, 18, 78, 122

Sims, Adm William L. 23, 24, 47, **125,** 134, 218, 222, 226, 227–228, 280, 281, 304, 317, 319–320
Smith, First Lt Bernard L. "Barny" 80, **85,** 85–87, **88,** 88–89, **89,** 90–92, **92, 93, 94, 99, 101, 102,**

106, 107, 112, **116,** 129–130, **155,** 160, 161, 170, **175,** 189
St-Inglevert aerodrome 306, 309
Sturtevant, Ensign Albert "Al" 226, 250–251, 252–253, **253**
Sweet, Lt George C. 22, 23, **23, 25**

Talbot, Second Lt Ralph 320–322, **321, 322, 323**
Tampico Affair (1914), the 24, 87, 106, **109,** 109–113, **116, 140,** 155, 254, **255**
Todd, Second Lt Charles B. 325–326, **331**
Towers, Lt Cmdr John H. "Jack" 7, 61–63, **62, 64, 65, 68,** 68–69, **71, 74,** 81, 82, 83, 84, 86, 89, 90, 95, 96, 99, **99,** 100, 102–103, **103,** 105, 106, 112, 129, **155,** 156, **159,** 159–160, 161, 166, 170, **174,** 183, 201, **202**

US Army, the 120, 304; Bureau of Ordnance and Fortifications 16, 18, 20
US naval base, Ponta Delgada, Azores **292,** 294, 295
US Navy, the 31, 50, 61, 78, 125, 149–150, 223, 304
   Bureau of Aeronautics 21, 58, 73, 191
   Bureau of Equipment 22–23
   Bureau of Navigation 21, 30, 47, 48, 58, 107, 170, 174, 182, 187, 334–335
   Bureau of Ordnance 21, 30, 58, 178
   Bureau of Yards and Docks 21

General Board 28, 29, 45, 49, 79, 119, 284, 285, 336
US ships
   Arkansas (BB-33) 100
   Birmingham (CL-2/CS-2?) 36, **36, 37, 38,** 38–39, 48, 111, 113
   California (ACR-6) 41
   Chester (CL-1) 27, 110
   Connecticut (BB-18) 87, 110
   Hancock (AP-3) 106, 107, 294, 295
   Jupiter (AC-3) 43, 226, **347**
   Louisiana (BB-19) 23, 86
   Minnesota (BB-22) 23, 110
   Mississippi (BB-23) 88, 106, 112, 113, **114, 117**
   Montana (ACR-13) 254
   Montgomery (C-9) 254
   Neptune (AC-8) 226
   New Jersey (BB-16) 81, 254
   North Dakota (BB-29) 87, 88, 158
   Pennsylvania (ACA-4) 39–40, **40,** 41, 43, **43, 44, 45, 46,** 48, **48,** 53, **54,** 57
   Tennessee (ACR-10) 160
   Vermont (BB-20) 98
   West Virginia (AC-55) 41, **76**
   Wisconsin (BB-9) 98

Whiting, Lt Kenneth 51, 52, 82, 154, 156, 170, **172, 175, 177,** 223, 226–227, 228, 233, 302
Wright brothers, the 13, 14–16, **16,** 17–20, **18, 19, 20, 21, 22,** 23–24, 31, 32, 33, 34, 96, 97, 343